MW01166095

VIOLATION
The Life of
Luisa Cannoli

VIOLATION

The Life of Luisa Cannoli

Luisa Cannoli

Publishing

Violation - The Life of Luisa Cannoli
Copyright © 2004 by Luisa Cannoli
All rights reserved

Cover Design by
Tim Phillips

Book Design by
Scott Willis

Publishing

ISBN 0-9754919-0-3

Published by
Cannoli Cultural Art Center, Inc.
P.O. Box 750458
Dayton, Oh 45475

This book is based on the author's perception of true events.
The names of characters, companies, and locations have been
changed to protect the identity of the parties involved.

PRINTED IN THE UNITED STATES OF AMERICA

ACKNOWLEDGMENTS

First, and foremost, to my parents. Their strength of character, and strong moral guidance helped me survive this long ordeal at the hands of those in power. And to the incredible outpouring of support from my friends, the churches, hospitals, and many others who have contributed to the development of this book.

I would like to thank Richard and Annie Moran for their many devoted hours and assistance in completing the book. Also, I cannot fully express my gratitude to the marketing team of Scott Willis and Audrey Willis. Their assistance provided this project with the final push it needed to reach publication.

AUTHOR'S NOTE

This book is also dedicated to the thousands of others suffering the same treatment at the hands of unethical insurance carriers, their extensive legal machine, and the doctors who conspire with them to hide the truth. This book is meant to provide a voice to these individuals, and perhaps some reassurance that they are not alone, and they can and will be heard and recognized.

Foreword

by Richard Moran

Here at last is a book that exposes the intrigue and nefarious tactics that all too many insurance companies resort to in their greedy drive to avoid paying rightful claims against their multi-billion dollar empires.

Within these pages, the author reveals the mental and physical torment inflicted on her by an insurance company devoid of ethics or compassion, a faceless corporate entity whose only guiding principle is the almighty buck.

Drawing on carefully-kept notes, medical and legal records, and her own vivid memories of the ordeal she suffered after a huge tractor-trailer smashed into her car on a mid-west freeway in July 1997, the author paints a riveting picture of a lone woman with limited resources struggling against an unscrupulous corporate giant.

Yet Violation is also a warm human story of a young woman growing up in an extended Italian family where love, laughter and hard work nurtured and shaped the author, and ultimately gave her the strength to triumph against all odds.

A former school teacher, the happily married mother of two beautiful daughters was a successful interior designer with her own flourishing business when an intoxicated truck driver crashed into her near-perfect world and sent her spiraling down into a hellish cauldron of physical pain, emotional anguish and near financial ruin.

The author's account of the sudden tragedy which befell her – and the torturous years that followed – will deeply impact all readers because this story could be anyone's story. We are all vulnerable to that horrible unforeseen event – an automobile accident, an unexpected physical calamity, and a terrorist attack – which could turn our happy lives into a vale of tears.

Justifiably concerned for her courageous stand against the insurance company she battled to help so many others with similar violations and to educate the world for those who do not know of such atrocities and tactics used to deny bona-fide claims, the author has chosen to write under the pseudonym of Luisa Cannoli. Written in the roman e clef format, the names of other people who were part of the real events described, as well as certain company names, have also been changed to protect those involved.

It can be revealed that Luisa is a 50-year-old artist, businesswoman and philanthropist living with her family in the mid-west. Although her initial legal action against the insurance company involved has been successfully settled, she is taking an active part in a proposed government investigation of the events surrounding her accident and the corporate persecution, which followed.

VIOLATION
The Life of
Luisa Cannoli

Chapter 1

The Crash

When Luisa Cannoli awoke at 7:00 a.m. on the morning of Tuesday, July 22, 1997, she had no way of knowing that this was the day her life would change forever.

As usual, her husband, Anton, had risen a half-hour before her and had already showered and shaved. He emerged from the steamy master bathroom with a towel wrapped around his middle. At age 51, he was a handsome man with dark hair and moustache only beginning to be flecked with gray. Many people – including Luisa – thought he looked like Tom Selleck. He worked out several times a week and carried his 175 pounds well on his 5'9" frame.

He bent to kiss the still sleepy Luisa good morning.

"I love you," she said with a soft smile.

"And I love you," Anton said, squeezing her hand. He crossed to the walk-in closet they shared and began getting dressed. "What are you up to today?"

"I have to be downtown by nine to see your Mom's attorney about Pappa's estate. He wants to talk about investment planning."

Family members had called Luisa's beloved late father-in-law, Paulos, Poppa. He had passed away four months before.

Luisa yawned. "Then I need to work on Ellis' design for a

new second floor office, spend an hour or so doing sofa and window treatments at the Design Center and after that meet Crissy, Marylee, Annette and Kath at Overseas Rugs. Then I'm taking Rosanna and Carmella to lunch at the Greyhorn Tavern."

"Give them a kiss from dad," Anton said, pulling on a dark blue sport shirt that complimented his gray slacks. "It seems like the older our girls get, the less I see them."

"You'll always think of them as your little girls, won't you," Luisa grinned. "Even though Rosanna's sixteen now and Carmella's a very independent ten-year-old."

Anton re-crossed the room and stood by the bed. "Guilty as charged. What's your afternoon look like?"

"Mostly returning phone calls and doing paper work. Ugh!" He kissed Luisa goodbye. "I'll see you around six. You cooking tonight or should I pick up a pizza?"

"Depends on what time I get home. Call me on my cell before you leave the office."

"Okay. Don't forget to kiss the girls for me."

"I won't. I'll even throw in a fatherly hug."

Anton laughed and headed for the door. Luisa could hear him begin to whistle as he bounced down the stairs.

She turned her head and stared in quiet rapture at the diffused sunlight streaming through the pale blue window shades.

The bedroom of their large English Tudor home faced south and the room was always bright in the morning. From beyond the windows she could hear the sounds of bluebirds, robins and yellow finches chirping in harmony from the branches of the stately oak trees on the front lawn.

Part of her early morning ritual was to spend an hour or so alone in bed saying her prayers and reading in solitude. She'd long ago discovered that this quiet time of communication with her God and contemplative reading helped her achieve a balance in her daily life, and an illuminating perspective on her interrelationships with her family, friends and colleagues at work.

Her daughter Rosanna was on her mind this morning, perhaps because Rosanna had just passed her driver's test and was exploring the new freedoms that a permanent driver's license made possible. Luisa said a silent prayer of gratitude to the Lord for the many natural gifts He had given her older daughter.

Carmella was equally as talented, and Luisa sometimes marveled that the Lord had blessed her with two daughters who were so adept at almost anything they put their minds to.

Yesterday Rosanna and Carmella had been getting ready to leave for their usual 3:30 to 5:00 PM Monday piano lessons when Rosanna had asked if she could drive herself and Carmella to the teacher's house instead of Luisa taking them as she usually did.

At first, Luisa was torn. After all, Rosanna was only 16 and had very little experience driving without her Mom or Dad sitting beside her. On the other hand, she was a good driver and had always shown herself to be responsible and mature for her age. Luisa took a deep breath and gave her permission.

As Rosanna did a little jig of joy, Luisa reminded her daughter to always stop completely at stop signs, not to speed, and to drive defensively, keeping an eye on the drivers around her. She also told Rosanna to take the back roads whenever possible.

Despite Luisa's fretting, the two girls made it to their piano lessons without a mishap. When they were finished, Carmella called her Mom on her cell phone and asked if she and Rosanna could drive over and visit their grandmother and their Aunt Sophia who had just had a baby girl.

Luisa agreed, but made Carmella promise that they would be very careful crossing the bridge over the Tennessee River to Kentucky. Luisa was most concerned that her daughters would be driving in heavy traffic just as dusk was falling.

The girls called Luisa to reassure her when they had safely crossed the bridge. Two hours later they called back to ask if they could spend the night at Grandma's. Luisa decided that it would be better if the girls didn't try to drive home after dark, and once again said okay.

Luisa stretched and brought her mind back to the present. She glanced over at the two books on her 18th century solid cherry nightstand, trying to decide whether to read an excerpt from *Simple Abundance* by Sarah Breathnah, or start the day with a selection from *Illuminati* by Mariann Willamson.

She chose *Illuminati* and turned to a passage titled, "*Neglect Not the Gifts within You.*" Twenty minutes later she put down the book, luxuriating in the sense of peace that the author's words had brought her.

After a moment, she reached for the phone and placed her usual morning call to her mother. They chatted about the girls for several minutes. Rosanna and Carmella had watched two movies Grandma had rented for them at Showcase Blockhouse then slept on the sleeper-sofa in the living room. The two were still asleep.

"They're going over to Sophia's house around ten to help her with her newborn and play with Jeanna. Lord, that is one active four-year-old. Always into something."

Luisa told her Mom her schedule for the day and asked her to remind the girls that they were having lunch together and to please be at the Horseshoe Tavern sharply at noon. She had a jam-packed afternoon. After promising her Mom that she would call back later that day, Luisa hung up and swung her feet out of bed.

She padded into the bathroom and turned on the water in the Jacuzzi for her morning bubble bath. She set her body lotions on her vanity, and then walked back into the bedroom to make the bed and straighten up the room. By the time she was finished, her bath was ready.

She liked her baths hot and clouds of steam rose above the Jacuzzi as she stepped in and sank slowly into the soothing bubbles. Fifteen minutes later the water had cooled and she stepped out and dried herself with a large fluffy lavender bath towel. She applied her favorite Lancôme body lotion then scrutinized her face in the mirror.

At age 45 she had a pretty freckled face that – her mother always said – reflected the goodness within her. Especially when she smiled. She was 5'7" and weighed 170 pounds, a fact that had prompted her to try at least a dozen different diets in recent years. She also swam regularly at either the Wood's Swim Club or the Mariner's Hotel pool in Clarksville where she had memberships.

As disturbing to her as her weight problem were the wrinkles that had begun to appear around her eyes and the corners of her mouth. She sighed resignedly and reached for her black velvet Fenton make-up bag to disguise the damage.

She first softened her skin with the natural-look lotions she liked, and then applied red Lancôme lipstick to complement the white ribbon cotton top and Susan Bristol red and gold paisley skirt she was going to wear today. The eye shadow on her upper eyelids came next, a light brown shade to brighten her green/hazel eyes, followed by an application of crème white beneath her eyes. She completed her make-up by applying black mascara to her long, curling Italian eyelashes.

Her hair came next. As she brushed her wavy strands, Luisa looked for any signs of graying. There were a few gray hairs around her ears and fringing her forehead and she made a mental note to schedule an appointment at Mitchell's, her favorite hair salon and spa, for later that week.

Luisa returned to the bedroom and selected taupe nylons and a white half-slip from her dresser, then put on her top and stepped into her skirt. She decided to wear her cream pearls, even though she was already wearing a gold chain necklace with her daughters' birthstones hanging below.

The necklace had been a gift from her Aunt Gwinnett, one of her favorite aunts, and she never took it off her neck. She choose medium brown leather Liz Claiborne dress shoes with low heels and checked herself out in the full-length mirror on the back of the closet door.

Satisfied – well, almost – with her appearance, she headed downstairs to have breakfast. Her favorite breakfast was a bowl of Wheaties and juice. Anton liked a cup of Amaretto coffee in the morning and the smell of the aromatic coffee still filled the kitchen.

She finished her Wheaties and filled a Styrofoam cup with juice to take with her in the car, then gathered up the two folders she would need that day: Nana's papers and Ellis's design for their new second floor office.

She walked through the dining room to their attached two-car garage and pushed the button to open the door. As the door slid up, she heard the neighbors' dogs barking as usual. The sky was a clear blue and the morning sun was shining brightly.

Her freshly washed grey '89 Toyota Cressida gleamed in the morning light. Luisa was determined to keep her car in pristine condition for she planned to drive it until she had 400,000 miles on the odometer – she was up to 120,000 miles so far – and then see if the Toyota Company wanted to use her car in a commercial.

She was so fanatical about maintaining her Toyota in like-new shape that she kept it garaged when she wasn't using it, never drove it in the rain or snow, and had it frequently washed and waxed by her friend Nick at the Power Klean Car Wash, or the always cheerful Don at the Village of Woods Car Wash.

In addition to keeping her beloved Toyota spotless, she paid close attention to the car's mechanical condition. She'd just had new brakes installed, and new tires from reliable Forever Safe Tires in Rockport.

She got behind the wheel, backed out and shut the garage door, and headed toward town. The entrance to the interstate was only a block from her neighborhood and, just as she'd thought, the post rush-hour traffic was moderate at most. As she turned onto the highway she turned on the radio. The Beatles' hit, When She

Fell in Love with You, was playing on her favorite oldies station, 103.5 FM.

The Beatles were her favorite group and she thought back to the Fabulous Four concert she and her grade school friends had gone to at Old Crosley Field in Clarksville back in 1964. As the music played, her mind wandered to thoughts of Anton and how tender and loving his good morning kiss had been.

I'm truly blessed, she thought. A wonderful husband and two great kids - what more could any woman want?

The drive to downtown Clarksville took only 20 minutes and, looking at the clock, Luisa knew that she would be on time for her first two appointments of the day. She approached the on-ramp for Donahue Avenue and eased into the third outside lane.

As she drove, she said a silent prayer of thanks to the Lord for watching over her family, especially her newly independent daughter, Rosanna. Luisa was also grateful that God had been there to protect her younger sister, Sophia – so recently a mother for the second time – during a recent accident on the expressway.

Six months before Sophia had barely escaped death when a 40,000-pound roll of steel had fallen off a tractor-trailer in front of her car as both vehicles rounded a bend on the interstate. Although Sophia had suffered only minor injuries, her classic BMW had been totally demolished.

Luisa's extended family, always close, had rallied behind Sophia. The memory of how loving and caring everyone had been to her sister always filled Luisa with a warm, safe feeling. She knew that if anything ever happened to her or Anton or the girls, her family would be there for them too.

As she thought of her loved ones, Luisa passed the Harrod's Avenue exit and neared the on-ramp on the other side of the overpass spanning four-lane I–75. The on-ramp emptied into a fifth lane that allowed cars entering the highway to gain speed before merging with the flow of traffic.

Suddenly Luisa became aware of a fast-moving tractor-trailer carrying steel beams and machinery parts attempting to cut into her lane from the left. A wave of fear washed over her as she realized that the truck driver had badly miscalculated the distance between the back of his rig and her car.

Her first instinct was to swerve to the right into the on-ramp lane but instantly realized that this was impossible because a second tractor-trailer hauling lumber had just entered the expressway from Coldiron Avenue and was accelerating fast to her right rear. The only thing she could do was jam on her brakes. The rapid deceleration from 55 MPH to O threw her painfully forward against the restraining seat belts.

Just as her Toyota screeched to an abrupt stop in the middle of the expressway, the outside right rear wheel of the truck on her left slammed into her front end and driver's door. Her cup of orange juice shot into the air, splattering the Toyota's interior, her necklace with her daughters birthstones flew off her neck, and her purse broke open against the dashboard, spilling the contents all over the floor.

The big rig was carrying a heavy load of machinery and the sudden impact crushed the entire front end of Luisa's Toyota, shattering the car's headlights and grill and buckling the hood. Beyond the windshield, she could see a blizzard of steel as parts of her car flew in all directions. For a split second the scene reminded her of the movie, Twister.

"Don't you see me down here!" Luisa screamed at the truck driver through the closed driver's side window. Luisa pressed on the horn non-stop with her sweat-soaked palms and wrists as the front of her car was thrust beneath the rusty yellow undercarriage of the lumber truck. A split second later the rig's left rear tire crushed the front wheel well and passenger door.

Although the driver obviously never heard her, he felt the impact and immediately applied his airbrakes, which only made matters worse. Luisa stared horror-stricken through the windshield as the braking truck slid to the right, pushing her Toyota into the on-ramp lane just the lumber truck that was passing her on the right.

As her car slid partially under the truck Luisa screamed out, *"Oh, Lord, I am being crushed!"*

Just then a brilliant white light engulfed her and a panorama of faces appeared before her eyes – as though she were looking at a crowd in a stadium. At that same moment her necklace flew up once again and the faces of her beautiful daughters floated before her.

Her hands were frozen to the wheel as a second impact thrust her '89 Cressida back onto the traffic lanes of the interstate.

Looking through the windshield at the crushed front end of her car she cried out in a quivering voice, *"Lord, I cannot believe I am still here!"*

Shaking, totally confused and unable to think, Luisa removed her leaden foot from the brake and gently depressed the accelerator, slowly guiding her car to the side of the interstate. As she looked around she noticed that several cars that had obviously been behind her had also stopped, as had the two trucks that had hit her.

During the accident her tortured body had been thrown violently first one way then the other. Her left side had slammed repeatedly into the driver's door while her right side had been continuously propelled against the hard console between the seats. At the same time, her upper body had been thrown first forward then back, snapping her neck and shoulders as if her torso were the end of a cracking whip.

Fighting not to slip into shock and lose consciousness, her mind flashed back to her vacation in Hilton Head with her best girl friends, Caroline and Suzanne, two weeks ago. They'd brought their kids and watched videos together all night long – including Twister.

Sitting immobilized behind the wheel, she realized that what had just happened to her was the same thing that had happened to the characters in the movie – she'd been powerless in the face of the sudden and total destruction of all around her.

Nauseated and confused, she fought not to scream as intense pain radiated from every part of her body – her head, neck, back, shoulders, arms, hands, legs and abdomen.

Her voice quivering, she said aloud, "I can't believe I'm still here." Then the terrible realization that none of her nurturing family was there swept over her and she whispered hoarsely, "I'm all alone. What am I to do?"

As she stared hopelessly through the windshield she noticed the driver of the first truck that had hit her climb down out of his cab and start toward her. His hair and beard were flecked with white and he looked to be in his 60s.

He was wearing a white tee shirt, blue jeans and brown cowboy boots. And he was swaying as he walked, as if he were drunk.

Using the last of her strength, Luisa peeled her right hand from the steering wheel and motioned for him to come help her.

"I can't breathe," she cried out. "I need help."

To her astonishment and shock, the truck driver shook his head no, turned on his heel and walked back to his rig. Luisa couldn't believe that anyone could be so cruel and uncaring.

The sound of yelling and people running toward her came from beyond the car windows and within moments several men were working to free her from the wreckage.

Although Luisa had no way of knowing it then, the worst consequences of her freak accident were yet to come. In the years ahead, she would wish more than once that she could be rescued yet again, not from a crushed car but from a life shattered by ruthless companies and unscrupulous men.

Luisa Cannoli's long descent into a living hell had only just begun.

Chapter 2

Beginnings

As the brilliant light enveloped her, Luisa's childhood life began to flash before her...

Luisa's parents, Joseph and Teresa Shappers were married on July 10, 1946. Joseph was a tall, slender, handsome man with thick dark wavy hair and green eyes. Teresa was attractive in a wholesome Midwest way. She had dark brown eyes, a round open face and, like Joseph, dark wavy hair. Although only 5' 2" and 107 pounds, she was buxom.

Not long after they were married the young couple rented a small, two-bedroom wood-frame house on Rosa Avenue in Western Cliff Hills, a working class section of Clarskville, Tennessee. The houses in the neighborhood were built close together – most barely three feet apart – and on warm evenings the residents would sit on their front porches and visit back and forth.

On December 5, 1950 Teresa gave birth to their first child, a healthy six-pound, eight-ounce girl with dark hair and hazel eyes they named Alexia. Two years later, on December 8, 1952, Luisa joined the family. Born with wavy brown hair and the same hue of hazel eyes as her older sister, Luisa was a chubby baby who at the age of nine months already weighed 30 pounds.

Given her mother's propensity for feeding Luisa whole milk out of beer bottles while she gurgled contentedly in her high chair, the baby's steady weight gain was not altogether surprising to family members and friends.

Joseph's mother and father had crossed the Atlantic from Holland, while Teresa's father had made the long sea voyage from Sicily, Italy. Her mother was born and raised in Clarksville, Tennessee. The different nationalities of their grandparents would later provide a rich cultural heritage for the Shappers girls.

While Alexia and Luisa were still very young, Joseph was studying toward a Master's degree in engineering at State University. He had graduated from the university's Department of Engineering in 1953 after serving in the Army during World War II. When Joseph studied at home at night, Teresa would make sure their young daughters played quietly in their bedroom.

Always conscious of his appearance, he wore crisp white cotton dress shirts, blue or brown wool trousers and color-coordinated ties.

Teresa ironed the family's clothes almost every day, pressing Joseph's shirts and embroidered handkerchiefs – she even ironed his baggy cotton underpants – and the girls' dresses.

On Sundays the family always attended the local Catholic Church. Before leaving for Mass, Teresa would meticulously dress her two beautiful daughters in matching outfits and adorn their dark, curly with big, flowing bows.

After church Teresa would cook her family a large breakfast and the mouthwatering aromas of scrambled eggs, sausage links, smoked ham and cinnamon toast would fill the tiny house. Every once in while on Sundays, Teresa would surprise her daughters with strawberry milk – their favorite drink – instead of the usual white milk they had with every meal.

Teresa was a nurturing and often playful mother. She would play paper dolls with the girls, taking the time to show them how to carefully cut out the dress patterns while leaving the tabs intact.

She also taught her young daughters how to make beautiful multi-colored potholders on a frame. It was a simple but sweetly satisfying way of life.

The thrifty couple saved whatever they could from Joseph's earnings and in 1951 they bought a black and white television with a solid mahogany wood cabinet. They liked watching family shows with their girls, especially Ed Sullivan and Lawrence Welk. The girls had their own favorites and rarely missed an episode of Howdy Doody, the Lone Ranger and Uncle Al. When Uncle Al was on, they would sing and dance along while the entertainer and his wife, Wendy, played songs.

The show played such a role in the girls' lives that Teresa got tickets for Alexia, Luisa and their many cousins to go see Big Al and Wendy in person. As Luisa watched the show, she experienced the first disillusionment of her young life when she discovered that Captain Wendy could not really fly. Instead, as a TV camera focused on her, Wendy stood on a platform with a fan blowing her dark hair, as if in the wind. Luisa learned that day that life was not always what it first appeared.

Joseph was an avid sports fan and he loved playing baseball with his two daughters. In his youth he had played first base with his brothers Edwin and Daniel and he taught Alexia and Luisa how to hit and field. The girls picked the game up fast and were soon among the best young baseball players in the neighborhood.

Teresa and Joseph had a soft spot for animals and took their daughters to visit the local zoo many times. They also surprised Alexia and Luisa one year with two rainbow-hued chickens. The girls had fun watching the chickens grow.

However, Teresa was not quite as sentimental about the two pampered pets as her daughters and one day while the girls were at school Teresa took the by-then full-grown chickens over to her mother's house where Nonni – as her granddaughters called her – promptly butchered them. Unbeknownst to the young girls, the main course at their Easter dinner in 1958 was the two chickens they had raised.

It was only after dinner that Alexia and Luisa were told that they had just eaten their little feathered friends. Tears and recriminations flowed, but it wasn't long before the girls realized that their mother had taught them a painful yet valuable lesson: sometimes life calls for sacrifice. It was a truism they never forgot.

Through the 1950s, the two young girls spent several weeks each summer visiting their maternal grandparents and seven cousins at their grandparents' home near Choctaw Lake in North Henderson, Clarksville. It was always fun. They would go to the nearby amusement park for rides and swimming, and there were always numerous other joyous things to do.

In the years to come, Luisa would often look back at these summers spent with her grandparents and cousins as among the happiest times of her life. The two families were very close and along with summers spent together they had numerous gatherings throughout the year.

In those days it was still safe for children growing up in the suburbs to venture out without parental supervision, and Alexia and Luisa were allowed considerable independence. They would frequently be given tokens and allowed to take the bus to their relatives' homes north of Clarksville.

The two sisters were competitive by nature, and Luisa would often find herself dominated by the older Alexia. The girls took tap and ballet lessons together and during one recital – with both dressed as sailors in navy blue uniforms and crisp white sailors' hats – Alexia's drive to be first asserted itself. During a rendition of Alexander's RagTime Band she tapped her way from the back row to the front, stepping ahead of a startled Luisa.

Alexia had the biggest smile on her face and her brown curls fairly danced on her shoulders as she tapped her black shoes to the beat of the Band. Although the audience clapped louder and louder, the stony faces of Joseph and Teresa reflected their displeasure at Alexia's coming out of formation to steal the show.

Even though the dance teacher considered Alexia her best   student – frequently rewarding her performances with photographs of the world's best tap dancers and ballet stars – and both Joseph and Teresa were very proud of their eldest daughter's prowess as a dancer, this grandstanding at the expense of Luisa and the other students was too much.

Joseph had a habit of raising his left eyebrow when he was irritated, and as Alexia tapped away his eyebrow shot up toward his hairline, a sure sign of his disapproval. After Alexia's selfish exhibition that evening, Luisa decided to stop taking tap dancing lessons with her sister.

Luisa compensated for giving up tap dancing by entertaining herself for hours on end with her green hula-hoop. She worked hard to perfect her talent at having the hula-hoop go from the top of her index finger, down her neck, over her chest, around her waist, down her ankles, and go all the way back up to her fingers while continuously taking small backward steps. She loved to take her hula-hoop wherever she went. Most of her cousins also had hula-hoops and at family gatherings Luisa would astonish them with her skill.

At ages six and eight, Luisa and Alexia were told they were going to have a new sibling. Both girls were excited by the news and impatiently waited the day when their new baby brother or sister would arrive.

After what seemed like an eternity, their new sister, Constella, finally arrived on a blistering hot day in late July 1958. The infant had curly amber hair that glowed like gold in the sun, beautiful green eyes and dimples when she smiled.

Luisa and Alexia would not learn until many years later that Teresa had miscarried a two-month girl at home eight months before Constella was born.

Luisa and Alexia treated their baby sister like a new doll. Although the older girls were usually careful with their tiny sibling, one day when Constella was five months old, they dropped her as they were handing her back and forth to each other in the living room.

Constella hit her head on the solid mahogany coffee table, causing a large bump to appear. When Teresa saw her injured infant she threw her arms up in the air and started shouting, "Mama Mia, my baby!"

Teresa was really mad at Luisa and Alexia. She picked up the wailing Constella and cuddled her tightly in her arms, then took the baby into the kitchen and put ice on her head. From that day on Luisa and Alexia realized the fragility of their baby sister.

At this time the Shappers were living on Joseph's meager income alone. He was more than qualified for better paying jobs, but taking a new position would interfere with his graduate school studies and he was determined to better himself so that he could give his growing family a good life and financial security.

Joseph and Teresa handled the finances together. Frugal to a fault, Teresa stretched every dollar as far as it would go. She mended clothes to make them last, took advantage of sales and bargains whenever she could, and never spent a frivolous penny on herself.

Joseph's father, Joseph Sr., was a talented artist, especially good at painting images of birds on wooden boards, but during the Depression and World War II his livelihood suffered and his family was poor. Because money was always scarce, Joseph's two brothers, Edwin and Daniel, joined a seminary, and his sister Rosemary entered a convent in order for them to obtain an education.

Despite the poverty that plagued him, Grandpa Shappers gave Luisa and Alexia shiny silver dollars for their birthdays every year for ten years. The girls delighted in their grandfather's gifts, and were fascinated by the detailed engraving on these late 1800s silver dollars.

During one hard time, Teresa asked her mother for a twenty-dollar bill in exchange for the twenty silver dollars her daughters had accumulated. To this day Teresa regrets the exchange she was forced to make. One of her brothers-in-law collected coins and he bought the silver dollars from Nonni. When he passed away, he bequeathed the coins to his daughter, who still possesses them.

Luisa and Alexia learned the value of frugality at a very young age. Their parents taught them that a penny saved is a penny earned, and that real joy in life did not depend on how much money one had.

Over the years Luisa had collected letters from the Shappers family elders in Holland. The letters were testimonials to the tough times that gripped Europe from World War I through the end of World War II. To survive meant to strive, and for generations their parents had taught younger members of the family that education and success went hand in hand. Fortunately, the strong German/Dutch work ethic was ingrained in the Shappers' bloodline.

Many of the Shappers who entered the religious sector lived long lives – some becoming Cardinals in their later years – while other family members spent decades devoted to God.

Teresa's family was neither as religious nor as educated as Joseph's forebearers. Her mother had been born to working class parents in New York City, while her father joined his uncles and cousins in the produce industry at age nine.

Although never formally educated, Louis Palmieri knew what it took to survive and soon became a workaholic, learning every aspect of the produce market. He married young and lost his first wife in childbirth, leaving him with a beautiful two-year-old daughter named Francisca to rear by himself.

A few years later, at age 30, Louis remarried. His second wife was a beautiful 18-year-old Italian girl from New York City named Maria Rose. His Italian good looks attracted many beautiful women, but he was true to his Marie Rose all his life.

Louis worked very hard and taught his three daughters and one son to work hard as well. He provided a very good life for his family, even building a home for them with his own hands. The house still stands today, a fitting memorial to a good man who won the love and loyalty of family and friends alike.

Louis was held in such high esteem in the local community that the city train in North Henderson, Tennessee, stopped running for a quarter of an hour to let his large funeral parade of family, friends and business acquaintances cross the tracks.

Luisa enjoyed her summer visits with Nonni and Grandpa Louis. Grandpa taught her how to play checkers and they would sit outside through the long hours of summer heat playing checkers with the neighbors. A quarter a game would go to the winner, and Grandpa won a lot.

He would proudly give his quarters to Luisa so that she could buy a big ice cream cone from the ice cream shop down the street. For a nickel she would get three big scoops of strawberry ice cream. The strawberries in the ice cream were huge. Luisa would carry two cones back, chocolate for Grandpa and vanilla for Nonni. When the cousins were there, they too, got huge nickel cones.

Grandpa liked to whittle pencils and when Luisa was in his market he would give her one and show her how to price vegetables and fruit at the market. He also taught her how to entice customers to buy his best-selling products, tomatoes and bananas, and the correct way to handle and bag his precious fruit and produce.

He always weighed purchases carefully and then good-naturedly negotiated the best price for his products. He knew that honesty, loyalty, and quality products would ensure that his customers came back again and again. Luisa learned so much from her Grandpa.

Nonni worked at the market three days a week and she and Grandpa would frequently speak Italian so that people around them wouldn't know what they were talking about. Often one of them would get annoyed at the other and they would shout at each other in flowing Italian. Luisa learned to pick up odd words and phrases, and after a while she was able to distinguish between polite conversation and slightly off-color language.

Grandpa was set in his ways. At home, he would put the daily newspaper on the porcelain kitchen table, then peel off the pages in order, putting one on top of another. After he'd carefully arranged the loose pages on the table, he would put his white ceramic bowl on top of the flat pile and open his box of Wheaties. He'd then pour the cereal into his bowl and add whole milk and slices of banana.

Never having had the chance to get an education and learn to read English, he could not understand the stories in the newspaper but nevertheless he put it to a useful purpose.

When all was ready, he'd sit down and contentedly eat his breakfast. While he was eating, he'd prop his rimless glasses on his nose and mark his note pad with a series of X's that recorded the previous day's sales at the market.

Nonni also had her rituals. She loved to watch her daily soap operas, and did not look kindly on any interruptions during her favorite shows. Every evening she would sit in her favorite chair in the front room crocheting sweaters, mittens, and hats for her grandchildren. Nonni taught Luisa how to crochet left-handed and also showed her granddaughter how to sew on her Necchi sewing machine.

At 10:00 p.m. all would go to their bedrooms. Grandpa slept in the back room. All the windows were open so that a breeze would cool the hot rooms. The city sounds rang throughout the night and Grandpa would snore so loudly that you could hear him streets away.

Nonni would exercise faithfully each night before going to sleep. When she was finished, she and Luisa would often sit down in front of Nonni's beautiful vanity dresser and play make-up with the numerous hairpins, hairnets and bottles of nail polish on top.

Nonni often read Italian poetry to Luisa before they went to sleep. Luisa's favorite poems came from The Treasury of Italian Love Poems, Quotations and Proverbs. The book contained poems and literary selections that spanned nine centuries from the 1100's to the early 1900's.

Nonni also taught Luisa a smattering of Italian words and sayings. One of the sayings Luisa's grandmother passed on to her was by Dante. It was *Amore, e 'l cor gentil son un cosa – Love and the gentle heart are the same things.* Through her acts of devotion to her husband, Nonni showed Luisa the meaning of Dante's words.

When Luisa's eyelids began to droop, Nonni would tuck the tired girl into bed beside her and the two would fall peacefully asleep listening to each other breathe. Luisa always felt so safe and loved lying next to her nurturing grandmother.

Among Nonni's many talents was gardening and, even decades later, the sight or smell of roses would instantly transport Luisa back to an image of her grandmother working in the beautiful rose garden she had planted in their small backyard.

For the rest of her life, Luisa would cherish the joyous memory of all she had learned from her grandparents, and how much fun she always had when she was with them.

Chapter 3

Bobby Socks and Curly Locks

The memories continued to flow as the white light grew brighter...

As Luisa, Alexia and Constella grew older, the Shappers began visiting Choctaw Lake 70 miles west of Clarksville. It was a large lake bordered by wooded cabins, play yards with swings, and baseball fields.

There they grilled hot dogs, played baseball, and swam in the lake. Luisa, as usual, brought along her hula-hoop and usually managed to gather an audience around her as she performed her tricks.

The old black and white Kodak photos in the worn family photo albums show Luisa and Alexia in bobsy curls, sleeveless cotton blouses, knickers, white bobby socks and gym shoes. Many of the pictures capture them cooling off after playing with large glasses of Kool-Aid.

When Luisa was 10 years old, Anna was born. The new baby had black hair, brown eyes and a full face. As an infant, Anna was sometimes prone to coughing spells. Teresa would hold her and rock her back to sleep. Alexia, Luisa, and Constella all helped their mother by playing with their new baby sister. Alexia would usually take the part of the mom, even dressing up and putting on makeup to assume the role.

Every Sunday, Teresa wore a full skirt and hat to go to church. She now had four daughters to dress for church as well. Joseph made sure his family had their missals, chapel veils and 25¢ each for the church service collections.

He was proud of his harem of girls, as he often called them. Joseph now had a crew-cut haircut and wore horn-rimmed glasses. He would often wear his favorite brown suit on Sundays, along with a crisp white cotton dress shirt and a conservative brown tie.

The family drove to church in their two-door 1959 Buick Bonneville'98. It was purple-pink and had a 450-horsepower engine that roared powerfully whenever Joseph stepped on the accelerator.

After church, Joseph would often take black and white photos of Teresa and the girls all decked out in their Sunday best standing in front of their home. Keenly aware of technological advances, Joseph had eagerly awaited the arrival of color film. When it finally came on the market, he switched over from black and white, and family photos from then on are all in living – if gradually fading – color.

Two years after Anna joined the family, the Shappers celebrated the birth of Sofia, the fifth and final daughter. The now 43-year-old Teresa went into labor very early in the morning and Joseph drove her to the hospital. Shortly after Teresa checked in, Sofia came into the world, delighting her parents with her curly brown hair and brown eyes.

Leaving Teresa and the new arrival at the hospital, Joseph took his four older daughters to a park north of their home for a picnic. After their lunch, Joseph could not find his keys to the Buick. Everyone searched everywhere. Finally, Joseph realized that he'd probably locked them in the trunk when he'd taken out the picnic basket and blanket. Determined to retrieve his keys, he began taking out the back seat.

The girls were fascinated with their father's fevered effort to get into the trunk. Each tug on the back seat was accompanied by a deep growl, and Luisa grinned to herself at the thought that her dad was making the same sounds as a dog tugging on a bone. Finally, the seat came loose and Joseph pulled it out the door.

He then turned to his girls with an appraising look, sizing each one up. Constella was the wiry one and she was selected to retrieve the keys. It was dark in the trunk, but Constella found them, and triumphantly handed the keys to her father.

Joseph reinstalled the back seat and they packed up the Buick and headed back to the hospital. Joseph drove to the front entry, pointed to a window on the second floor and told the girls that was the room where their Mom and baby sister were staying. He then explained to them that it was against hospital rules for young children to visit, and that they would have to wait to see their new sister until Mom brought Sofia home.

Over the next two days, the older Shappers girls helped their proud father get the house ready for the arrival of their mother and Sofia. Out came the broom, out came the mop, out came the vacuum, and away went the toys.

The big day finally came, and both the adults and children in the neighborhood shared the jubilation of the Shappers. The women brought over cakes and cookies and cooed over the baby, the men continuously slapped Joseph on the back and prodded him out the back door for sips from a dark brown bottle being passed around, and the excited children danced through the house leaving trails of cookie crumbs.

In the days that followed, Alexia, Luisa, and Constella spent endless hours playing with both their little sisters. The kids in the neighborhood joined in and the Shappers house echoed with the sweet sounds of laughing children at play.

Teresa had her hands full. The now seven members of the Shappers family generated endless amounts of laundry, and she could simply not keep up with all of the washing and ironing.

Joseph realized what a heavy workload his wife was bearing, and hired an ironing lady to help.

Later that month, the Shappers family received the surprise of their life. Every month without fail Joseph bought a ticket for the church raffle, hoping but never really expecting to win one of the $100, $250 or $500 prizes.

Sofia must have brought the family luck because for the first time they won – and it was the grand prize of $500! Joseph and Teresa were elated, for after years of frugality they finally had some money they could spend any way they wanted. They decided to surprise the older girls with a trip to the Smokey Mountains.

As for Anna and Sofia, their Aunt Gwinnette, Teresa's eldest sister, offered to take care of them for the week. Aunt Gwinnette was Luisa's favorite aunt. Five foot four and 130 pounds, she had the carriage and manor of an Italian aristocrat. Her coiffeur, clothes and nails were always perfect, and she wore tons of jewelry, especially diamonds.

Aunt Gwinnette was very artistic and, over the years, she imbued Luisa with a knowledge and appreciation of art. She also taught her eager niece how to cook gourmet dishes. When Luisa was growing up, Aunt Gwinnette became like a second mother to her, and the young girl delighted in taking the bus to faraway Lake Choctaw in North Henderson, Tennessee – her little blue suitcase in hand – to spend several weeks with her aunt each summer.

Teresa and her helper spent hours ironing her family's clothes for the trip. The day of their departure soon arrived, and they packed up their suitcases and loaded the Buick for a week of adventures in Gatlinburg.

Before leaving the Clarksville area, they stopped at AAA to get a detailed roadmap of the county roads in Tennessee. Joseph drove as Teresa relaxed beside him, and the girls stretched out in the large backseat. By evening they had reached Knoxville,

Tennessee.

The next morning, the family got up early for breakfast. After devouring stacks of pancakes drowning in maple syrup, they hopped into the car and this time Teresa took the wheel. Although the mountain roads were steep and twisting, she drove at the speed limit.

The Buick was big, heavy, and powerful, and handled the mountain twists and turns with ease. When they arrived in Gatlinburg later that day, they discovered that the streets were crowded with people and lined with shops of all kinds.

Joseph suggested going to the hotel first, and everybody agreed that it was a good idea. Off they went to Howard Johnson to check in. Alexia, Luisa and Constella were immediately interested in the pool and the boys, and hurried to unload the car and change clothes. The three sisters spent hours at the pool that first day while Joseph and Teresa toured the local shops.

That evening they all ate McDonald's hamburgers for dinner, then – tired from their long drive – turned in early and slept like logs through the cricket-serenaded night. The week that followed was filled with walks in the mountains – where they saw their first black bears – hours spent boy watching at the sunlit pool, and light shopping. It was fun and relaxing, and all were somewhat saddened when it was time to pack up the Buick for the return trip. Two days later they arrived home and began planning for the new school year.

In the late 1950s, Joseph earned his Master's in Engineering. His postgraduate degree allowed him to earn a better salary, and he and Teresa decided it was time to buy a house in the suburbs where they could give their growing daughters a better way of life.

Their timing was perfect since mortgage interest rates were at a low four to six percent. Joseph and Teresa went to see a real estate agent and before long found a beautiful three-bedroom home.

They moved in and began a life that Luisa would later remember as idyllic. Every day brought new rewards, but their

Christmases were really special. They each received one carefully chosen gift for themselves, and were also given gifts to share. The year Luisa turned eight she received a red vinyl Her Treasures box.

The gift thrilled her. The box had a little girl dressed in blue and white on the cover with the words "Her Treasures" printed below. It even had a lock and key, and Luisa locked her most prized possessions – little figurines dressed in costumes from cultures all over the world – in the box.

The girls' shared Christmas gifts that year were a record player and a turquoise green and white Eldorado bicycle, which they cherished for many years. Luisa would buff and shine it every time she went for a ride, and used the bike to explore far and wide.

Luisa loved school. She even played school with Alexia, teaching imaginary students when she came home. Joseph also had a pretend friend he brought home from work. He named his invisible pal, Harvey, after the imaginary character in the Jimmy Stewart movie of the same name.

Along with playing school, Luisa enjoyed playing baseball with the neighborhood children. They organized their own teams, and even had their own baseball cards and batting averages. Joseph loved to join in the games when he got home from work.

Luisa's entrepreneurial talents were evident at an early age. She was still making her potholders; however, now she was selling them to the neighbors for 25¢ apiece. She also organized daily activities for the younger children in the neighborhood and charged 25¢ a week for each child. She read stories aloud and played 4-square, Jacks, marbles, and checkers with them. She even fixed picnic lunches for the children in her charge.

When Luisa became a teenager, she used most of the money she earned to buy 45 RPM records and soon amassed a large collection of songs by her favorite stars, including Ricky Nelson, the Everly Brothers, the Four Seasons, the Beach Boys, and the Beatles.

In August 1964 she and her grade school friends stood in line for hours to buy tickets to a coming Beatles concert in Cincinnati after the man then considered the greatest DJ in the Midwest - Dusty Rhodes, a local DJ with WSAI AM radio station - was able to bring the Beatles to Cincinnati.

The entire city pulsed with excitement. When the special day finally arrived, the star-struck teenagers took a bus to Old Crosley Field and found their seats behind the dugout on the third base side of the stadium.

It seemed like everyone from his or her school was there too. The teenagers all clapped and screamed and jumped up and down as the high voltage music shook the stadium. When the show was over, Luisa experienced yet another thrill when her friend Jamie McCartney got to hug Paul McCartney – who, unfortunately, was no relation – as the gray-suited Beatles ran into the dugout on their way to their dressing rooms.

Luisa took black and white photos of the "Fab Four" both during the performance and as they ran past the section where she was seated. When the pictures were developed, Luisa locked them and her concert ticket in her Treasures box.

A week after the Beatles concert, Joseph surprised Luisa and her sisters by announcing that the family was going to take a vacation in Florida. Joseph had just traded in their old Buick Bonneville for a brand new maroon and white 1964 Buick Bonneville and he was looking forward to the drive south.

Joseph had heard about a wonderful family resort called Lago Mar in Ft. Lauderdale. Owned by Walter Banks Sr. and his family, the resort boasted beautiful landscaping, waterways, sailboats, yachts and a view of incoming and departing ocean liners.

The entire Shappers family was excited, as they never had been to Florida before. Tingling with anticipation, Teresa and the girls sorted their clothing for the ten-day trip. Their luggage also included yellow rafts, sand toys, and buckets with shovels, multi-colored beach balls and a ton of towels. They even had beach hats.

When the car was fully loaded, Joseph whistled for his "harem of girls" – as he called them – to hop into the newly washed and waxed Buick. They were all so comfortable in the car. Joseph, Teresa and two-year-old Sofia sat up front while Luisa, Alexia, Constella and Anna nestled together in the back seat.

The Shappers were off to sunny and hot Florida for ten days of fun in the sun.

Driving steadily, they soon reached Knoxville, which was the first milestone on the long drive. Along the way the girls played car games, which made the time, pass quickly. Tiring of games, Luisa and Alexia polished both their own toes and nails and the toes and nails of their younger sisters. The two older girls also styled their siblings hair so the little ones would look gorgeous later on.

They sang songs together and sang along with songs on the radio as well. With the recent Beatles concert still fresh in her mind, Luisa led the others in spirited renditions of the mopheads' most popular releases.

As the Shappers reached the Florida state line, they saw a sign that welcomed them to the sunshine state and invited all to stop to sample the cold delicious orange juice. Joseph drove into the Welcome Rest Area. He parked the car. All his Harem girls were ready to have their picture taken at the Florida Welcome sign. After their brief break, they all loaded back into the car to head to St. Augustine.

The Shappers reached the old historic city of St. Augustine later that day and found a motel for the night. They rose early the next day and drove on down A1A to Ft. Lauderdale. Along the way, the attention of the girls was riveted on the beautiful Atlantic Ocean on their left.

Joseph stopped periodically to show his family the different beach areas. They saw crabs crossing the road and heard crushing sounds as cars drove over the crabs. That early evening they reached Lago Mar. The sky-blue/turquoise resort sign stood out boldly against the white facade of the resort complex.

The intercoastal waterway flowed in front of the resort and the Shappers drove over the bridge to the entrance. Lago Mar was even more beautiful than the pictures in the brochure Joseph had shown the family.

The resort was both elegant and casual; a secluded, tropical oasis nestled on the largest private beach in Fort Lauderdale's exclusive Harbor Beach neighborhood. Lago Mar was often called "the hidden treasure of the Gold Coast" because it combined old-world ambiance with contemporary luxury.

The handsome well-tanned porters wearing tropical shirts and crisp white slacks met the Shappers. Joseph checked his family into the Resort. Their rooms had an oceanfront View. The girls and Teresa commented about the beauty of the Lago Mar foyer with its hanging chandelier and beautiful flooring.

They felt like they were in Hollywood. Luisa and Alexia remarked that this was like watching Troy Donahue and Connie Stevens in Where the Boys Are. The porters even looked like the actor.

Luisa's dad had arranged for Luisa and Alexia to have their own room, which adjoined the suite where the rest of the family was staying. He also established a budget for their stay and gave $20 each to Luisa and Alexia for their weekly allowance.

After the family had settled in, Teresa went to the grocery store, for they had planned to be frugal and eat all their meals in the kitchen in their room. Even though the eating arrangements might be just like home, the atmosphere of Florida made everyone continuously aware that they were in a tropical paradise.

The girls loved playing in the blue-green Atlantic Ocean waters. They made figurines in the clean white sand with their beach toys. Joseph blew up the yellow rafts and multi-colored beach balls until he was almost blue in the face.

Teresa was concerned that her girls might get sunburned and came prepared with Noxzema cream and sunscreen. Sofia found the Noxzema and coated her body with the cream from head to toe. Her entire body was covered with a white frosting. It was so very funny to all the Shappers. Teresa brought out her Brownie color camera and took a picture.

Two-year-old Sofia did not want to wear anything else but her tiger-striped black and white bathing suit. A typical toddler, she even wanted to take her baths and sleep in it.

That evening, Luisa helped change Sofia into her nightclothes. Sofia resisted at first but Luisa patiently calmed her and told her that it was time to wash her tiger bathing suit. When the two-year-old took off her bathing suit her dark Sicilian skin was covered with a tiger-striped tan pattern. This discovery was so funny for all to see. Luisa tried her best to reassure her two-year-old sister that she could put on her suit the next morning.

The week brought new adventures for the Shappers that they had never experienced before. They met people from Europe and different parts of the United States and shared stories about their vacations.

Thirteen-year-old Luisa had read all about room service and – without asking her parents' permission – at mid-week she called down and ordered a glass of freshly squeezed orange juice. Shortly after her order was placed, there was a knock at the door. She opened it to find a handsome dark-haired, blue-eyed waiter with shining white teeth.

He was wearing a colorful shirt and white slacks and holding a round tray with her glass of orange juice. Luisa knew the juice cost $3. She only had her $20 bill. She proudly handed the $20 to the nice attendant.

He smiled and graciously said, "Thank you very much!" and left.

Luisa shut the door to drink her $3 glass of orange juice that had cost her $20. Later that day, Luisa told her dad about her room service experience.

Joseph slowly raised his left eyebrow and said, "That twenty dollars was your budget for the week and you've just spent it all on a glass of orange juice. When are you going to learn to be frugal and make your money last?"

Joseph was gentle but firm, much like Theodore Roosevelt saying, "Speak softly but carry a stick." This was a lesson for life.

The sunny weather lasted all week with crystal clear blue skies. Finally, like all good things, the family vacation ended and the Shappers packed to head home with forever-lasting memories. On the way back north they once again explored cities on the way.

When they reached West Palm Beach they drove past huge and beautiful mansions surrounded by blooming azaleas, rhododendrons and palm trees. They visited the space center at Cape Canaveral and stopped to watch cars driving on Daytona Beach's hard sandy beaches.

In St. Augustine, they visited an Alligator Exhibit and watched a man wrestle with a large alligator in a ring surrounded by gaping tourists. Luisa was enthralled by the danger involved in the event, and the scene stayed in her mind for days to come. The rest of the trip home went smoothly.

The Vietnam War was raging when Luisa was in high school and some of the boys she knew from her neighborhood were drafted into the Army. Luisa really missed her friends and she would write to them often. She even fashioned a helmeted soldier's head out of ceramic and wrote a poem on the base.

She gave the statuette to her friend, Anthony Jones, when he came home from his tour of duty in Vietnam. Anthony was changed after his military service overseas. He was more serious and pensive and did not want to talk about his Army experiences. To this day they are still friends.

Luisa took college preparatory courses in high school, including an advanced art program. Having taken private art lessons through grade school, she was highly qualified for the course and her creative and artistic talents soon surfaced. Her art teacher was especially impressed with her ability to work with equal ease in watercolors, ceramics, clay, and oil.

During this time Joseph was working full time and also studying for his Ph.D. Despite his busy schedule, he somehow found time to play sports with his beautiful daughters and help them study. He also took care of the yard work and helped the local church organize festivals and church councils.

Teresa volunteered at school and chaired the cookie committee for her daughters' Girl Scout Troop. In all she did, Teresa demonstrated her dedication to perfection and good Christian fellowship.

She continuously set a superb example for her five daughters, and as the girls matured they followed in their mother's footsteps.

Chapter 4

The Farm

As the car spun about, Luisa remembered fond memories of her father...

For many years Joseph toyed with building a new home for his growing family. He had long realized the value of real estate as an investment, and in 1958 he purchased hundreds of acres of rural farmland in Withering East, Indiana. A sharp businessman, he paid less than three thousand dollars for the property.

The farmland had abundant groves of cherry and walnut trees, and – it later turned out – sat on an oil deposit that added considerably to the value of the property. Joseph worked the farm on weekends, helped by Teresa and the children. When the chores were done, the family loved to walk the rolling fields, picking wild raspberries.

Joseph put in two lakes, one for family recreation and one for the cows to drink from. Wisely choosing to diversify his crops, he planted tobacco, soybeans, alfalfa, corn and hay fields. After much thought, he decided to rent out the small farmhouse, barn, garage and storage buildings.

His philosophy was to find someone he could trust and charge a low rent. For many years Joseph had loyal tenants named Joe and Karen Robinson, who lived on the farm with their two children, Victoria and Charlie.

Joseph treated the Robinsons like family. He made sure the rental house was always in good repair, and even built a new indoor bathroom to replace the existing outhouse. The tenant – a good, hardworking man – recognized and appreciated the opportunity Joseph was providing to him.

Ever the artist, Luisa painted many scenes of life on the farm during her visits. She even did a painting of the old outhouse shortly before it was torn down.

Luisa learned designing and engineering skills from her father. She had helped him convert the bare basement of their suburban home into a very nice recreation room with a bar, and had become familiar with tools, architectural plans and building materials during construction.

During visits to the farm, Luisa and her dad would huddle together, drawing up plans for both the farm buildings and their future home. In the years to come, she would put the skills her father taught her to good use.

In 1970, Joseph decided it was time to build their new home and chose a large lot in a newly developed residential neighborhood in southern Valley of Greenville, Kentucky. The house he designed was huge. It contained 16 rooms, including separate bedrooms for each of his five daughters.

The architectural style was Colonial and the front of the house was graced with a striking row of stately white pillars that soared to the roof. When the house was finished, Joseph proudly proclaimed that their new home was the Franco family version of Thomas Jefferson's Monticello.

The move to Valley of Greenville was quite an adjustment for the Shappers. It was difficult to leave family and old friends behind. It was especially painful for the girls to have to say goodbye to their schoolmates and to friends in the neighborhood they had known for years.

Adding to the girls' unease was the fact that the private schools they were about to enter were more advanced scholastically than the public schools they were departing.

Alexia was the only one who didn't have to go through changing schools. She was now attending Our Lady of the City College where she was studying biology and chemistry. She was also working in a lab, as well as a retail department store. Luisa was a senior in high school, while Constella was in the seventh grade, Anna was in the fourth grade, and Sofia was in second grade.

Despite her trepidation about switching schools, Luisa quickly made new friends and came to like her new teachers at Our Lady of the Rosary. In addition to the usual senior year curriculum, her advisor recommended that she take typing on her own, with a teacher personally checking on her progress.

Her courses included physics, chemistry and astrology, and Luisa found each subject exciting. Her English teacher taught her how to create colorful stories, which Luisa would read aloud. She soon came to like her English instructor, as well as the small class size. And the girls in the class made her feel welcome, even though she was a newcomer, and most had known each other for years.

The three younger Shappers sisters went to a local church school. Despite that they always had a lot of homework to do, they enjoyed their classes and reenacted their school day daily, even to the southern accent of the teachers. While their siblings played school, Luisa and Constella took piano and organ lessons.

The art class Luisa was in focused on free-hand drawing. The students used pastels to do their projects. Luisa had done this type of art years before and she shared some of her previous work with her teacher, who was impressed with the quality of her paintings. Luisa also helped other girls prepare their art portfolios for that spring's National and Local Scholastic Art Contest and Expedition.

She assembled her own portfolio of ink drawings,

watercolors and oils, along with her faceless ceramic statue of the Virgin Mary.

The teacher entered her students' portfolios in the contest and a few weeks later the winner was announced. Luisa won the Blue Ribbon award and recognition for her Virgin Mary statue. It was the most cherished award she had ever garnered. Her teacher explained that the statue would go on to enter National Competition.

Before long Luisa was notified that she was one of the top prizewinners in the National Competition. For an entire year, her statue traveled the country as the Scholastic Art winner, and then was put on exhibition at the Guggenheim Museum in New York.

The School Art Committee announced that they would make slides of Luisa's Virgin Mary statue available to schools across the country in the years to come to help art teachers prepare for the Annual Competition. Luisa was both honored and grateful that her art teacher had submitted her creative work for others to see. Today the statue occupies a place of honor in her home.

Luisa took college preparatory courses during her senior year at Our Lady of the Rosary. She was very popular with her fellow students and much enjoyed the many social functions she was invited to. Her graduation in 1971 was a source of great pride to her family, and her parents took endless pictures of her in her long white formal gown and matching white hat.

The following fall Luisa entered Village College in Valley of Greenville, Kentucky where she concentrated on the study of history and economics. Not long after entering college, she met a fellow student named Anton Cannoli.

Four years older than Luisa, Anton was 5-foot ten-inches tall and had a muscular 150-pound build. He had curly dark brown hair, brown eyes, chiseled cheekbones and a neatly trimmed mustache. He tended to wear preppy clothes and was meticulous about his appearance.

Anton had served in Vietnam from 1960 to 1965

and was going to school on his savings and the GI Bill, majoring in Computer Science. They had the same English and Biology courses and before long they started dating. Although their relationship was still casual, Anton was obviously smitten with the attractive co-ed from Tennessee and he would often leave notes and BC cartoons for her on the library table where they both studied between classes.

Although neither Luisa nor Anton could have guessed it at the time, as it turned out their relationship was to last not only through their college years but for the rest of their lives.

At that point in her life, however, Luisa was reluctant to commit herself and she continued to see other men – especially fraternity men – socially at the same time she was dating Anton. One of those men was a post-grad student in his last year of law school named Tom W. Freeby. Her friend Marie, who had met Tom through her boyfriend, Will, introduced Luisa to Tom.

Tom was a big man on campus in more ways than one. He was six-foot seven-inches tall and weighed slightly over 200 pounds. He had blue eyes, a pointed nose and chin, and a complexion so fair that after only an hour or so out in the sun his skin would turn rosy red.

A skilled communicator, Tom was very charismatic and had a sweet compassionate side to him. Like Anton, he favored preppy attire, even when he was busy washing his cherished navy blue '57 Chevy.

Luisa quickly realized that Tom was driven to succeed and had vision, passion and values. Before long, Luisa found herself enthralled with him. She did not want to hurt Anton, but at the same time she felt that she had to decide if he were the man she wanted to spend the rest of her life with.

While Luisa was earning both a History Degree and a Secondary Education Degree, she worked in the home furnishings department of a nearby retail department store. She enjoyed her work very much.

Constella worked at the same store as Luisa, as had Alexia before them. Alexia went into retail work after her college graduation. She later took some time off and traveled to Europe, which she loved. She never went back to work in hospital labs.

After college graduation, Luisa quit her retail job and entered the world of education. She got a teaching job at Peace High School in Newland, Tennessee and taught history to students ranging from freshman to seniors. Later she established a private tutoring program for those students who needed extra help.

Although she was only earning a modest salary, Luisa began to save for her first car. Anton encouraged her frugality, for he strongly believed you only appreciated what you earned for yourself. It took awhile but Luisa finally accumulated six hundred dollars and – after having Anton check the car out thoroughly – bought a red 1967 Volkswagen with a sunroof.

During her first year at Peace Academy, Luisa met a math teacher named Rita Sue. The two hit it off immediately and Rita Sue soon became like a fifth sister to Luisa, as well as a treasured friend of the Shappers' family.

The fast friends shared their innermost thoughts and Luisa revealed that she was torn between the two men she was dating. She told Rita Sue that she had long loved Anton, yet now found herself also falling in love with Tom.

What was she to do? Anton was content with their relationship yet seldom talked of a future together. He seemed equally reluctant to discuss either her goals and dreams or his own.

On the other hand, Tom talked openly to Luisa about his goals after graduating. He told her that he knew exactly what he wanted. Luisa confided to Rita Sue that her conflicting emotions about the two men in her life were getting more and more difficult for her to handle.

As she saw more and more of Tom, she told Rita Sue, her feelings for him were becoming more intense. They had begun making plans together for their future. Tom even wanted to build them a custom home near his parents' house to live in after they were married.

At the same time that she was dealing with her dating dilemma, Luisa was trying to decide whether to go to graduate school. Her father was very much in favor of her continuing her higher education, and offered to give her five acres of farmland if she earned her masters.

Luisa talked to Tom about her plans for graduate school, and he encouraged her to take the test to pursue a master's degree. Motivated by his enthusiasm, she began preparing for the test. Taking tests were difficult for Luisa because she had a fear of failure that sometimes almost overpowered her.

She turned to Tom for support and he provided a strong shoulder for her to lean on. On the evening before taking the MSAT, Tom hugged her tightly, pushing her long hair back behind her ears. He kissed her long and passionately and softly reassured her that she would pass the MSAT.

Luisa melted in Tom's strong arms and – after kissing him goodnight as they stood on the patio under a radiant moon – she went home with renewed confidence. That night, for the first time in weeks, she slept like a baby.

The next morning when she went in to take the MSAT she focused on Tom's encouraging words. When the test results were released a week later, Luisa was speechless with joy. She had passed with flying colors. When she rushed over to Tom's house to share the wonderful news, he was elated too. He helped her fill out her application for graduate school at Northern Rivers University, and several weeks later she was accepted.

Luisa and Tom were now spending more and more time together. Their dates consisted of playing tennis, talking for hours, going to concerts in the park, and attending gatherings at his family's home. Despite her growing involvement with Tom, she continued to date Anton as well. Juggling between the two men was putting Luisa on an emotional roller coaster ride. Just who was "Mr. Right?"

By permission of John L. Hart FLP, and Creative Syndicate, Inc.

Hoping to resolve the conflict raging inside her, Luisa finally decided that it was time for Tom and Anton to know about each other. She knew that she simply couldn't continue to date two men she had grown to love equally.

She realized that Tom was assertive and Anton was not, yet she wasn't sure whether this counted heavily in Tom's favor. Especially after her dad told her "still waters run deep," referring to Anton. She began to believe that Anton simply kept his emotions inside himself and Tom, as a soon-to-be lawyer, needed to be more aggressive to achieve success in his field.

Luisa carefully chose the moment to tell Tom about Anton. It came after a wonderful time at a University of Black Mountains football game. Following the game, they had dinner with Tom's parents and partied with his law school friends for a while, then went to Tom's apartment.

They sat on the sofa together and began kissing, and were soon quite aroused. Tom moved his strong yet gentle fingers under Luisa's blouse and began to fondle her swelling breasts. As he started to unbutton her blouse, she pulled back and looked him in his beautiful blue eyes.

Taking a deep, calming breath, she told Tom that she was also dating someone else, a man named Anton, and that she cared for Anton as much as she did him. Luisa would never forget the pained expression that came over Tom's face upon hearing her words.

He quickly removed his hand from her breasts and after a moment of shocked silence told her that she should probably go back to Rita Sue's house that night. He walked her to Rita Sue's front door and gave her a gentle if tentative kiss goodbye. As Luisa lay in bed that night, she felt like she had betrayed Tom. Perhaps she had betrayed Anton, too. After a sleepless night, she returned home the next morning, saddened, reflective and confused.

Anton called later that week and – although she was on the brink of asking him to come over so that she could tell him about Tom – she lost her nerve and put her confession off. After all, she reasoned to herself, her confession to Tom had obviously ended their relationship, and perhaps Anton would have the same reaction.

Although she would keep the memory of Tom within her for the rest of her life, a memory is a poor substitute for a flesh and blood man, and she dared not risk reducing Anton to a memory as well.

In February 1976, Anton proposed to Luisa and a wedding was planned for that August. To Luisa's relief, in the days and weeks that followed the young couple finally began to talk of their future together. The bride-to-be would later reflect that her relationship with Tom had taught her the importance of looking ahead and setting goals.

Luisa and Anton were both delighted when Father Charles Ralph, the pastor of the parish where Luisa taught school, offered them the use of his church and hall as a wedding present. Father Oscar Rubin, who was Tom Freeby's uncle, would assist Father Ralph at the ceremony.

Shortly after Luisa and Anton's wedding, Tom also got married. Today, 27 years later, he is still married to the same woman, and runs a successful law firm.

Anton and Luisa traveled to Ft. Lauderdale, Florida, for their honeymoon. After an idyllic seven days in the sun, they settled in Southlawn, Tennessee, and began their married life together.

After they had settled in, Luisa switched from teaching high school to teaching math, religion, science, history and art to seventh and eight grade students at St. Sebastian Catholic School in the rolling hills of northern Tennessee.

Luisa enjoyed teaching all subjects, but she especially liked imbuing an appreciation of art in her students. She involved the pupils in her classes in a wide range of art projects, including her favorite, silk-screening.

One of the most popular projects she introduced was the design of a class shirt. All the students submitted concepts, and when the votes were tallied a bunny rabbit design had won. Luisa had her pupils add preservatives to their paints so that the design would not wash out and to this day the surviving shirts look brand new.

Most of the children she taught put forth their best efforts, and she rewarded their hard work with good grades. One year she had a friend that knew a Cincinnati Slugger baseball player and arranged for the 1976 World champion baseball team to autograph official baseballs for her students.

Later in life, Luisa crossed paths with many of her former students in the business world, and discovered that few of them had forgotten her. It warmed her heart when several of the boys she had taught told her that they had always cherished the baseballs they received from the Hustlers. They kept the baseballs under glass domes and shared them with their children.

Math was easily the most difficult subject for her students to absorb. Determined to prepare each pupil fully for pre-algebra, she instituted individualized instruction for the math class and divided the students into nine levels, depending on their aptitude.

Throughout the week she rotated the teaching of each of those groups. She knew that math concepts build upon each other and wanted her students to learn how they arrived at their answers step-by-step.

To be certain that she was employing the most proven methods to teach math, she consulted with her sister, Constella, who taught math and English at a prestigious private school for boys. She also sought the advice of other high school math teachers. All agreed that it was critical for grade school students to have a solid foundation in math before beginning the study of algebra.

Luisa's conscientious teaching methods paid off and at the end of each school year almost all her students had mastered the subjects she taught and were fully prepared to move on to more advanced courses. To Luisa, her success as a teacher was measured in the success of her pupils.

In late 1977 Luisa faced a hard decision. At that time gasoline prices were rising rapidly due to the crisis in the Mid-East and every school day she had to drive 120 miles round-trip between her home in Clarksville and St. Sebastian far out in the Tennessee countryside.

Providentially, as Luisa worried about how to pay her ever increasing gas costs on her meager Catholic school salary, she was offered another teaching job at St. Anthony Francis Catholic grade school in Village of Woods, Tennessee, only twenty miles from her home.

The school's principal, Sister Mary Rose Brasilton, was familiar with Luisa's teaching methods and felt that she would be an excellent choice to teach the sixth, seventh and eighth grades at St. Anthony Francis. The timing was right, and Luisa decided to take the new job.

She was given a choice of subjects to teach and chose math, social studies, science and art. She individualized her math classes to help each of her 30 students learn pre-algebra and made her social studies classes interesting by staging historical plays and preparing authentic Thanksgiving meals.

Luisa loved biographies of American Inventors and had her students come up with concepts for inventions like the telephone, light bulb, water pump and cotton mill. Under Luisa's watchful eye, the students also made authentic period costumes. Twice a year the students would don their costumes and present their invention ideas to assemblies of students and parents in the school auditorium.

Luisa also had the students in her art classes make latch hook rugs, mold ceramics and paint pictures with watercolors. The students also made fruit baskets and lamps from Popsicle sticks. At Christmas time the students would fill the baskets with fruit and give them to the principal, teachers and school assistants.

The next two years were a tranquil and rewarding time in Luisa's life. She enjoyed her teaching job and her marriage to Anton was flourishing. Then a dark cloud blocked out the sunshine that had been bathing her life when her beloved father died at the all-too-young age of 54 in January 1978.

In February 1977, Joseph had gone to a dentist to have his wisdom teeth pulled. He emerged from the procedure with slurred speech and frequent dizziness. Hoping that his condition would improve, Joseph put off seeing a doctor for the next four months.

Finally – convinced that something was seriously wrong – he went to see Dr. Robert Balsam, a top neurosurgeon in the area. The surgeon immediately admitted Joseph to the hospital and ordered a CAT Scan. The test revealed a large blood cyst at the base of his cerebellum. The cyst was pressing against his brain.

As his family raced to the hospital, Joseph was wheeled into surgery for the delicate and dangerous operation to remove the cyst. Recovering in the ICU after the surgery, he was visited by each of his adoring daughters, who prayed beside their father's bed for his recovery.

Against all odds, Joseph did recover, and left the hospital a month after the operation. However, yet another medical ordeal was ahead, and this time not even his strong constitution and indomitable will to live would be able to pull him through.

The surgeon who had performed his operation had used metal clamps to close his sutures, and the ionized clamps led to blood poisoning and the formation of clots. The damage to Joseph's body was irreversible, and he died on February 13, 1980 on the way to his office.

Luisa had just arrived home when her mother called with the awful news. "He's gone," Teresa said in a hollow voice, causing Luisa to spill the box of oats in her hand all over the kitchen counter top. Devastated, Luisa did her best to console her mother, then hung up and called her neighbor, Olivia to come over and comfort her. Olivia did her best, but there was to be little serenity for Luisa that terrible day.

Joseph's death was all the more tragic because it came as the result of a terrible medical mistake that might easily have been prevented. Sister Mary Rose – as well as Louisa's teacher friends – consoled Louisa and helped her get through the ordeal of losing her father.

In the days and weeks that followed, Luisa did all she could to help her grieving mother through the ordeal. She took on many of the responsibilities that Joseph had borne, and spent as much time as she could with Teresa.

The sudden death of her dad hit her hard. He had died so young, and his passing made Luisa realize how short life was. She and Anton had been putting off starting a family until they had achieved a measure of financial stability. Now she wondered if it wasn't time to begin having children.

Before they could even think about the patter of little feet, though, they had to solve the problem of a suitable family home. They had planned to build an English Tudor house on a lot they had purchased in a newly developed subdivision. Unfortunately, the builder they selected had spread himself too thin and had gotten only as far as the foundation.

Luisa and Anton contacted a real estate attorney named David Harre, who advised them to put a lien on the property. Adding urgency to the matter, mortgage interest rates were rising rapidly, approaching double digits.

To finance their lien battle, the builder asked the Cannolis to apply the $14,000 deposit they had put down to have their home built to a model home already constructed. They agreed, and purchased the model home for $48,000.

In June 1980 Anton and Luisa tried to start a family, but Luisa failed to get pregnant over the next three months. Luisa sought advice from her dear neighbor, Olivia, who had given birth to five children. Olivia gave her a book on the Rhythm Method so that Luisa could better understand her biological clock.

With a Basal Thermometer and a calendar in hand, she recorded her temperature daily. This simple task recorded her ovulation peak time. It took a couple of months and then BINGO! The pregnancy test proved positive. Anton and Luisa were very excited.

During her months of pregnancy, Luisa felt the changes taking place within her body. One of her neighbors, a nurse named Mary, gave Luisa a stethoscope to hear all the growing baby sounds – including hiccups and body movements.

Anton had been a psychology major in college, and during one of his many fascinating experiments he had studied the movement of plant leaves in response to music. When he happened to mention the experiment to Luisa one day, she became fascinated and decided to play music for the baby growing within her.

She would listen to the baby's response while she played classical, religious, jazz, pop and rock. Much to her delight, the baby kicked differently to the sounds of the diverse music. Luisa continued playing both vocal and instrumental arrangements to her unborn child, praying that the prenatal experience would develop a love of music in her baby.

As it turned out, her prayers were answered. Her first child, Rosanna took an interest in music at an early age and later developed a gift for both the piano and guitar. Luisa also exposed her second daughter to music while she was still in the womb, and Carmella turned out to be a talented musician as well.

During her first pregnancy Luisa gained so much weight that one day while talking on the phone she sat down in a blue recliner and couldn't get back up. Much to her embarrassment, she had to call her neighbor and friend, Eve, to help her up. To this day, the two women still laugh about the day Luisa and her enormous belly got stuck in the recliner.

Following the birth of Rosanna, Luisa decided to leave teaching and care for her daughter full time at home. Although her income had been low, the money had allowed her and Anton to take vacations and go out to dinner frequently with her friends and families, and both soon missed their leisure activities.

It wasn't long before Luisa's teacher's salary was missed in other ways. The country had slipped into a recession and the steel frame company Anton worked for hit hard times. His yearly bonus of $8,000 was cut off and the new parents were suddenly faced with a greatly reduced income of $22,500 a year.

As that summer faded into fall, Luisa and Anton discussed ways to supplement the money coming in. Anton, an Engineer, liked the new outdoor furniture made from PVC (Polyvinyl Chloride).

Luisa's entrepreneurial talents rose to the surface and she proposed that the two of them design and market their own outdoor furniture line. Anton quickly agreed. He used his engineering skills to design frame sizes and fabrication methods while Luisa figured out sling and cushion sizes for the frames.

They founded a company called Deck and Patio PVC Furniture and set up a small factory in their garage. Once the company was established, Luisa's sisters helped them get their furniture line into the Homerama homes of established builders the following spring.

Luisa and Anton also designed a unique company brochure featuring hand-drawings of patio furniture and began marketing their products through local garden centers and swimming pool companies.

Since Anton still worked at the steel company during the day – and their market was seasonal – they both labored late into the night during the spring and summer, turning out as much PVC furniture as they could while the demand remained high.

Somehow Luisa managed to juggle motherhood and work. When things got too frantic, she would often ask her neighbor, Olivia, to help with some of the fabrications and sewing. Their hard work paid off and they were soon selling 50 sets of furniture or more each season.

For the Cannolis, it was the beginning of a cottage business that helped them over their financial hump and taught them that there was little in this world they couldn't accomplish together.

Chapter 5

Adventures at Lure Lodge

Visions of friends in colorful clothing applauding, and children laughing appeared before Luisa...

There were at least 20 children in the Sunrise Hills subdivision where the Cannolis now lived, many of them around the same age. In fact, between September and November of 1986, nine babies were born within walking distance of the Cannoli home.

Luisa and Anton went to so many baby showers they joked that either the water was causing all the pregnancies or they must have all gotten drunk at the neighborhood New Year's Eve Party.

One of the wonderful things about the neighborhood was that everyone partied together. They had Halloween parties, Tupperware parties, Longenberger Basket parties, Pampered Chef parties and birthday parties. Individual families also hosted cookouts.

Families in the neighborhood had numerous yard sales, as well, with everyone helping each other. When it was Luisa and Anton's turn to have a sale, nearby neighbors would rush over with items to sell. One year the thrifty lady that lived across the street even sold her underwear!

At one of their sales Luisa learned that there's a buyer for literally anything. A stranger stopped by and spotted a stack of broken garage door sections in the back of their garage. He asked how much Luisa wanted for them. Dumbfounded – the door parts weren't even for sale and were in fact on their way to the dump – she regained her composure and told him $75.00. The man quickly agreed to the price and lugged the heavy wooden sections out to his truck.

The parties and garage sales helped unite the neighborhood and to this day – even though many families have since moved away – whenever the old neighbors run into each other they exchange fond memories of the happy times they shared in their Mr. Rodgers neighborhood.

As Luisa's daughters grew, she began taking them to beauty salons to have their hair done. The beauticians loved styling the girls' hair and doing their nails. Rosanna, now five years old, and Carmella, age one, grew especially fond of a hairdresser named Liza.

Liza french-braided Rosanna and Carmella's hair. Even though Rosanna was only five, she watched what Liza was doing closely and soon learned how to braid her own hair.

The girls' 11-year-old cousin, Laurie, was always over at the Cannoli house and she often went to the beauty shop with Rosanna and Carmella. The stylists got a kick out of Laurie because she would walk into the beauty shop with her white parakeet perched on her shoulder.

Luisa believed that introducing Rosanna and Carmella to varied experiences would stimulate their minds and she took them to parks, museums, zoos, festivals, and on excursions to downtown Clarksville.

The Cannoli women were especially active around the holidays. At Christmas they went to see live reindeer in a holiday corral on Fountain Square in downtown Clarksville, and later stared in awe at the Square's gigantic Christmas tree.

During other excursions the girls rode elephants, camels and horses, discovered the thrill of Ferris Wheel, roller coaster and carousel rides – Luisa was especially enamored of carousels – and listened to music at open air concerts. Listening to the music and the laughter of her daughters having a good time made Luisa's heart soar.

Their trips to Disney World and Magic Kingdom were awesome. There were long lines but no one cared. It was well worth the wait for the imaginative rides that transported them to faraway fantasy worlds. They also collected the autographs of all the Disney characters they encountered and got their pictures taken with Mickey, Donald, Snow White and a dozen other cartoon stars.

During their trips to the Disney theme parks, Luisa and Anton spoiled their girls shamelessly, allowing them to fill up on cotton candy, snow cones and multi-colored lollipops between rides. They also permitted Rosanna and Carmella to stay up late watching television in the Disney hotels they stayed at.

The parental indulgence was a way for Luisa and Anton to reward their daughters for being so good the rest of the year. The arrangement made their trips fun for everyone, and produced wondrous memories that are preserved in the well-thumbed Cannoli family photo albums.

The Cannolis also spent many vacations with family members and friends. These were delightful times when Rosanna and Carmella got to have fun with their cousins, Phillip and Laurie and their parents' friends, Seth, Lynne, Arnold and Diana. Family and friends would spend their days singing, playing cards, swimming, fishing, and riding bikes. At night, while the children watched videos, Luisa and Diana would drink Bloody Marys until they were bleary-eyed.

Although the Cannoli family always had a wonderful time on their vacations, Luisa and Anton also had to pay the bills and they both worked hard at their vocations. Luisa paid close attention to the design needs and preferred styles of the builders she worked for. She also conscientiously began to establish relationships with contractors and suppliers.

In her college years Luisa had studied history and economics and she possessed an impressive knowledge of the world economy. She had also used part of her salary as a teacher to invest in the stock market and was familiar with the ways of Wall Street. She and Anton had their eye on a lot they wanted to buy, and Luisa decided that investing was a good way to earn the down payment.

Before they could move up to a better home, they knew that they would have to sell their existing property and Luisa and Anton set to work to fix up their small split-level home. Finally, the interest rates fell into single digits. It was time to pursue their goal to move.

For nine years Luisa had planned this project. The first thing she did was to contact a builder that she had worked for five years before and arranged with him to build an English Tudor shell. She would handle the interior construction and completion. However, the builder wanted an unreasonable $200,000 to build the shell, and Anton and Luisa declined.

The next approach was for the Cannolis to act as their own general contractors. Anton took real estate courses while Luisa studied construction books. They also interviewed Henry Delage from Green Builders who agreed to build the shell of their new home at a fair price. Mr. Delage advised the Cannolis on what supplies to buy and how to hire other subcontractors to assist in the construction of their home.

The Cannolis decided not to build on the original lot they had picked out. Instead, Henry assisted in helping them find another lot to build the English Tudor. Now Luisa had to get a construction loan. Being female and inexperienced as a builder, it was difficult to obtain a loan. Finally, the Cannolis obtained the loan at a nine-percent interest rate.

Luisa hired her long time friend, Nina, as a file clerk to assist in organizing their construction file. Nina wrote the work orders for each contractor and followed them up with start dates and schedules for each job.

The project had to be completed in six months. Luisa and Anton selected their products, brick and shingles. The bidding process took one month to complete, with Luisa obtaining bids from subcontractors for each phase of construction.

The project began on time and was on schedule the whole way. Henry built the Cannolis a beautiful English Tudor and the subcontractors honored their commitments to do the work as scheduled. Building their own home gave the Cannolis much satisfaction.

Their English Tudor home dearly demonstrated Luisa's design capabilities to potential clients. As her company grew, word spread of her ability to be a general construction consultant with reasonable rates.

Luisa had always believed that excellence was worth the effort put forth, and – whether the project she was working on was a new home, a remodel or a decorating job – her credo was reflected in the consistently superlative work she did for her clients.

Her motto was, "Do your best no matter what. Be honest and fair in pricing and you will succeed."

Her company, Luisa's Interiors, grew steadily over the years and she eventually employed three full-time remodeling crews. Her work – and professional ethics – were so esteemed that she maintained 30 large clients for many years.

Luisa's life – both professionally and personally – was now going well. She attributed much of her success to the fact that she had her priorities in order. She held dear the Lord, her family and her friends, and she lived her life guided by Christian values.

In June 1990, Luisa and two of her friends, Caroline and Suzanne, decided to take their six kids and three other children of friends to the Cumberland State Park in Kentucky for a four-day stay at the Lure Lodge. Several years before Luisa had fallen in love with the park while on a boating vacation with Anton and his sister and her husband.

The three adults and nine children squeezed into a Ford Club station wagon with a bag of snacks and a soda for each kid. The plan was for the moms to relax around the pool while the kids played.

Their visit to the Lure Lodge was always an adventure. On one visit the fire alarm went off in the middle of the night and all the guests had to rush outside. The women had their nighties on and the kids clutched their tattered security blankets. Little Julie cried for her dolly, which was at home five hours away. Caroline, who was with her through it all, settled her down.

The moms were on a tight budget of $60 each for the four-day holiday and this had to cover food, entertainment and lodging. To keep within their budget they stayed in one room.

With three adults and nine kids packed into the room, just finding space to sit down was a challenge. Somehow – using both the two full beds in the room and the assortment of sleeping bags they had brought along – everyone managed to find a place to sleep.

Luisa, Caroline, and little Carmella slept in one twin bed while Suzanne and Madison shared the other. Chris, Rosanna, Mary, Stu, Jason, Kim and JoAnn slept in sleeping bags on the floor.

One night as Carmella tossed and turned her toes ended up in Caroline's nose! It was too much for Caroline and she abandoned the bed and found solace on the floor between the beds.

As she tossed and turned on the floor, the sound-asleep Caroline worked her way toward the nightstand and ended up with her head inside. She awoke with a startle and screamed, "I'm blind! I can't see!"

Her cries woke everyone up and both mothers and children broke into hilarious laughter upon seeing Caroline with her head inside the nightstand. To this day everyone still laughs loudly when remembering the humorous sight.

On the second day they decided to take out a pontoon boat and go fishing, all nine of them. However, the dockhand said there were only eight life jackets per pontoon. It seemed an unsolvable dilemma until Luisa had a sudden inspiration.

She led the gaggle of gawking moms and kids some distance away and explained her plan. They would empty the large red and white cooler they had with them and hide three-year-old Carmella inside. Now down to eight, they would then board the boat, don their life jackets and motor out beyond sight of the dock, and then let Carmella out.

The plan worked flawlessly and ten minutes later they reached the middle of the fish-laden lake and a widely grinning Carmella hopped out of the cooler midst a round of laughter.

The kids couldn't wait to start fishing. Their poles weren't the best but the fish were biting and the boat soon echoed with excited shouts of "I've got one!" The three moms spent most of their time putting worms on hooks and untangling lines.

It was a gorgeous day and when the youngsters tired of fishing they took turns driving the pontoon boat on the sunlit lake. They stayed out until lunchtime, and then went back to the dock – Carmella once again hidden in the cooler – and got ready for lunch.

That evening they went to the lodge and lined up for dinner. Caroline looked over the menu and asked the kids if they'd like corndogs for dinner. Little Carmella looked hard at Caroline – her dark brown eyes reflecting revulsion – and announced, "I don't eat dog bones!"

Everyone cracked up. Luisa explained to her youngest what corndogs were, and Carmella relented – although she remained wary until their meal actually arrived. Everyone ended up having corndogs and fries and after dinner they all went outside to watch the local raccoons eating leftovers. The kids were in awe at the number of raccoons there were, and how they varied in size.

It happened that one of Luisa's friends owned a T-shirt shop near the lodge and she generously provided shirts for all to wear. The boys' shirts featured images of Lamborghini cars while the girls' shirts displayed pictures of famous gymnasts. To the amusement of all, several guests at the Lodge asked the girls if they were in training for the Olympics.

The group spent the remainder of their stay enjoying the many recreational opportunities available at the lodge and park, including horseback riding, swimming, hiking and animal watching.

When it was time to leave Lure Lodge and return home, everyone reluctantly piled into the car. No one had wanted the fun to end. Still, both adults and children had stored away wonderful memories – and recorded others on film – and in the years to come all would look back fondly on their stay at the park.

For the Cannoli family, August meant anniversaries and birthdays. Luisa and Anton's wedding anniversary was August 7 and Luisa's parents' anniversary followed a few weeks later in September.

Sofia's birthday was on August 20th, Anton's birthday arrived on August 23rd, and Teresa's birthday was on August 25th. In addition, many of their friends also had birthdays in August. Luisa thought it would be a good idea to have a single large party to celebrate all the many anniversaries and birthdays at once.

Her high school had organized a scholarship fundraiser in the mid 1980's called Lobsterfest and she decided to ask her family if they would like to organize a similar event at the Cannoli home to celebrate everyone's big day. All agreed that it would be a great idea.

Each family member chipped in to buy the lobsters, and everyone also brought a dish. Luisa and Anton set up colorfully decorated tables and chairs, provided abundant drinks for both adults and children and – with the help of other family members – organized entertainment.

Several of Luisa's cousins helped out at the party. The women dropped the live lobsters into big pots of boiling water set on charcoal grills in the backyard and a few minutes later the men fished the crustaceans out and steamed them on the grill. Along with the lobsters the family dug into shrimp, scallops and steak.

The scrumptious spread also included both spinach and fruit salad, several vegetables, and a wide variety of fresh fruits. Anyone who still had room in their stomach could choose cheesecake, pineapple-upside-down cake, brownies or Amaretto orange cake for dessert.

After dinner, the women sipped wine and talked about fashion and child raising while the men – cold beers in hand – huddled around the television to watch sports and howl at the jokes of the two comedians in the group, Poom-Baw Eddie Luella and Richie Margale.

Although only a handful of family members and friends came to the Cannolis' first lobsterfest, in the years to come the event would expand into an annual neighborhood celebration attended by over 100 people.

Chapter 6

The Passing of Poppa

Luisa screamed " Oh Lord, I am being crushed!" as she heard a horrendous crashing sound, and the car shuddered to an abrupt halt… As she drifted into unconsciousness, she remembered the sudden passing of her father-in-law.

Through the mid-1990s, Luisa, Anton and the girls flourished as never before. Everything was going well at work, at school and in their family life together. Nineteen ninety-seven rolled around and Luisa and Anton decided to plan a family vacation in Aruba after buying a timeshare at the Blue True Resort on Lake Buena Vista, Florida.

Before making arrangements to travel to Aruba, they bought a membership in Internal International Travel Club because the cost of their island vacation – as well as other vacations in future – would be so much more affordable if they were members of the highly regarded club.

Interval International was affiliated with five-star resorts all around the world. The Cannolis' trip to Aruba would be their first travel adventure outside the U.S. and they excitedly planned their vacation for the April/May school spring break.

The cost was only $1500 for airfare and five-star accommodations for the family of four for a week. Luisa contacted Aruba's Chamber of Commerce and obtained a list of scheduled events and favored places to visit on the beautiful island.

Concerned about the health risks of international travel, Anton contacted the Disease Control Center to inquire whether his family needed any shots or should take any other health precautions during their stay in Aruba. He was informed that the whole family had to take the drug, Larium, for three days prior to leaving to guard against contracting malaria.

Unfortunately, even as Luisa and Anton planned their well-deserved vacation, a black cloud hovered over the family. Anton's father – who was now 89 years old – was suffering from increasingly severe congestive heart failure.

A self-sufficient native of old-world Sicily – where men considered going to the doctor to be a mark of weakness – Poppa had neglected needed medical care for years. Instead, he focused on maintaining his home and garden. Now neither he nor the family could any longer ignore his rapidly failing health.

Anton's brother Mercede, a medical doctor who lived and practiced in California, cancelled his upcoming appointments and flew east to visit Poppa at his home in Clarksville, Tennessse. Mercede was immediately alarmed by his father's worsening condition.

Mercede was a firm believer in Holistic healing and practiced many of the natural Chinese and Japanese methods for curing illnesses. He had long been sending Anton and their mother, Mela, literature about vitamins and natural remedies for illnesses. They, as well as Luisa, followed Mercede's advice and took the vitamins he had recommended. Luisa considered him to be ahead of his time in the practice of medicine.

Among Poppa's physical problems was a loss of hearing. For years the family had been trying to persuade him to get a hearing aid. Now – just about on his deathbed – he unexpectedly asked Luisa to take him to get a hearing aid.

The next day Luisa took Poppa to a hearing specialist to be fitted for a hearing aid. A problem arose when the specialist informed Poppa that the cost of the test and the hearing aid would come to $700. Pappa had Medicare but no private health insurance and very little money. Luisa called Anton about the problem and he told her to give the specialist a check and he would split the cost with his siblings.

When they left the doctor's office, a big smile came over Poppa's face and he surprised Luisa by telling her that he could hear birds chirping. It was the first time he had heard the sweet sound in years.

Luisa called Anton back to share the moment, and then handed the phone to an excited Poppa. Poppa's eyes lit up for he could actually hear Anton on the phone.

Another first!

Her father-in-law's happiness at being able to hear again renewed Luisa's conviction that there is no joy greater than helping someone in need.

That took care of the hearing aid, but the family now faced the thorny issue of how they would pay for Poppa's inevitable hospitalization.

Luisa called her closest cousin, Alice – who had mentored her in child rearing and was familiar with health care plans – and asked her advice on what to do about Poppa's medical needs. It turned out that Alice had some useful contacts and she put Luisa in touch with a nurse who helped the elderly receive better Medicare coverage through United Healthcare Insurance.

Louisa called United Healthcare immediately and arranged for Pappa, Mela and herself to meet with a company representative to set up coverage. Within days Poppa was covered. Everyone in the family breathed a sigh of relief as Poppa's health was steadily declining.

Luisa felt that the trip to Aruba should be cancelled so that the family could remain at home near Poppa. They had insurance that would reimburse the trip cost. Anton did not see the need to change their plans and insisted that they did not give up their sorely needed vacation.

Luisa was uncomfortable with Anton's decision. In addition to Poppa's health problems, she was very busy with her work. She was finishing a huge project that involved the design and construction of a residential/commercial building for a lawyer. She had nearly completed the project and the lawyer was ready to move in. The furniture had been ordered the previous fall and was waiting for delivery.

A week before they were to leave, Poppa began having chest pains and Luisa picked him up at his home to drive him to the hospital. She explained that she had to pick Rosanna and Carmella up at school on the way.

On the way to the girls' school, Poppa said, "My feet are ice cold. They feel like I've been walking barefoot through the snow."

Luisa gave him a worried look, thinking that the old man looked as ill as she'd ever seen him. A few minutes after they'd picked up Rosanna and Carmella, Poppa suddenly announced that he was thirsty.

"Would you like a malt?" Louisa asked.

"Sure would," Poppa said.

Louisa glanced in the mirror at the girls in the back seat. "We're going to stop at the ice cream parlor," she said. "What would you two like?"

"Cones!" Rosanna and Carmella said in unison.

Poppa savored every drop of his malt like it was his last drink. Watching him out of the corner of her eye, Luisa's eyes welled up with tears.

Finally, they arrived at the hospital and after a quick examination the ER nurse announced that Poppa was in cardiac arrest. He was immediately admitted to the Cardiac Care Unit.

Now Luisa knew the trip to Aruba simply had to be cancelled. They were to leave the next morning, which was Good Friday.

She called Anton and he rushed over to the hospital, arriving with tears in his eyes. The doctor advised the family that Poppa was stable but that his insurance only covered a three-day stay in the hospital. After that he would have to be moved to a nursing home.

Poppa simply didn't have the money to pay the hospital bills that his insurance didn't cover. What was going to happen? Anton's niece, Madison, who was in charge of Poppa's medical care, told Luisa and Anton that she would look into options for Poppa's care and that the family should continue with their plans to go to Aruba.

Having done all they could for the moment to straighten out Poppa's medical insurance, Luisa and Anton went to his room to see how he was doing. The dinner on his tray was untouched. Luisa picked up a fork and carefully started to feed him.

Poor Anton could only stare at his father in grief. Stealing a glance at her husband's stricken face, Luisa knew in her heart that this would be the last time he would see his dad alive.

"We've got to do as much as we can for him," Anton said, his voice cracking.

In an effort to take Poppa's mind off his condition, Luisa spoke of their plans to go to Sicily in a few years to visit his birthplace.

His face softened as he reminisced about his home village of Mineo. He spoke of how beautiful the olive gardens were in his beloved Sicily and how he had missed his home village all these years.

Soon after Luisa finished feeding Poppa, the nurse came in and told them it was time for the old man to rest. Luisa went and got Rosanna and Carmella from the waiting room so that they could tell their grandfather how much they loved him and say goodbye.

As Luisa and the girls left Poppa's hospital room, they all knew that death was near. Anton stayed with his dad for a few more minutes, and then joined them in the parking lot. Tears filled his eyes and once again Luisa tried to talk him into canceling their trip to Aruba. Anton shook his head no and said that missing their vacation wouldn't help Poppa. It was better to simply go on with life.

Anton had driven himself to the hospital so they returned home in separate cars. A pall shrouded the Cannoli home that night and few words were spoken. Everyone had already packed for the trip and the family went to bed early, their hearts heavy with worry about Poppa even as their minds whirled with thoughts of the exciting island adventure that awaited them.

The next morning they got up early and drove straight through to Atlanta to catch their flight to Miami. Luisa called their niece, Christina, and was told that Poppa was stable. Reassured, the Cannolis boarded the plane to Miami.

Luisa called Christina again from the Miami airport and learned that Poppa was still in stable condition. The family breathed a sigh of relief and boarded the plane for Aruba.

The Air Aruba flight over the Caribbean was smooth. While Anton napped, Luisa talked to some of the other passengers, Rosanna put on earphones and listened to music, and Carmella played with her Gameboy. As the plane descended toward Aruba, the pilot circled the island, describing the various points of interest.

They breezed through Customs and then headed for the car rental booth, passing colorful stalls where boisterous vendors were hawking wares in a language unique to the island.

Anton rented a white Mazda for $400 a week – which he considered reasonable – and they packed their luggage into the trunk and drove to the Royal Caribbean Beach Resort where they had reservations.

The family was soon settled into a spacious condo. Luisa and the girls were anxious to take a dip in the warm emerald sea and they quickly changed into their bathing suits. Although Anton had been putting on a brave front since they'd left home, he was obviously suffering inside and Luisa understood when he announced that he wanted to take a walk by himself.

After a while Anton joined Luisa and the girls on the beach and the family spent several hours enjoying the sun and the surf. When everyone started to redden from the warm rays, Anton suggested that they take a drive around the island.

Luisa and the girls agreed and they set off to explore their vacation paradise. They drove first to the oldest chapel on Aruba where they stopped to say prayers for Poppa. They then began to circle the island, admiring the breathtaking beauty of the tropical wonderland. Luisa videotaped every scene, including the wild goats grazing on the hillsides.

They discovered a golf course, a lighthouse and several beautiful beaches. After exploring for a couple of hours, they headed back to town. They had decided to eat out that evening and went to a local restaurant that the resort had recommended.

Along with delicious food, the restaurant provided musical entertainment, and everyone thoroughly enjoyed their dinner that night, although the $210 tab seemed a bit stiff to the thrifty Anton. After dinner they drove back to the condo where Anton, Luisa and the girls – exhausted after their long, busy day – all went to bed early.

At midnight the telephone rang in the condo. Luisa answered and listened wordlessly as Christina told her that Poppa had passed away a half-hour before. Although the news broke Luisa's heart, she was not surprised. Her elderly father-in-law had simply been too ill to last long.

She chose not to awaken Anton. She knew the days ahead would be draining for him, and – tonight at least – she was determined that he get some much-needed sleep. As for herself, she tossed and turned half the night.

At dawn, she woke Anton and broke the sad news. He merely nodded, then got dressed and went off by himself. While he was gone, Luisa called down to the front desk to make arrangements to go home. Unfortunately, it was Easter morning and there were no scheduled flights going in or out of Aruba.

Luisa looked up Mass times at the local Catholic Church and when Anton returned she and the girls got dressed and they all went off to the beautiful island church to pray for Poppa's soul.

After Mass, they found a restaurant on the shore and ate breakfast on the patio, then returned to the condo. Luisa made arrangements with Delta for the family to fly home the next day. Their flights to Miami and Atlanta went smoothly. On the flight Luisa and Anton decided that it would be best if he flew the rest of the way home while Luisa and the girls followed in the car they had left at the Atlanta airport.

After Anton took off, Luisa and the girls started their drive home. They were tired, however, and decided not to make the entire road trip in one day. Instead, they stopped overnight in Knoxville, which meant that they would reach home on Tuesday.

Unbeknownst to Luisa, Anton's sister, Virginia, had planned Poppa's funeral for Tuesday. When Anton told Luisa the news during their phone call Monday night, she realized that they would have to leave Knoxville very early the next morning if they were going to make the service.

The drive home from Knoxville went smoothly and Luisa and the girls quickly got dressed for the funeral that started at 4:00pm. Luisa looked rested and relaxed, but inside she was stressed out.

She kept thinking, How could Virginia have scheduled the funeral only two days after Poppa's death when they had been in Aruba and other relatives lived out of town?

The funeral mass was the next day and it went smoothly.

During the rest of the week the Cannolis struggled to recover from the stress brought on by Poppa's death. Luisa kept her mind off things by helping her mother-in-law, Mela straighten out her precarious finances. Poppa had never believed in long range planning and as a result he never accumulated much in savings.

Luisa had time to help Mela as her construction project for her lawyer client was now 95% complete. Her company had some small projects to attend to – window treatments, carpets, paint, and furniture – but nothing overwhelming.

The lull in her business responsibilities would also give Luisa the chance to go to Disneyland with their best friends Arnold, Diana, Seth, and Lynne to see Lynne march in a parade with her flag core group. Unfortunately, Anton was too busy at work to go along.

Although the summer school vacation had just ended, Luisa wanted Rosanna and Carmella to enjoy Disneyland with her and she took them out of school the Friday before the trip so that they could have a three-day weekend at the theme park.

They arrived in Orlando and stayed at their timeshare, Blue Tree Resorts at Lake Buenos Vista, which was only minutes from Disneyland. That first night they met Diana for dinner at the rustic Wilderness Lodge then took a boat over to Magic Kingdom. Lynne went with her flag core group to practice for the afternoon parade at MGM.

Suddenly a thunder and lightning storm erupted overhead and torrents of rain poured down, flooding much of the park. The director of Lynne's Flag Core group was notified by Disneyworld officials that the parade would have to be canceled due to the flooding.

The disappointing news put everyone in a blue mood. Still, the group had come to Disneyworld to have fun and they decided to don their yellow Mickey Mouse ponchos and enjoy the sodden park as best they could.

That evening Diana suggested that they have dinner at Epcot to see the fireworks. Everyone agreed and they dined at the French restaurant by the lighted lake, which offered a perfect view of the fireworks.

After a delicious dessert of French pastries and hot chocolate, they said goodbye to each other – they all had separate early flights out the next morning – and called it a night. It had been a weekend they would all long remember.

During the month that followed the trip to Disneyworld, Luisa continued to help Mela with her finances and healthcare concerns. She arranged with a SLM financial advisor for non risks funds so that the elderly lady would earn at least a little interest on the money that she had.

Luisa had now finished her large project for the lawyer and all had gone well. The client was happy with his new office and furnishings, and he spoke of potential additional projects for Luisa in the future.

Luisa had another project nearing completion. Her client, Hasson, had hired her to update their first floor furniture, window treatments, wallpaper, and paintings. Most of their items ordered were in storage and ready for delivery.

Luisa liked to have three to four weeks for design projects because of the myriad details inherent in organizing all the steps in the design and selection process. As this project came closer to wrapping up, Luisa switched her attention to planning a Hilton Head vacation with Caroline and Suzanne and their kids during the coming school summer vacation.

Before leaving, she scheduled an appointment with her physician for her annual physical examination. She had been feeling rather stressed out lately, and she knew the reason for her tension: Rosanna.

Although Rosanna was very bright and – on the whole – a wonderful daughter, she was also a teenager experiencing all the changes that go with the transition from child to young adult. Like her friends, 16-year-old Rosanna wanted to party and "hang-out," and that meant drinking. The alcohol issue had caused several confrontations between mother and daughter.

During Luisa's examination, her physician, Dr. Grizzly diagnosed a very mild case of hypertension and ordered a stress test to insure that she didn't have any heart problems that needed treatment.

Dr. Grizzly sent her to the Cardiac Care Institute for the test. Physicians at the Institute discovered that she was suffering from a Mitral Valve Prolapse and gave her nitroglycerin to take should she ever experience a serious heart problem.

During the third week of June, Luisa, Suzanne, Caroline and their nine kids climbed into three minivans and headed for a vacation in Hilton Head, South Carolina. The minivans were packed to the roofs with beach chairs, floats, duffel bags, tennis and badminton rackets, munching food and drinks.

During the ride down, the teenage girls with drivers' licenses constantly badgered their mothers to let them drive. By the time they reached Knoxville, the teenagers had browbeat Luisa, Suzanne and Caroline into agreeing to the switch.

When the girls were at the wheel, Caroline reached for her Valium, Suzanne prayed hard to St. Jude – the patron saint of lost causes – and Luisa hoped that she wouldn't need her nitroglycerine.

The three Moms needn't have worried for the girls drove fine. They were quite confident, and the women used the cell phones in the minivans to keep everyone together during the journey.

After a conference call between cars, they decided to stop in Charleston for the night. The stay would leave only a three-hour hop to Hilton Head the next morning. They found a Motel 8 on the outskirts of town with a $25.00 room rate that fit their tight budgets.

After checking into their rooms, the group found a truck stop restaurant called the Green Lizard. The kids were starving and hurriedly ordered juicy hamburgers, chips and cokes. After dinner they went back to the hotel for the night.

They all slept well and the next morning the group drove into Charleston to do some sightseeing. After a self-guided tour of the beautiful city, they ate lunch together at an outdoor café and then headed for Hilton Head.

Everyone had a wonderful vacation at the beach, highlighted when the older kids got their picture taken by a newspaper photographer while they were surfing. To the delight of all, the picture appeared the next day on the front page of the South Carolina News. The paper mailed Luisa the original photo and to this day it hangs proudly in the Cannoli home.

When their vacation in Hilton Head ended, Luisa, Suzanne and Caroline rounded up their sunburned kids – all long-faced at the thought of leaving the beautiful beach – and headed home. As on the way down, the older girls drove, with Rosanna at the wheel of Luisa's '89 Toyota Cressida.

The gray car hummed effortlessly up the freeway, its highly polished exterior gleaming in the South Carolina sun. Luisa was proud of the pristine condition the Toyota was in. The constant care had been a lot of work, but she felt the effort had been well worth it.

Had she been able to see the future, Luisa would have cherished this moment of pride, for in under a month her beloved Toyota would be a twisted mass of metal by the side of the road.

And she would be trapped inside.

Chapter 7

Trapped and Terrified

Luisa and Anton Cannoli were comfortably settled into a lifestyle they had worked hard to achieve. Their days were filled with a happy blend of family life and careers. Rosanna and Carmella were maturing into fine young women. Family and friends were near and dear. And so life went on – and would likely have continued that way – until that horrible day in July 1997 that changed their lives forever.

The accident had been both sudden and violent. One moment Luisa Cannoli was driving peacefully down Route I-75 South on her way to a Monday morning appointment, the next two huge tractor trailers had struck her car – one from each side – crushing her Toyota as if it were a beer can in a vice.

In her unconscious state of mind, after crying out to the Lord, ***"Oh, Lord I am being crushed!"***, a brilliant white radiant light engulfed her with hundreds of faces in living color. Her necklace with her daughter's birthstones flew up, and visions of her beautiful daughter's faces came forward as if to kiss her scarlet red lipstick covered lips.

Her totaled car ended back onto the expressway as she cried aloud, trembling as her frozen hands were on the steering wheel, 'Lord, I cannot believe that I am still here!!!' She moved her frozen right foot from the brake to the accelerator and slowly hobbled the severely damaged car to the safety lane. Unknown to her in her state of mind the other cars on the expressway had stopped. She sat in the car frozen and in total shock fighting not to pass out. Crying aloud, "*I feel alone. I cannot breathe'!*" as she peeled her baby finger, ring finger and middle finger on her right hand motioning for the weaving driver to help her. He shook his head no and walked away from her desperate plea for help.

She was vaguely aware that traffic was rushing past her on the freeway, and that she should try to get out of the mangled wreck that had finally come to rest in the right lane. But she was deep in shock – frozen behind the steering wheel – her numbed mind unable to process what was happening to her.

Even the terrible pain that engulfed her seemed abstract, as if it were coming from far away. Then, as if in a dream, she slowly became aware that there were people outside, and that they were trying to help her.

An African-American man in his 30's ran up to her driver's door and said through the half open window, "I saw the accident. I called nine-one-one. My little girl is in the car so I can't stay. But help will be here soon."

With an anguished look on his face, the man turned and ran back toward his car.

Against all odds, a moment later a woman Luisa knew appeared. Luisa recognized her face but was too deep in shock to remember her name. The woman saw the confused look on Luisa's face and said, "It's me, Luisa, Lori Kork. Don't worry; I'll stay right here with you until the ambulance gets here."

A second woman arrived with a cell phone in hand. "My name is Renée Jones," she said. "I called nine-one-one. Do you want to use my phone?"

Luisa nodded weakly and said, "Yes." Her body was shaking so badly by now that she could barely control her fingers on the keypad as she dialed her mother's number. When her mother answered, Luisa told her in a quivering voice that she'd just been hit by two tractor-trailers. "The car is totaled," she said.

She suddenly remembered that her daughters were both still at her sister's house in Tennessee, and that they would be driving back later that morning. In the fear and confusion that gripped her, she associated driving with danger and she said, "Tell Rosanna and Carmella to stay at Sophia's. And call Anton."

Her mother agreed to make the calls, and Luisa hung up and handed the cell phone back to Renée Jones. Renée noticed a police car zoom by with the flow of traffic and said, "Why aren't they stopping to help us? I'm calling nine-one-one again."

She did, and was told that an officer was on the way. Less than a minute later a police car pulled up and a highway patrolman in his 60's got out and hurried across to the side of Luisa's car. In a calming voice he told Luisa not to move, and asked her how she felt.

"I hurt all over," Luisa said, "and I'm really nauseous."

The sound of a siren signaled the arrival of a team of Emergency Medical Technicians. One of the EMTs checked Luisa's blood pressure and told her in a worried voice that it was over 250. Blood pressure that high is extremely dangerous and the technician quickly administered oxygen to slow down her breathing.

The technician then told Luisa that he would try to get her out of the wrecked Toyota. Normally another EMT would assist the delicate extraction maneuver from the passenger side but the hinges on the right front door were crushed and the door couldn't be opened.

Moving slowly and carefully, the EMTs eased Luisa out the driver's door, put her in a neck harness and laid her on a bed board. Still in shock and moaning from her agonizing injuries, she was carried to an ambulance where EMTs continued to administer oxygen and monitor her vital signs during the trip to the hospital.

After what seemed like an eternity to Luisa, the ambulance

arrived at the Good Heart Hospital Emergency Room. She was quickly wheeled into an examination room where a team of doctors and nurses began a thorough examination.

The most obvious exterior injuries were deep red welts across her chest and middle caused by her seat belt during impact. She also had a cut – probably caused by a metal part of the belt – on the right side of her stomach.

The X-rays that followed pointed to a neck injury – possibly serious – and the attending physician recommended that Luisa see her own internist as soon as possible that day.

Her husband Anton arrived, a look of shock on his face on seeing Luisa lying on the hospital bed in obvious pain. As Anton tenderly held her hand, Lori Kork entered the room. She had stayed behind at the crash scene to gather information about the driver of the truck that had caused the accident.

His name was Frank Walker, and he drove for the Oceanic Land Transportation Company of Birmingham, Alabama. Freedom Insurance insured the company's trucks. Lori added that the police had thoroughly interrogated Walker and closed the expressway for two hours while they investigated the accident scene.

Lori relayed all the information she had on the accident to Anton and told him where Luisa's car had been towed. Lori added that the police had kept Frank Walker in his truck for two hours; the length of time the expressway had been closed.

Lori had been a passenger in the car of the second witness, Renée Jones, who was a caseworker for the State of Tennessee, and she gave Anton Renée's phone number and work address.

Although both Anton and the doctor were concerned that Luisa's neck injury required attention, she insisted on going home, promising she would see her own doctor later that day.

After dropping Lori at her apartment, Anton and Luisa drove to Renée Jones' workplace to thank the caseworker for stopping to help Luisa that morning. Anton then explained that Luisa was still confused about the details of the accident, and asked Renée if she could draw a diagram of the crash scene.

Renée agreed and replicated the positions of the vehicles involved on memo paper. She said the driver of the first truck was weaving before he hit Luisa's car. "I knew he was going to hit someone," Renée added. "You did an incredible job keeping control of your car."

Anton and Louisa thanked Renée and left.

Anton decided that they should take a look at what was left of Luisa's Toyota, and they drove to the tow lot. The wreck was a sobering sight to both of them, and they left quickly to go get the girls.

Early that afternoon, Rosanna drove Luisa to her doctor's office at North Medical Hospital in Rockport, Tennessee where Dr. Ted Grizzly, an internist, saw her. After a thorough examination, Dr. Grizzly told Luisa that her blood pressure was still alarmingly high and that she remained in a state of shock.

He also warned her that her pain and signs of muscle strain would likely worsen over the next 24 hours. The physician prescribed painkillers, muscle relaxants and a medicine to lower Luisa's blood pressure.

By the time they got home, Luisa was in severe pain. Anton got her prescriptions filled and Luisa took the Darvon, Methocarbamol and Relafen the doctor had prescribed. That night was filled with pain and horror. She fell into an agonized sleep only to awaken – her nightgown soaked with sweat – in the throes of a hideous nightmare.

Lying in bed gasping for breath she could still see the monster trucks coming at her and the metal parts flying off her car on impact. She could hear the scream of metal being torn apart, and the sound of her tires screeching on the pavement as she jammed on her brakes. She could even smell the crash scene – the burning rubber, the diesel exhaust of the trucks, her own sour fear sweat.

The nightmare had been so real, so terrifying, so filled with pain. Tears streaming down her cheeks, Luisa prayed to her Dad to help her get through her ordeal.

The next morning she decided to fight her fear by getting an understanding of exactly what had happened to her body during the accident. Logic told her that a scientist would likely be her best source of information.

Already feeling better that she was doing something positive, Luisa looked up the phone number for the State College Department of Engineering and spoke to the department head, a Doctor Green.

After listening to Luisa's account of the accident, the professor carefully explained that body parts undergo severe shaking when a person abruptly decelerates within the confines of a car. He then offered to have some of his graduate students re-enact the accident scene. Luisa thanked the professor and told him that she would relay his offer to her attorney, Michael Wright.

After Luisa hung up, she took a deep calming breath and thought about the future. She knew that the accident had changed her life forever. She had stared death in the face, and she could still feel the eyes of the grim reaper upon her.

It suddenly occurred to her that the medical bills she was likely to incur in the weeks and months ahead – not to mention lost wages during treatment – could amount to a great deal of money.

The unexpected expenses could jeopardize her family's finances – everything from mortgage and car payments to her daughters' college fund. Alarmed that she and Anton could lose everything, she called Michael Wright for advice.

After speaking with her attorney, Luisa called Dr. Grizzly to get his advice on what she could do to alleviate her pain. He advised her to start physical therapy with Dr. Peta Bronz, a local psychiatrist.

When she called Dr. Bronz, he recommended that she begin her therapy as soon as possible. He told her that he would set up appointments for her for at Spirit of Body Healing Hospital three times a week. Her treatments would consist of ultrasound, massage, and moist heat/steam applied to 75% of her injured body.

When Luisa agreed to the treatments, she had no idea that it was going to be an agonizing five-year rehabilitation process.

During the days that followed, bruises appeared on her groin and left hip, her right thigh throbbed and her physical pain steadily increased. She could not raise her arms nor rotate her head; any movement brought pain to her thoracic area, and injuries to her head, jaw, neck, chest and left ankle caused her constant agony. She started taking narcotics for pain and applied both hot and cold compresses to the injured areas.

Luisa knew that her physical therapy would take up a lot of her time and she was determined to start the process of filing an insurance claim against the trucker who had caused the accident before beginning her rehabilitation.

She called Ocean Land Transportation to get the name and phone number of their insurance company, then phoned the carrier, Freedom Insurance. Although the woman who answered the phone at Freedom was pleasant – asking how she was feeling – Luisa ran into problems right off the bat.

When she asked about a rental car to replace her totaled Toyota, she was told that it would take ten days for Enter Car Rental to get her a car. She then requested a Toyota, and learned that no Toyotas were available and she would have to settle for a Chevy Blazer.

And her troubles didn't stop there. When the Blazer was finally delivered to her home on August 2 it had practically no gas in it. Later that day – when she attempted to drive the Blazer to an appointment with a client – the SUV abruptly lurched forward when she pressed the gas pedal down. The sudden acceleration startled the already anxious Luisa, and she quickly pulled to the side of the road.

Two men driving by stopped to help her. When she explained

the situation, one of the men got behind the wheel of the Blazer and drove her to a gas station where she filled the tank.

As the men pulled away, Luisa broke down and cried. Why was this happening to her? Refusing to give in to the panic attack that threatened to immobilize her, Luisa took a deep breath and forced herself to drive.

Just keeping the car on the road was a constant battle for she was tortured by constant flashbacks of Tuesday's impact and Walker walking away from her, shaking his head no as she screamed for his help.

How was she to deal with these painful flashbacks? The vivid memories were so emotionally crippling. Summoning up all her willpower, she finally made it to her appointment. As if from faraway, she listened to her client's wish list for his new kitchen. When she had finished jotting down his design requests, she took measurements and scheduled a follow-up meeting in three weeks.

Later that August, an Enter Car Rental clerk called Luisa and left a message on her answering machine telling her that there had been a "car settlement" and Enter wanted their car back.

When Luisa called the clerk back to ask what was going on, she was told to "Call your attorney." Luisa did just that, only to be told by Michael Wright that Freedom Insurance had not offered any settlement for the replacement cost of her Toyota Cressida.

Luisa did not like the Blazer she had been given. It handled poorly and the driver's seat was uncomfortable. After a week of misery, Luisa called Enter to come pick up their car.

Luisa really wanted another Toyota to replace her totaled Cressida. She had called the National Headquarters of Toyota and described her accident to their representative. When she mentioned that all of the car parts had flown away from the windshield, the representative explained that this was exactly the way the car was designed to react in a sudden impact.

After that call, Luisa knew that she would never really feel safe driving unless she was behind the wheel of a Toyota. Besides, the

Cannolis had purchased Toyotas since 1976 – the year they'd read a glowing report on the car in Consumer Reports.

At first, Anton and Luisa tried to find another Toyota Cressida. There were only three listed in the local newspaper classifieds. They looked at all three but none measured up to Luisa's original Toyota – which had been in immaculate condition before the accident – and they decided against buying any one of them.

They now faced a dilemma. Although the 1989 Toyota Cressida had been highly rated in Consumer Reports, Toyota had stopped manufacturing the car in 1990. The superb sedan had been replaced by the LS 400 Lexus, which was as highly rated as the Cressida.

Luisa and Anton discussed whether to buy a Lexus. Although they were convinced that it was a quality car that they could rely on, the cost was more than they had planned on spending.

Luisa called a client friend, Marcus, who had just purchased a LS400 Lexus and asked his advice. He spoke highly of the car and the Performance Lexus dealership where he had purchased it. He added that he had dealt with a car salesman named Lou and recommended that Luisa ask for him when she went to the dealership.

The next day Luisa visited Performance and met with Lou. She told him about her accident and explained that she could not afford to spend more than $20,000 on a new car. The car would be financed by a loan.

Lou showed her a 1993 ES300 for $24,000, but she was sure that the car's lavender color would not appeal to Anton. She told Lou that she needed her husband with her to help her make the decision. They would stop by that weekend.

During this time Luisa began extensive rehabilitation treatment as an outpatient at Spirit of Body Healing Hospital. She went to physical therapy three times a week at the hospital, and followed this up with four days of therapeutic exercises at home. Her 20-35 hours of rehab each week consisted of stretching, massage therapy, cold therapy, and ultra sound. Her treatment at Spirit of Body Healing Hospital lasted for four months.

Her daily schedule was completely altered. She tried to juggle family and job responsibilities between treatments, but the inevitable conflicts arose. To add to her misery, her pain was getting worse and she suffered constant nightmares.

Dr. Clark, her rehab specialist, and Dr. Grizzly, her internist, observed that Luisa was showing signs of severe post-traumatic stress and ordered psychological counseling.

Family and friends rallied around the suffering Luisa, bringing over meals and sending encouraging notes and cards. An old friend, Lori Kork – who was scheduled to leave for Puerto Rico on July 30 to accompany her husband on a yearlong work assignment on the island – stopped by and volunteered to help Luisa with insurance matters. She also invited Luisa to visit her in Puerto Rico.

Although Luisa flirted with the idea of visiting Lori and her husband in Puerto Rico, she and her family decided instead to go back to Hilton Head in August. The family had vacationed there often and they found the setting relaxing and enjoyable.

Through the weeks that followed, Luisa's mental and physical pain was constant. She also suffered anxiety attacks when riding in a car – whether she was the driver or a passenger – and her extreme nervousness when Anton was driving was causing tension between them.

Both Luisa and Anton recognized that the smorgasbord of medications that she was now taking undoubtedly heightened her agitation. These included Relafen, Darvon, Methocarbamol, Zantac, Oxycondin, Sulfameth, Buspar, Ranitidine, Trazodone, Promethazine, Roxicet, Hydrocodone, Cipro, Guaifenesen, Paxil, Prevacid, Lorazepam, Prevacid, and Neurontin.

In order to spare Anton, whenever possible Luisa asked friends to drive her to doctor appointments and client meetings. Her schedule was extremely tight, for in addition to her intensive therapy sessions with Dr. Bronz she had two design projects going at the same time.

The first was a kitchen for a client named Harden, and the second was a one-room plan for a customer named Ellis that included a custom office corner, a reading area, a storage glen and a game area.

Although Luisa could handle the Harden project by simply showing her client door samples and hand drawings, the Ellis job required that she and her customer view materials at various showrooms. Ellis was very helpful to Luisa – driving her around to pick out cabinets and other furnishings – and the project went smoothly.

Despite Luisa being chauffeured around by friends and clients, it was becoming more demanding on the Cannolis to have only one car. Anton needed his car for work, Rosanna needed transportation for her part-time job, and Luisa needed Rosanna to drive her to medical treatments and client meetings.

Although the Cannoli transportation problem had become acute, the always-cautious Anton told Luisa that they should wait for the insurance settlement before contemplating a car purchase.

Although she longed for a new Lexus, Luisa saw the logic in Anton's reasoning and switched her focus to the family's coming vacation in Hilton Head.

At 11:00 PM the next night Luisa had just fallen asleep when the sudden ringing of the telephone in her bedroom jolted her awake. She'd had nightmares about the accident for several days running – waking up in the middle of the night with her nightgown, hair and body soaked with sweat – and she desperately needed sleep.

The late caller told Luisa that he was with the Neilson Rating and asked her what television shows she watched, suggesting that she probably watched soap operas. She told him adamantly that she did not.

"I prefer Sixty Minutes, Twenty-Twenty and Dateline," she

said.

"Well, I want to tell you that you've been selected by the Neilson Rating to participate in our television show tracking service," he said. "I'll send you the information."

Several days later she received an envelope from Nielsen and promptly threw it in the garbage.

Thinking back Luisa recalled that Lori had called the week before and told Luisa that her family had been selected by Neilson Rating to document their television shows. Lori explained to Luisa that Nielsen supplied a box that went on top of their television and recorded shows, times, and length of watching. Lori taped soap operas when she was gone. She told Luisa that she would be paid for letting Nielsen record her viewing preferences.

The next morning as Luisa was leaving for a medical appointment, she noticed an older crème white and green Buick parked at the end of her driveway. A heavy-set balding man in his 60's with a round face and black-rimmed glasses sat in the driver's seat. He was holding a laptop computer against the steering wheel with one hand and had a pen in the other.

Luisa wondered what the man in the old Buick was doing parked so close to her home. Her neighborhood was private and her street normally had very little traffic. Still a bit unnerved by the strange late night call from the "Nielson Rating Service" the night before, she decided to get into her car and drive around the neighborhood for about ten minutes and then return home and see if he was still there.

Completing a circuit of her neighborhood, she drove back home and discovered the man in the Buick taking pictures of her house with a small camera. As she slowly pulled into her driveway, he yanked the camera down out of sight.

She decided to go into her home and watch him through her office window. Five minutes went by without the man making a move. Finally Luisa looked at her watch and realized that she had to leave for her medical appointment or she would be late.

As she pulled out of her driveway, she memorized the man's fat round face. Not surprisingly, when the doctor examined her 45 minutes later he found that her blood pressure was elevated.

That afternoon Luisa called her Aunt Gwinnete and told her about the strange Nielson rating call and the old Buick with the fat man in it. Gwinnete suggested that Luisa go with her to the Grand Victoria Casino and Resort in Indiana for that evening to get her mind off these disturbing incidents. Luisa agreed and her aunt picked her up that evening and drove her to the casino.

Aunt Gwinnete was a whiz at playing quarter slot machines and by the end of the night she had turned her original $50.00 stake into $75.00. Luisa was also lucky and managed to win $40.00. The evening was a much-needed change of pace for Luisa.

The next day she put her worries out of her mind and began to concentrate on their coming trip to South Carolina. Perhaps, she thought wistfully, she would find some relief from her anguish and pain midst the sun and surf of the tropics.

Chapter 8

Hilton Head Vacation

The Cannolis arrived at their vacation condo in Hilton Head on August 4, 1997. While they were there, Anton and Luisa planned to celebrate their 23rd anniversary on August 7.

Both their vacation and anniversary plans were soon shattered, however, for on their first day in Hilton Head Luisa noticed blood in her urine. Her groin area was also extremely painful. She called her primary doctor in Clarksville who ordered her to go to the Hilton Head Hospital immediately.

Anton drove Luisa to the hospital where an ER doctor ordered a CAT scan for internal injuries. The x-ray technician injected a dye into a vein in Luisa's right arm for the test. The excruciating pain in her arm and shoulder limited her range of motion for the test.

Luisa endured the pain to get the test over with quickly. The test results revealed internal bleeding from an unknown source and also showed that her blood count was at an anemic level. The findings were sent to a staff physician for further analysis, and Luisa was told to call the next morning for an appointment.

After leaving the hospital that morning, Luisa went back to the condo to rest. Shortly after lying down, she experienced severe pain in her right arm and noticed that it had started swelling.

Anton and Luisa decided to place a second call to her

doctor in Clarksville. He also advised Luisa to follow up with the local hospital. Anton called the Hilton Head ER and they recommended that Luisa put ice on her arm and keep it elevated. If the swelling continued they were to return to the hospital immediately.

That evening, the family celebrated Anton and Luisa's anniversary by eating dinner at a restaurant on the beach. By now, Luisa's arm looked enormous. The swelling was obviously not going down so after dinner Anton took Luisa back to the ER.

After several tests lasting four hours, the doctor told them that Luisa had experienced an allergic reaction to the dye from the CAT scan. The ER technicians did a sonogram to confirm there was no blood clot, and then announced that Luisa could leave.

She was to apply ice on her arm and to keep it elevated until she saw a doctor the next morning. That night Luisa suffered agonizing pain in her arm and got almost no sleep.

The next morning Luisa saw the physician who had first treated her the day before. He prescribed Cipro to prevent any bacterial infection, and advised her to continue to ice her arm.

Before leaving Clarksville, Luisa had arranged to continue her physical therapy at the Hilton Head Hospital and after seeing the doctor she went for ultrasound and heat treatments.

At this point Luisa wished she had stayed home. With all her medical problems, this was not really a vacation for anyone. She told Anton how she felt and when they got back to the condo they broke the news to the girls that they would be leaving.

Anton drove Luisa to Savannah and stayed with her until her plane took off to Clarksville, then he, Rosanna and Carmella drove home. During her flight home, Luisa thought about what happened and felt deep gratitude toward Anton for his tender nurturing during her ordeal.

She remembered a passage from one of Dante's poems that Nonnie had read her years before: Amore, elcor gentil son un cosa - Love and the gentle heart are the same things.

Once home, Luisa's troubles continued. Freedom Insurance failed to provide the car Luisa had requested to replace the Blazer, her medical treatments were eating into her work time, and her medical bills were mounting alarmingly.

The need to purchase a car was now becoming critical. Anton contacted Michael Wright to see what he was doing to collect the property damage settlement for Luisa's totaled Toyota. The attorney told Anton that Freedom Insurance was only offering $6750.

Anton collected newspaper ads to compare prices for 89' Toyota Cressidas and found that the average sale price was between $8,500 and $10,000. Luisa contacted Toyota Towne – where she'd bought her Cressida – to establish a value for the car. Toyota Towne's used car manager gave Luisa a letter on company stationary stating that the value of her car before the accident had been $9200.

Finally, Luisa and Anton decided that they could no longer delay buying another car and on a fall weekend in early October they went down to Lexus. As luck would have it, the lavender car Luisa had liked had been sold the day before.

Anton spotted a jade green ES300 with a tan interior that he liked, but the cost was $30,000. In any case, the color did not appeal to Luisa. Lou appeared and showed Anton and Luisa a 1990 gray LS400 that had just come in. It had a sunroof and was very similar to Luisa's 1989 Toyota Cressida.

Luisa preferred cars with sunroofs and was leaning toward buying the gray Lexus. However, Anton was hesitant about any purchase that day. Luisa countered by bringing up the difficulties they were facing with Rosanna now driving to work and school using the family's '93 Nissan Quest.

After much discussion, the Cannolis decided to see what the Lexus would cost. Luisa told Lou that they could not afford to spend any more than $18,000. The sticker on the window showed $33,000 but Lou told the Cannolis he would see what he could do.

The salesman spoke to his general manager and returned to say that they could have the Lexus for $20,000. Luisa and Anton immediately accepted the offer. When Luisa asked Lou why the general manager had shaved so much money off the cost of the Lexus, the salesman replied that everyone at the dealership understood the terrible ordeal that Luisa had been through and wanted to help her.

Their car loan was secured on their home equity line of credit, although the sudden increase in personal debt concerned Luisa. She had always paid for her company cars and personal car out of her earnings from her design jobs. Now, she'd had to ask Anton to help her with this expense.

Anton reluctantly agreed to help Luisa pay for her replacement car. This would be a turning point in their financial relationship and made Luisa realize that sharing financial burdens was also an important part of marriage.

Neither Luisa nor Anton knew it at the time, but the purchase of her Lexus was the beginning of a journey that would greatly strengthen bonds.

The transaction also gained Luisa several new friends at Lexus, including Franco, the service manager, and Dutch, his assistant. Car buyers genuinely liked both men because they always treated their customers right.

Franco – with his full face, dark beard and jolly laugh – had a relaxing way about him that put his customers at ease when they came in for service. Dutch made sure that each customer's Lexus was serviced properly and did so with a warm smile and a pleasant demeanor.

Shortly after buying her Lexus, Luisa called Michael Wright to ask about the pending settlement of their claim with Freedom Insurance. The lawyer told Luisa that there was still no settlement and that he was continuing to negotiate with the carrier.

Although Luisa was as busy as ever, both at home and at work, her shoulder, neck, groin and thoracic pain were not responding to medication and she continued her physical therapy with Dr. Clark. Although her therapy sessions seemed to help Luisa, she continued to experience pain and Dr. Clark referred her to a local chiropractor named Dr. Silver who he believed might help her further.

Unfortunately, due to slow insurance company payments, Dr. Silver would only accept full payment in cash. Even though the chiropractic sessions would eat up most of her income from her company, Luisa decided that she had to do all that was possible to get well again.

Her decision had almost immediate repercussions. She found herself using credit cards to pay for gas for her car and other essentials. Worse, she wasn't sure how she would come up with the money she had to spend up front whenever she started a new client project.

Nevertheless, Luisa didn't think she had a choice. After a thorough examination, Dr. Silver set her up with three two-hour appointments a week. Luisa had to adjust her business appointments to fit her new therapy schedule.

Dr. Silver's treatment included electro stimulation, ultra sound and physical manipulation of the right leg and left angle, head, neck and both arms. In addition to being treated by Dr. Silver, Luisa was still taking medications for muscle injury, nerve damage and severe pain. She was also seeing a pain psychologist, Dr. Chuck Stuart, who had been recommended by Dr. Bronz.

Although Luisa was spending a lot of time attending to her medical needs, work on her design projects was progressing smoothly. The Harden project was going especially well. The scheduled completion date was Thanksgiving.

While working on the Harden project, Luisa got some chilling news. After carefully observing Luisa over the course of many chiropractic sessions, Dr. Silver confirmed that she had suffered permanent injuries. He also told her that the weight gain she was experiencing was a direct result of all the medications she was taking.

So many negative events were assaulting Luisa that she made up her mind to take back control of her life and make positive things start to happen too. The first thing she did was to write Michael Wright a detailed letter asking him to provide answers to several important questions.

She wanted to know if Frank Walker should be charged with vehicular assault for the serious injuries she had suffered. She also asked Wright if it would be appropriate for the city prosecutor to take action against the police for failure to enforce the 1984 Federal Law stipulating that a breathalyzer test be administered to the defendant in a motor vehicle accident in which injuries had been sustained.

She went on to point out that Walker had been weaving before the accident – an indication that he might well have been drinking – and that this surely should have set off warning bells for the police who investigated her accident.

In her letter, Luisa added that she had had difficulties even getting Freedom Insurance to arrange for a suitable rental car and asked Wright if they should file a complaint with the State of Tennessee Department of Insurance. She also requested that Wright obtain copies of both the 911 calls alerting police to the accident and tapes of the television and radio news reports of the tragedy.

Luisa went on to ask Wright why he had demanded that she furnish copies of her medical reports when it was clearly his job to obtain these.

She also pointed out to Wright that Walker had taken a long time to get out of his truck after the accident, and had then refused to come to her aid – even though she was screaming for help – as she sat trapped in her car.

Within a week, Luisa received Michael Wright's reply to her detailed letter. As she read his words, Luisa was shocked at how heartless and uncaring he was. He told her that it was just an accident, adding that he was not a criminal lawyer and therefore was not prepared to take any action against Walker. He also advised against contacting either the city attorney or the Department of Insurance.

Greatly distressed by Wright's reply, Luisa sought solace in a call to Dr. Stuart. He listened and advised that this huge insurance industry was a mighty tall mountain to climb. He advised her to seek release from her stress by reading poetry and using imagery to relax and conjure up positive thoughts.

Taking the physician's advice, Luisa was able to achieve a positive attitude, which encompassed her spiritual life. She started each day in prayer and then spent a half-hour or so reading excerpts from *Simple Abundance*, a book full of wisdom and inspiration.

One passage in particular – *Getting from Here to There: When you Haven't a Clue of What to Do* – helped her find a semblance of peace. She especially related to the words, *"You want to go forward but find yourself standing still, overwhelmed by the options or the risks."*

Friends frequently brought her other inspirational books, including *Embraced by Lite* by Debbie Diane Dirrs and *Trilogy, Walk to Remember, The Notebook* and *Message in a bottle*, all by Richard Sparks.

Luisa's positive approach to the physical and emotional problems that plagued her began to show results. Her passion to use her creativity to help others resurfaced and a new vitality became evident in her design work.

The horrible accident on July 22, 1997 had almost taken her life. Yet she had survived – rising from the ashes like Phoenix – and despite the severe pain she still suffered, she was determined to make herself whole again.

Chapter 9

Hiring a Private Investigator

As Luisa sat in her office in October 1997 looking through the Yellow Pages for a private investigator, she said a prayer aloud that she would find a Christian. Without knowing why, she focused in on an ad for Marshall Kent & Associates.

She took a deep breath, dialed the number and was put through to Mr. Kent. Luisa explained her situation and asked if he would take her case. He said he would need more information before he could make a decision, and suggested they meet. Luisa agreed, and they scheduled an appointment at her home the   following morning.

Mr. Kent arrived promptly at 10:00 AM. A gray-haired man in his mid-sixties, he had an air of self-assurance about him and spoke with authority.

Luisa began their conversation by telling Kent about the terrible car accident she'd been involved in two months before. She then went on to describe an unsettling incident that had occurred the previous month.

"I was dusting the living room when I suddenly heard voices outside," Luisa said. "We're well back from the road, you know, so I knew it wasn't a couple of people walking down the street. I looked out the front window and there was a couple standing in our driveway. They were both heavyset and dressed like farmers."

Kent knotted his eyebrows thoughtfully. "Did you confront them?"

"I sure did. I went out and asked them what they were doing in my driveway."

"What was their response?"

"They said in unison, 'We came to look at your outdoor furniture.' I hadn't advertised any outdoor furniture for sale and I had no idea what they were talking about. I told them firmly to get off my property, and they walked away up the street."

Kent frowned. "No car?"

"None that I could see."

"Had you ever seen either one of them before?"

"No, never. I know everyone in this neighborhood and I assure you that those two were not from around here."

"Go on," Kent said.

"Well, immediately after that strange couple appeared in our driveway I began to hear clicking sounds on our phone," Luisa said, shuddering slightly at the memory. "I'm certainly not an expert on eavesdropping devices but I've done some research and learned that those clicks I keep hearing could mean that couple may have planted a bug on our telephone line."

Kent said, "It's certainly something we need to investigate."

"And that wasn't the only strange thing that's happened since the car crash," Luisa said. "A few days after the clicking sounds started on the phone I was about to leave for a medical appointment when I noticed a fat balding man – in his sixties, I'd guess – sitting in an old Buick parked a few yards from our driveway. I drove around the neighborhood and the man was still there when I returned."

"Did you get a license number?" Kent asked.

Luisa shook her head. "No. I was too rattled. I just drove away."

"To be frank, Luisa, without names or a license number it's

going to be hard to track down the people you just told me about."

Luisa nodded. "I know. I wish I could tell you more."

"Okay, let's move on to the truck driver that caused your accident. What was his name again?"

"Walker. Frank Walker."

"What can you tell me about him?"

"Not a heck of a lot. My attorney, Michael Wright, has been trying to track him down but apparently he has two addresses listed with the trucking company he works for. I can tell you that I'm convinced he was driving drunk when he hit me."

"I'll do a background check on Walker and get a report to you as soon as possible," Kent said.

Luisa and Kent went over other details of her case for the next twenty minutes, then the PI closed his notebook, told Luisa that he would be in touch, and left. Luisa felt reassured by Marshall Kent's professionalism, and the fact that she finally had someone on her side.

A few days later Kent dropped off a file at Luisa's home, containing detailed information on Walker. Luisa paid the PI's $1,000 fee and dove into the material. Not surprisingly, she read that Walker had several past DUI convictions. The last one had cost the truck driver 180 days in jail. She passed the information on to Michael Wright.

Luisa was still having anxiety attacks whenever she drove so they hired a man named William Starr to drive her around. He also chauffeured Carmella, helped with domestic chores, and did maintenance on the house.

William witnessed many of Luisa's anxiety attacks – as well as her ongoing battle with Post Traumatic Stress Disorder (PTSD) – and his reassuring voice and presence did much to help her get through her ongoing ordeal.

Despite William's help, Luisa's life was getting more complex with each passing day. It was hard enough to balance being a wife, a mother, and the owner of a design studio without having to deal with massive health problems. On top of all this she was also involved in a private investigation into the strange events that had been plaguing the Cannolis the past few weeks.

One of the medical problems plaguing her was PTSD. The debilitating malady forced her to have William drive her to most of her medical and professional appointments. It was quite expensive to employ William as a driver and home-helper, and Luisa was forced to take out charge card and home equity loans.

In addition, her design company had taken on some large projects that involved extra overhead and her accountant, Mark Schneider, advised her to raise her retail prices to pay for the additional expenses.

Frustrated that she had become so dependent on William, Luisa gradually tried driving again. At first, she would only trust herself behind the wheel on side roads during the relatively low-traffic mid-morning.

Despite avoiding the busy freeways, driving continued to be difficult for Luisa. She kept seeing black skid marks on the pavement and that would bring on heart palpitations, trouble breathing and sweaty hands. Often, her accident would replay itself before her horrified eyes.

Ironically, when she tried to wean herself from some of her medications, she started getting speeding tickets. The first traffic citation came when she stopped taking Paxil.

A midsize truck had come up beside her car on a city street. It appeared to be right next to her driver's door. A flight response suddenly kicked in and – trying desperately to escape the threatening truck – she hit the accelerator and sped down the street ten miles over the speed limit.

By the time she slowed down, there was a policeman behind her with his blue lights on. Without Luisa saying anything, the officer guessed that she was having an anxiety attack. He said that his wife suffered from the same condition and she was taking

Paxil to help her.

Her experience that day convinced Luisa that an anxiety attack could strike at any time. She told her doctors what had happened, and they recommended that she continue all her medications, including Paxil.

Even as Luisa was struggling to regain control of her life, the pain in her groin was steadily worsening and her periods were irregular. Concerned, her doctors ordered both an MRI and an ultrasound of her uterus.

After studying the results of the tests, her rehab specialist Dr. Clark recommended that she see Dr. Cary Mark, an abdominal surgeon. After examining Luisa, Dr. Mark decided to do exploratory surgery in May 1998.

Although the operation was exploratory, it was also a major procedure – there would even be miniature medical cameras inside her during the surgery – with potentially life-threatening consequences.

During the surgery Dr. Mark discovered that her right ovary – which was attached to her ileopsoas muscle – had been stretched four inches. The ileopsoas muscle can radiate pain that is felt deep in the lumbar spine but which also may appear in the groin.

The muscle itself is difficult to find, lying deep in the abdomen and virtually hidden under the muscles of the anterior thigh, making self-examination difficult. The pain caused by this muscle can be completely incapacitating.

At one point during the surgery, Luisa's blood pressure dropped so low that Dr. Mark feared she would die on the operating table. By the narrowest of margins, she survived the operation. As she slowly returned to consciousness in the recovery room, she gained an insight into how serious her injuries had been when she overheard two nurses talking about her condition.

"I can't believe her ovaries were stretched four inches," one nurse said.

The second nurse replied, "She's been bleeding internally for four months and she's dangerously anemic. It's a miracle that she's even alive."

A few days after the operation Dr. Mark gave Luisa photos of her injury both prior to and after her surgery. He also provided her with a detailed medical explanation of the blunt trauma that she had suffered.

Although Luisa was still recovering from her surgery during the spring and summer of 1998, she continued her   physical rehabilitation. She also kept up her counseling sessions with her psychologist, Dr. Chuck Stuart. Dr. Stuart taught her pain management and advised her to keep a journal to help her focus better.

In early November 1998 Luisa prepared for shoulder surgery. She was not so much worried about the actual operation as she was about the strong narcotics – such as Oxycondin – she would be required to take during her recovery.

Anton and her girls were already worried that the medications she was taking were adversely affecting her emotional state. They told her that she was acting differently, yelling at them for little or no reason and showing intolerance for things that never used to bother her before.

In an effort to understand what was happening to the woman he loved, Anton started reading books on chemical imbalances in the brain. He kept telling her that her doctors were prescribing too many medications and that she ought to think about finding an alternative means of treatment.

To add to Luisa's problems, her weight was going up. She tried to lose weight by exercising while watching Richard Simmons and Bob Greene tapes, but when she attempted to repeat the calisthenics she saw on the screen her pain level went up, severely limiting her workouts. In an attempt to relax between exercise sessions, she watched Oprah Winfrey on television – drawing strength from the talk show host's shows on self-esteem.

At this time, Dr. Stuart told Luisa that he preferred not to schedule her for the P.A.S.T (Pain and Stress Treatment) Program he wanted her to take part in until her insurance case was settled and she could concentrate on her health recovery without having to worry about legal matters.

Luisa confided in Dr. Stuart about the conflicts she was facing both at home and at work. She told him of her problems with Michael Wright, and added that the attorney's apparent lack of commitment to their case was contributing to Anton's frustration with their growing financial difficulties.

Dr. Stuart told Luisa that in his years of counseling he had treated many clients who suffered severe stress while dealing with insurance company settlements. He explained that insurance adjusters were compensated according to how much they saved their companies in insurance claims.

Dr. Stuart's words confirmed all the bad things Luisa had heard about insurance companies. She left her session with the pain psychologist feeling apprehensive about her own case.

Despite the turmoil in the Cannoli family caused by Luisa's accident, Luisa and Anton went ahead with plans for their summer vacation in June. They had purchased a timeshare week at Blue Tree Resort, Lake Buena Vista, Florida, just a half-mile from Epcot Center and Disney Village.

Luisa was still suffering from severe post-traumatic stress that would have made the long drive from Tennessee to Florida torture to her, so she and her mom flew down the same day Anton and the girls left by car.

Luisa and Teresa arrived safely in Orlando where they rented a Toyota. Since they were both having medical problems that inhibited their ability to get around unassisted, they also rented two wheelchairs. After dinner they settled into their rented condo to await Anton and the girls, who arrived around 2 AM.

The next morning Luisa rose early so that she could spend some time alone with Anton. Over the past several months their relationship had been severely strained by the medical problems and financial worries caused by Luisa's accident.

Since Rosanna was born, they seldom went anywhere by themselves. Their lives were centered on their girls, and being alone was a special treat for the weary couple. Anton was especially helpful and caring that early crisp June morning as he happily pushed Luisa along in her wheelchair.

Just to talk to Anton with no interruptions was a gift to Luisa and she tried to add romance to her words. Anton was equally loving and they had a wonderful time enjoying the park together. Luisa thought of those lovely poems, Quotation and Proverbs and Proverbs, in the Treasure of Italian Love so often recited to her by her grandmother and mother. The words that came to mind were *Gli amori nuovo fanno dimenticae I veccchi* – New love soon expels an old love.

They started off their romantic adventure by having breakfast together. They then went on the Safari ride – where they enjoyed the sight of dozens of exotic African animals – and afterward visited several exhibits and shops. It was a very relaxing and refreshing outing – their first "date" in a long time – and both took away fond memories of their special morning together.

When they returned to the condo they found grandma and the girls dressed and ready to go. They spent the rest of the day at the MGM Studio. Teresa, now in her 80's, enjoyed talking to the actors and actresses who played movie stars on the streets, especially actors impersonating characters from old movies.

Through the remainder of the week they visited as many other Disney World attractions as they could. They also enjoyed the parades and nightly fireworks. The trip helped to take Luisa's mind off her terrible accident. At least throughout the day it did.

Nighttime was a different story. Even at relaxing Disney World, Luisa was having difficulty sleeping. Flashbacks of the crash scene would wake her up at all hours of the night and she would find the blankets twisted, the sheets in a ball and her hair and nightgown soaked with fear sweat.

Luisa wondered if her medications might be causing her terrible nightmares. She was now taking Relafen, Oxycondin, Neurotin, Paxil, Traxodine, Tenormin, and Prevacid – drugs that were known to have a variety of side effects.

Her nightmares of the accident were always clear as day when she awoke. She was in her crushed car moments after the accident, motioning frantically to the gray-bearded truck driver for him to come help her. But all he did was turn his back and walk away. Luisa could not understand how anyone could be so cruel and uncaring.

The last night of her vacation was the worst of all for Luisa. When she awoke from her nightmare she suddenly noticed that her arms, hands, thighs, and fingers were white as a sheet. She was also trembling with chills, unable to get warm despite having a pile of blankets over her.

She awoke her mom. Teresa took one look at her daughter's ghost-white face and trembling limbs and threw her arms around Luisa, comforting her as only a mother can.

"I don't know what's happening to me!" Luisa cried out plaintively.

Anton woke up and he and Teresa suggested that Luisa call her doctor in Clarksville. When Luisa got through, the doctor listened to her symptoms and told her that he didn't believe that her condition had been caused by complications following her surgery a few weeks before.

The doctor recommended that she see a physician as soon as possible. Since the family was going home the next day, Luisa decided to wait and be examined by her doctors in Clarksville.

Anton and the girls left early the next morning for their long drive home. Luisa and her mom were to fly home later that day. Then Luisa had a sudden inspiration. Her friend, Diana, lived in Atlanta, which was only a short flight from Orlando – and Diana's husband, was a doctor. Perhaps he could help her.

She called Great Wings Airlines and arranged a flight to Atlanta, then phoned Diana back and got directions from the airport to the nearest hospital. When they got to Atlanta, they went directly to the hospital.

Unfortunately, Diana's physician husband was tied up with an emergency case when they arrived and was unable to see Luisa. Instead a specialist in stress disorders examined Luisa's blanched body and diagnosed her as having a severe panic attack.

When Luisa revealed the chilling details of her accident and all the terrible things that had been happening to her ever since, the physician told her that the stress she was under had undoubtedly caused her latest attack.

The doctor conferred with her physicians in Clarksville and they agreed that what she needed most of all was rest. She had not had a good night's sleep since the day of the accident. As if to confirm the doctors' diagnosis, Luisa collapsed on her hospital bed and was out for three hours. Her mom arranged for them to fly to Clarksville the next day.

Upon arriving home, she saw her doctors who advised her to begin pacing herself more to lessen the stress she was under. Luisa knew the doctors were right, and made the traumatic decision to shut down her interior design business for the remainder of 1998.

Now that she had more time to devote to healing her injured body and psyche, Luisa dedicated herself to gaining a fuller understanding of exactly what was happening to her.

She gained a valuable insight into the root of her nightmares when her pain counselor told her that they were the result of bottled up anger and emotional scaring caused by her accident.

Her counselor advised her that what the truck driver had done to her was similar to rape. He had invaded her body and mind, causing her severe injuries and then leaving her alone and helpless on the freeway. Knowing that Luisa harbored a terrible rage toward the truck driver, the counselor gave her literature on anger management to study.

Luisa also decided that it was time she talked to her priest, for she simply could not forgive the truck driver for the pain and misery he had caused her. Her priest reassured Luisa that it was okay for her to not yet be able to forgive the man who had caused her so much physical and mental anguish. He also promised her he would pray that – over time – she would find a way to let go of her anger.

Part of Luisa's inability to forgive Frank Walker was the physical pain she continued to suffer as a direct result of the accident he had caused. According to biofeedback machines, her pain level was higher than 48. The arm on the machine went to the top.

The specialist told her, "My test confirms that you have severe and debilitating pain."

The computerized biofeedback machine had proven to Luisa and everyone else that her pain was not psychosomatic. It was real! Yet it was not the only pain she suffered. Her mental anguish was equally as debilitating.

Luisa had spoken to other patients who were being treated for pain management and she knew that her suffering was not going to cease anytime soon. One woman in her sixties confided to Luisa that her muscles were still extremely painful despite years of therapy.

The woman's words were very discouraging to Luisa, for they forced her to face the fact that overcoming her injuries would   involve a long and agonizing battle. She now began to understand what her doctors really meant when they said her recovery would "take time."

Luisa's own torn muscles were now forming scar tissue and she soon found herself being prepped for shoulder surgery to correct the problem. The only way Luisa could deal with her the myriad problems life had heaped upon her plate was to take one day at a time. Her medical expenses continued to soar and she had no income with which to pay gasoline bills and physicians' co-pays.

She was falling into depression and felt like her world was collapsing around her. All her free time was spent undergoing medical treatments. Her closest friends called her and tried to help her refocus. They also sent cards and inspirational books such as *Embraced by the Light*.

She also read *Simple Abundance* by Sarah Ban Breathnach and *Bloom Where You're Planted* by Jacques Weisal. In Weisal's book she found a quote from Frank Ward O'Malley that read, "*Life is just one damned thing after another.*"

O'Malley's words could have been written about her, Luisa had reflected ruefully.

She was inspired, as well, by the words of Raine Marie Rulhe who wrote, "*The future enters into us, in order to transform itself in us, long before it happens.*"

Luisa got a further indication of just how unscrupulous Freedom Insurance was when she ran into a man who was also battling with the company. A truck insured by Freedom had run into the man's truck. He had suffered severe injuries that were permanent and was now enduring chronic and debilitating pain. He told Luisa of the underhanded games the insurance company had played on him, including canceling their last trial date. He added that he had been receiving harassing phone calls.

His case had now dragged on for four long years with no end in sight. Despite his constant pain, the lack of a settlement had forced him to work during his rehabilitation.

As Luisa continued with medical treatments in the fall of 1998, the doctors prepared her for right shoulder surgery that would involve cutting away one inch of clavicle to create space between the clavicle and the humerus. They would also repair the torn cartilage in that area.

Knowing that Luisa had found it hard to take care of herself at home after her first operation, this time the doctor ordered home nursing care and kept her in the hospital for two days after surgery.

In the fall of 1998 Luisa felt her stress level rising and she knew she was pushing herself too much. She spoke to her doctors about the advisability of taking a trip to Europe – something she had planned for the past 10 years – in the summer of 1999.

The doctors agreed it was a good idea and pledged that in the coming months they would help prepare her for the trip by scheduling additional physical therapy to build up her stamina and her ability to deal with her chronic pain. They also made sure that she would be taking the correct medications with her.

Luisa's company had hardly any sales during the entire year of 1998. In November, she did do a design project. The weather that winter was mild and the client decided she would take advantage of the unseasonable temperatures by having her old deck torn down and a new one built.

Being an accountant, the client was determined to have her deck completed within her budget. Luisa got the bid process started only to discover that Nicholas DeVinci – the subcontractor she normally hired to build decks – was building his own home and would not be accepting outside work for a few months.

Luisa would have to hire someone else to do the work. She went to a local lumberyard and spoke to the supervisor, David Wooden. He told her that he and his brothers built decks and showed her pictures of some of the decks they had constructed.

Luisa hired Wooden on his word, but was soon sorry she had trusted him. He was going through a divorce and his personal problems took precedence over his professional obligation to Luisa. Wooden got only as far as framing the substructure of the deck before abandoning the job.

Luisa was beside herself for her reputation was at stake. Fortunately, severe cold and heavy snow gripped the Midwest for the next two and one half months and the client did not expect the work on the deck to be completed during such inclement weather.

In March of 1999 Luisa was finally able to hire Nicholas DeVinci and his crew to finish the deck. William Starr was hired to speed the job up. William was both amiable and hardworking and was well liked by the client.

In January 1999, Luisa did a renovation job for a client named Mary Sue Morris. The project included the installation of cherry wood cabinets and a matching hardwood floor. It also entailed the hanging of off-white wallpaper with maroon, butter yellow and sky blue flowers, and the selection of matching furniture in the same colors.

During the work, Mary Sue revealed to Luisa that a truck driver had killed her mother-in-law. Union Insurance had represented the trucker and had stalled and delayed payment to them. Her brother-in-law had finally hired a lawyer and they'd eventually received a begrudging out-of-court settlement. Luisa thanked Mary Sue for the information, and filed it away. Would her own insurance case also turn out to require litigation?

A few days later Mary Sue called Luisa and asked her to design a home addition. Luisa gladly accepted, even though she knew the job would run through the end of the year and further strain her already tight schedule.

The project meant she would have to coordinate a host of subcontractors, including a structural engineer, an architect, a landscaper, a heating and air conditioning contractor and an electrician. As if the Morris project weren't work enough, Luisa was also directing several smaller projects that involved kitchen updates, bathroom remodeling and deck designs.

Even as Luisa's workload grew heavier, her physical condition continued to worsen. One day in late January Anton stayed home from work to help Luisa and to spend some time with her. He had asked Dr. Mark about her limitations and the physician had cautioned Anton that his wife must avoid going up and down stairs. Late in the afternoon Luisa went upstairs to lie down.

Luisa fell into a deep sleep and did not awaken until 1:00 PM the next day. Still groggy, she struggled down the stairs and found Anton sitting at the kitchen table reading the paper. He looked at her but said nothing. Exasperated, Luisa stared back.

Finally Anton asked, "Do you need any help?"

"For one thing you can open the penicillin soup for me," she said, pointing at the four-gallon container of chicken broth and noodles that her friend Caroline had brought over for her.

Her neck and shoulder injuries made it impossible for her to exert the torque required to unscrew the large top on the container – something she felt Anton should have known.

Anton didn't answer her. He simply went back to reading his newspaper without opening the soup. Luisa threw up her hands in exasperation and returned wearily to bed. She would ask Carmella to open the soup when she got home from school.

Several days later Luisa had regained her strength and was back at work when she had a most revealing conversation with a client named Marguerite Pisano. Marguerite, who was several months pregnant, had suffered back and neck injuries in a car accident.

Attorneys represented the defendant in her case in court from Grant Insurance, the company that had issued the insurance policy on his vehicle.

With tears in her eyes, Marguerite told Luisa how the unscrupulous insurance company had tried to convince the judge that her injuries did not exist except in Marguerite's imagination. The nefarious legal maneuver had caused Marguerite a great deal of emotional distress.

She confided in Luisa that a good friend, Bob Martin, had been killed in a second automobile accident during the same week her car had been struck. A truck had crossed the median on I-275 and crashed into Bob's car.

Marguerite went on to tell Luisa that her friend's brother Kevin, a funeral director with a great deal of knowledge about human anatomy, had handled Bob's funeral. Marguerite suggested that Luisa talk to Kevin and see if he could help her understand the nature of her injuries.

Luisa subsequently called Kevin and described her accident, carefully listing the injuries she had sustained. Kevin was very forthcoming, and explained to Luisa that almost all the car crashes fatalities that came through his funeral home had injuries to the right side of their bodies. He added that right leg damage was prevalent because the victims usually slammed on the brakes with their right foot in the course of a collision.

Kevin's explanation allowed Luisa to finally understand the bruising pattern on her hips and why she had sustained such serious injuries to her abdomen and internal organs.

Kevin went on to suggest that Luisa contact Dr. Donald Bruno, a mortuary instructor at State Mortuary College who was an expert in accident injuries. Luisa thanked Kevin and quickly called Dr. Bruno. The instructor suggested a meeting at Luisa's home, and asked her to assemble all her medical files.

Dr. Bruno was a husky man in his 40s. He had light brown hair and spoke loudly about his ability to use his anatomical knowledge to "slam-dunk" guilty defendants. He told Luisa that his fee would be based either on the time he spent on the case or on a percentage of the final settlement.

Luisa contacted Michael Wright to tell him of her meeting with Dr. Bruno. The attorney explained that this type of specialist routinely charged $10,000.00 for his testimony.

The astronomical figure gave Luisa pause, and she decided to give a lot of thought to whether Dr. Bruno would be able to justify his high fee by successfully making a jury understand the true extent of her injuries.

During this time, their legal case was going nowhere. On top of that, Michael Wright was not keeping them apprised of what was going on. To Luisa and Anton, it seemed like their settlement negotiations with Freedom Insurance had disappeared into a black hole.

Then Luisa started noticing more noises on her telephone. It sounded like call-waiting sounds – click, click, click. She thought that the problem lay with her telephone so she replaced it. In fact, she ended up having her phone replaced three times in total. Anton also bought a new fax machine, as the old one could not receive incoming faxes.

She also called Midwest Bell to see if the problem was being caused by her call waiting service. A Midwest Bell technician checked her call waiting and told Luisa that it was working properly.

With plans for their European trip finalizing, Luisa put the phone problem on the back burner and focused on making sure that all her design projects would continue while she was gone. She contracted with another designer, Alicia Jones, to do the work on a new kitchen for one of her clients and instructed William to pick up supplies for the project.

Then – just when Luisa thought she had all her jobs under control – a high school classmate of hers asked her to update her kitchen in time for her daughter's graduation in May 1999.

Luisa's doctors advised her that her stress level was rising due to her increased workload and prescribed several strong new medications. At the time she suspected that she might be taking too many drugs and that they were affecting her behavior, but she had no idea that she was rapidly becoming addicted.

Although her physicians agreed to let her go on her long-planned European vacation, they also insisted that she purchase a $1,000 Hometrac Pneumatic Cervical Unit to take with her. The Hometrac unit was engineered to release pressure on the bulging discs off her spinal cord by stretching her neck. The process called for Luisa to lie flat on the floor with Velcro straps running from a pneumatic pull on the unit to her head.

The result of this 20-minute ritual was that Luisa's pain level would be reduced from a 10 to a far more manageable five. The doctors also prescribed enough medication for Luisa's planned 4-6 week stay in Europe.

Luisa was now ready for their long awaited European trip. The budget was set at $17 a day for each person, and everyone stuck to the budget. This included food, transportation and housing.

Luisa, Carmella and her mom planned to board a plane for Rome in early June. Rosanna would leave with her class – which was also going to Europe – in mid-June and Anton would join the family in London late June.

Luisa and Anton asked several dear and trusted friends to join them, including Josh, Lynne, Arnold, and Diana and Diana's parents.

As she looked forward to her European trip Luisa thought, *I've been trapped in a web of pain and emotional trauma for months now. Maybe visiting exciting new places and meeting interesting new people will be just the escape I've been searching for.*

It was a thread of hope the long-suffering Luisa desperately needed.

Chapter 10

European Vacation

Luisa and her mother, Teresa packed for at least a month-long trip to Europe. Along with an excited Carmella, they departed from Tennessee International on June 6, 1999. In New York, they transferred to a connecting flight to Rome, where they caught a third plane for the final leg of their flight to Palermo, Sicily.

When they reached Palermo they checked into the beautiful Hotel Astoria. Its architecture bespoke understated elegance. At the front entrance a soaring archway and stately pillars welcomed guests to the splendid foyer. The mahogany-paneled walls of the lobby were hung with magnificent artwork, and everywhere one looked, subtle touches of European sophistication adorned the interior.

The well-dressed porters greeted them warmly and their suites were tastefully furnished with mahogany beds, gold-gilded furniture and beautiful oil paintings.

They would only be in Palermo for three days so after a brief rest from their long flight they ventured out to explore the historic city. To their surprise, there were few people other than tourists on the streets. Later they would discover that Sicilians traditionally stay home and rest during the hot midday hours.

By now Luisa, Teresa and Carmella were all hungry so they

went to a local restaurant where they ordered spaghetti and meatballs. The meal was delicious and the service could not have been better.

After lunch they decided to walk around and were rewarded with the discovery of centuries-old buildings, beautiful fountains and gardens ablaze with bright colored flowers.

While preparing for the trip, Luisa had learned that they would need European cell phones. She felt that they needed the cell phones so they could keep in touch with Rosanna and her friends, who would be arriving in Rome in mid-June on their school trip.

It would be more economical for them to purchase the cell phones in Palermo so their first stop was the cell phone shop. Luisa's high school Latin and college Spanish helped her communicate with the salesman. They soon completed their purchase and headed for an outdoor café up the street where the two women ordered homegrown grape wine and Carmella had a soda.

As they enjoyed their drinks a gray-haired street vendor pedaled up on his bicycle and stopped before their table. His bicycle was loaded down with baskets of beautiful lace goods and Luisa and Teresa inquired about his tablecloths.

He proudly told them that the elderly women out in the countryside made these beautiful items. The cost of their labor was low and he was able to sell his lace goods for very little. They thanked him but decided not to buy anything. He returned their thanks and peddled away toward the city.

At 4:00 PM all the streets suddenly became filled with hundreds of Sicilian people – all tanned and beautiful. Luisa never had seen so many people talking on cell phones. They'd had a delightful day but jet lag was catching up to them all and they reluctantly headed back to their hotel room to rest.

That evening they went to the hotel's restaurant for dinner. The seven-course meal was most filling – so many appetizers and entrees to choose from – and they relished every delicious bite.

That night they went to bed early and slept soundly – even Luisa – in their ornate mahogany beds.

The next morning after breakfast they met their bilingual tour guide, Vincente, in the hotel lobby. He was both charming and good-looking with ash blonde hair, blue eyes and a well-muscled build.

Luisa had planned a visit to Termini – an ancient city on the coast that was also the ancestral home of her Italian forebears. After getting acquainted, Vincente escorted them out to his air-conditioned Mercedes and graciously opened the doors. Teresa preferred the front seat so she got in next to Vincente and Luisa and Carmella sat in the back.

Vincente drove them out into the rolling countryside along the coast, stopping several times to allow his passengers to take pictures of the flowered hillsides and deep blue sea. After they had driven for a couple of hours, they stopped at a quaint café where Luisa treated Vincente to lunch.

After lunch they continued their journey to Termini. Built on a hillside, the city consisted mainly of yellow clay buildings latticed with centuries of cracks. The streets were narrow and quite bumpy.

It was a Sunday afternoon and all of the women were dressed in their Sunday best, including colorful flowered hats. The men sported suits and shiny shoes, and the children were decked out in their dressiest clothes.

The scene reminded Luisa of Sunday afternoon gatherings at her grandparents' home when she was a child. The memory of the delicious meals her grandmother had served – especially the Gelato and Cannolis she made for dessert – made her mouth water.

After exploring the city by car, Vincente drove them to the town's cemetery. Beautiful fresh flowers surrounded the raised marble headstones. What struck Luisa most were the pictures of the deceased on the headstones. She also recognized many of the names on the stones – Tue, Dattilo, Palmsono, Campbelli, Casteunni, Matracia, Tedesco, Costo, Re, Francisco, Pacino, Montecarlo, Manatrica, Castelinni, Mercurio, Galo, Rosatto, Palmiero - for they were the family names of the fruit and vegetable men her grandfather had worked with in the marketplace back home.

Luisa's Italian ancestry was important to her and she cherished every minute they spent at the cemetery. Yet the highlight of their visit was when they found her great grandfather's grave.

The face on the tombstone was the same one that had stared back from a picture on her grandparents' parlor wall. His face was oval and he sported a long beard. Luisa's cousin, Viniete, resembled their great grandfather so closely that he looked like his twin.

Teresa was jubilant to be in the birthplace of her ancestors and to be standing there before her grandfather's grave. Luisa could see that Carmella was also enthralled with her first glimpse of her roots.

After visiting the graveyard, Vincente drove the three to the crowded market area. As they worked their way through the throngs of Sunday shoppers, Luisa spotted a miniature statue of a centuries-old Sicilian soldier dressed in full armor. She was immediately taken by the piece – especially the soldier's feather-adorned helmet – and bought it on the spot.

After stopping to buy some Gelato – which went down smoothly on that sultry Sunday afternoon – they continued their window shopping and sightseeing until it was time to return to Palermo.

In the car on the way back, Luisa felt rejuvenated. This had been her best day since her terrible accident nearly two years before. Teresa was happy too. Her long-held dream to visit her father's hometown had finally come true. She told Luisa that she felt blessed, and said a prayer of thanks to the Lord.

"This is the trip of a lifetime," 12-year-old Carmella said, as moved as her grandmother by her day in Termini. "I'm going to write all about our trip in my journal."

As they drove through the picturesque countryside, Luisa and her mother began talking about Anton's Sicilian relatives, who lived in Palermo. To their surprise, Vincente knew the families. In fact, he lived next door to them!

He volunteered to set up a meeting and when they reached the hotel, he put through a call and arranged for Anton's relatives to meet them there that evening. Luisa called the concierge and ordered appetizers of fruit, cheese and wine for the family reunion.

At 9:00 PM Anton's smiling relatives, the Romanos, arrived and they all exchanged happy hugs and kisses. Although Luisa had met Anton's aunt and uncle – now deceased – years before, this was her first meeting with the couple's daughter, Rosa, and son-in-law, Pauli, and their daughter, Lana.

Pauli was a wealthy businessman and diplomat and was fluent in many languages. His swarthy Italian features made him an exceptionally handsome man and his easy charm marked him as a sophisticated gentleman. Rosa and her daughter were also most attractive, each possessing an exquisite Italian beauty.

The other relatives were Anton's cousins Lena, Roberto and Stoffi De Stalloni. They, too, were quite good looking and well off, having inherited the family's ancestral villa and olive groves.

They all ate, laughed and shared family stories together well into the evening. Then – although it was now rather late – the relatives insisted that they all go out and see Palermo at night.

It was to be a night that Luisa, Teresa and Carmella would never forget. In front of the hotel, they split into two groups and got into the relatives' two large Mercedes. Then they were off for a whirlwind tour of the city, driving up and down cobblestone streets and slowing to gaze into shop windows displaying tempting Sicilian goods.

During the tour Teresa spotted a jewelry store with her maiden name on it and vowed to come back and buy a momento before they left Palermo.

After they had explored the city, they all went to Romano's hillside home for refreshments. Luisa, Teresa and Carmella were entranced by the beautiful flowers blooming on the balcony that warm June evening and the art treasures from all over the world that graced their beautiful villa overlooking Palermo.

As they sat in the living room, the Romanos surprised them by bringing out platters laden with all kinds of Italian desserts. Carmella's dark brown eyes lit up when she saw the delectable treats.

After enjoying the desserts, they drove to the family villa of Roberto and Lana. The villa was on a hillside overlooking Palermo and Luisa, Teresa and Carmella gazed down, enraptured at the spellbinding sight of the city lights sparkling below.

In the courtyard of the villa was the family tombstone. On the stone were different spellings of their name – the vowels at the end switching from "i" to "o" to "a". The Sicilian relatives didn't explain why the spelling had changed, and – overwhelmed by the exciting events of the evening – their American visitors never thought to ask.

The enchanted evening finally came to an end and the relatives drove Luisa, Teresa and Carmella back to their hotel. They were leaving early the next morning and had only four hours to sleep before they had to check out and head for the airport.

Luisa left Palermo feeling entirely at peace. Their visit had been just the tonic she needed after so many months of turmoil. Their flight to Rome was smooth and they checked into their hotel one day before they were to meet their tour group.

Shortly after checking in Luisa received a fax from home. It seemed that the client on her last project didn't want to pay the balance of his bill until he spoke to her. The shot back to reality was not received well by Luisa. Who in their right mind would bother you with such an issue when you were thousands of miles away? It reminded Luisa of a telephone call that she received many years ago after childbirth. The client called her in the maternity ward to see where her order was.

Luisa thought, don't these people realize that sometimes you just need a break from the real world?

She answered the fax, "Resolve when I get back!"

Rosanna and her schoolmates were leaving for Rome in a few days and Luisa hoped that her daughter had remembered to pick up the cell phone she had arranged for her to use while in Europe.

The next day Luisa, Teresa and Carmella awoke early eager to explore Rome. They were to meet the Global Tour group for dinner at 6:00 PM and then spend the next 21 days with the group visiting places throughout Europe.

For today, however, they were on their own and the three women set out to see the Eternal City. Somehow Teresa got separated from Luisa and Carmella in Vatican Square. Luckily both Teresa and Luisa had the address of the restaurant where they were meeting the Global Tour and the family reunited there at 6:00 PM.

The restaurant where they met the Tour group was called El Toula. It had a cozy atmosphere with antique furniture and beautiful flowers and fruit on every table. The bar by the front entrance served a procesecco e fagiola (pasta and bean soup) risotto with radicchio and the delicious fegato alla veneziana (calves' liver with onions). The sounds of Andre Bocelli singing Mistero Dell' Amore were heard throughout the dinner.

Soon after they sat down at a table, Luisa discovered that she had left her cell phone in the cab she and Carmella had taken to the restaurant. She lamely told Teresa that she had forgotten the cell phone because she had so many other things on her mind.

The wise Teresa shook her head no. "It's the drugs, Luisa. They're making you addled."

Luisa knew her mother was right. By the time she, Teresa and Carmella had left for Europe she was taking an astounding 27 medications.

These included Darvon, Methocarbamol, Relafen, Tylenol #4, Zantax, Oxycondin, Sulfameth, Buspar, Ranitidine, Trazodone, Promethazine, Roxicet, Hydrocodone, Cipro, Guaifenesen, Paxil, Prevacid, Lorazepam, Neurontin, Lipitor, Dulcolax, Lotrel, Ativan, Hydrocholorothiazide, Restoril, Zyprexa, and Rhineocert.

For several moments Luisa was crestfallen. With a few simple words her mother had put her finger on a mushrooming problem that Luisa had tried hard to deny to herself even existed.

She sighed inside and thought about what to do. They were about to embark on a three-week tour with a busload of strangers. There was little she could do about her drug dependency until she returned home and had a chance to consult with her doctors.

Recognizing that it was pointless to dwell on her problem now, she looked around the table at the other diners. Sitting next to her was a heavyset man named Mr. Green. He was dressed somewhat shabbily and was muttering under his breath. Across from her sat Teresa and Carmella. The four others at the table appeared to be middle-class Americans with no agenda other than to enjoy a tour of Europe.

Then, as Luisa was starting her meal, she suddenly remembered that she had the number of her cell phone and that she had left it on. She asked the waiter to bring a phone to their table and when she dialed her cell phone number the cab driver answered. She asked him to bring her cell to the restaurant and – rightly anticipating a tip – he did. Finally Luisa could settle down and enjoy her meal.

The next day they toured Rome with the group, visiting well-known sites that included the Vatican, the Sistine Chapel, the Roman Coliseum, the Catacombs and the Spanish Steps. Throughout the tour Luisa snapped pictures.

That evening they had dinner at La Terrazza dell'Eden, one of the best restaurants in Rome with a breathtaking view of the city. Afterward they went to the famous Trevi Fountain where

Carmella threw her lira into the pond and made a wish.

That evening Luisa took a taxi to the hotel where Rosanna and her friends would be staying and dropped off the cell phone she had purchased for her.

The next morning they journeyed to Florence. Their tour guide, Stefan, was an Austrian. He was affable and articulate. He explained the importance of compatibility within the group, pointing out that they would be traveling and dining together for the next 21 days. The rules for the tour were simple: be punctual and listen to Stefan.

Luisa decided to stake a claim to the long seat that ran from wall to wall in the rear of the tour bus. Here she could stretch out and peacefully read during their hours on the road. As the bus left Rome she nestled in with her *Foder Tour* Book and her copy of *Simple Abundance*.

Carmella sat next to her grandmother – who was entertaining herself by playing cards – and played her Gameboy.

After a while, a girl named Cindy rose from the seat she had been in and plopped down next to Luisa. She told Luisa that she had decided to come on the tour at the last minute, adding that her mother was wealthy and had paid for her trip.

Cindy asked Luisa who had paid for her trip, a question Luisa found rather strange. She replied that she had paid her own way. Thinking the girl was lonely and wanted to make conversation, Luisa went on to tell Cindy that she had been in a terrible car accident and that she had signed up for the European tour to escape the stress at home.

Cindy mentioned that she had suffered a jaw injury in a car accident but had forgotten to bring her pain medication along on the tour. Cindy then asked Luisa if she could have some of Luisa's pain pills.

"I'm afraid I can't give you any prescription medicine," Luisa said. "It's against the law."

Despite Luisa's refusal, Cindy asked for narcotics again. Once more, Luisa said no. The girl then revealed that her traveling partner was the same Mr. Green that Luisa had sat next to at dinner the night before.

"We're both from Miami," Cindy said. "Mr. Green owns several beachfront hotels there."

By now somewhat leery of the girl and her strange questions, Luisa made small talk until Cindy finally went back to her seat. As Luisa watched her walk down the aisle of the bus, she thought, she's as shabbily dressed as Mr. Green. I wonder what their real story is.

As the bus trip wore on, Luisa discovered that the pair were both loud and obnoxious – often yelling and cursing at each other. They were so annoying that an ever-increasing number of the other tour group members refused to associate with them.

By the time the bus finally arrived in Florence, Mr. Green and Cindy were totally isolated from the others. Their offensive behavior even irritated the tour group leader.

Luisa was determined not to let the bad-mannered Floridians spoil their tour. After all, most of the group was both pleasant and friendly. There were couples celebrating their wedding anniversaries, men recovering from heart attacks, widows on their first trip by themselves, and mother/daughter teams.

Not surprisingly, Carmella was popular with the people on the tour. They admired her cheerful personality and good manners, and the way she was attentive to her mother and   grandmother.

They toured Florence for two days. As a History major who had taught European cultures for many years, Luisa was thrilled to be in Florence. Many of the buildings had been built in the 11th and 12th centuries. One of the most beautiful buildings they visited was the Piazza della Signoria designed by Lorenzo Ghiberti. The structure's most famous feature was the renowned gilded bronze east portal, which Michangelo called the "Gates of Paradise."

From there, Teresa, Carmella and Luisa toured the Mueo

dell'Opera del Duomo, home of the unfinished "Pieta" by Michangelo. Then they walked the Piazza della Signoria where Michangelo's statue of David stood. The Piazza was also the home of Cellini's famous bronze Perseus Holding the Head of Medusa.

After visiting the Piazza the group took some time to browse the nearby shops and Luisa located a jewelry store where she bought a necklace with a gold cross and her daughters' birthstones.

The tour group then headed back to the Villa Azalee hotel where they were staying. The bedroom that Luisa, Teresa and Carmella shared was spacious and featured copies of Michelangelo's paintings on the walls. Gild-gilded red velvet drapes framed the windows and the carved Italian mahogany furniture lent an air of elegance to the room.

The surrounding garden in full blossom reminded Teresa and Luisa of Nonni's beautiful Rose gardens. Luisa suddenly remembered a poem by Jacopo da Lentini, which captured her feelings as she gazed out the window of her room at the Eternal City, sprawled out below.

> *I have it in my heart to serve God so*
> *That into Paradise I shall repair,*
> *The holy place through which everywhere*
> *I have heard say the joy and solace flow,*
> *Without my lady I were loath to go,-*
> *She who has the bright face and the bright hair;*
> *Because if she were absent, I being there,*
> *My pleasure would be less than nought, I know.*
> *Look you, I say not this to such intent*
> *As that I there would deal in any sin:*
> *I only would behold her gracious mien,*
> *And beautiful soft eyes, and lovely eyes,*
> *That so it should be my complete content*

To see my lady joyful in her place.

The next morning the tour group boarded the bus for the trip to Venice. Teresa especially looked forward to seeing Venice for, in addition to its canals and historic sites; the city was famous for its collectibles, including exquisite Murano glassware.

Luisa fell in love with Venice. Italians called the beautiful canal-laced city La Serenissima, the Most Serene. The gondola ride they took through the canals was awesome. Luisa videotaped their journey and for years afterward family and friends enjoyed the video of the historic buildings and bridges along the canal.

While in Venice they also took a tour of the Murano glassworks and learned that the glassblowing techniques employed by the artisans had been handed down for generations. Luisa decided to purchase some crystal vases for the design studio she dreamed she would have some day.

The vases – gilded in 24K gold – were a rainbow of colors that included azure blue, crimson red, amber gold, hunter green, and amethyst. Teresa also bought some crystal. Later they would both give some of their purchases to family members and friends as gifts.

The Murano salesman, Marc, was so appreciative of their patronage that he offered to take Luisa, Teresa and Carmella to lunch. They told Marc that they had planned to go to Sunday Mass at Basilica di San Marco and he graciously escorted them to the basilica and promised to meet them after the Mass.

The Basilica di San Marco was unique in that it was half church and half mosque. The richly decorated façade of the building featured four gilded horses and inside the church was a 10th century gold and silver altarpiece inlaid with precious gems and emeralds.

The Mass was beautiful. The church was ancient, and its architecture and marble statues both massive and impressive.

As promised, Marc met them after Mass and surprised them by

taking them to La Caravella – a storied Venetian restaurant – for lunch. When they were seated, they let him guide them through the menu.

Like the Italian gentleman that he was, Marc made excellent recommendations and they dined on granseola (crab), scampi Ca d'Oro (shrimp in cognac sauce, served with rice), Spaghetti, and Past e fagioli.

Marc invited them to visit him again. In fact, he wrote them a letter inviting them to stay at a friend's condo in Venice. Luisa saved this letter just in case they traveled to Venice again.

Lunch was a leisurely affair and Luisa's mom was worried about the time. They were to meet the tour group at 3:00 p.m. Marc assured them that they would not be late. Unable to finish their rich desserts, they opted to take the treats with them. Before they left, they thanked Marc with Italian hugs and kisses.

They made it back to their tour bus by 3:00 p.m. Although they hadn't gotten to see much of Venice, they'd had a wonderful time shopping, and their stomachs were full from the seven-course lunch.

Unlike Luisa, Teresa and Carmella, the tour group had been so busy sightseeing that they hadn't had time to get anything to eat. They were not happy with the tour guide and his tight schedule.

Realizing that food was a sore subject, Luisa was reluctant to tell the others about their sumptuous luncheon. However, their white lunch bags and large red leather menu gave them away and the tale of their storybook luncheon was soon making the rounds of the bus.

The next day the tour continued on to Pisa. Unfortunately, Luisa had tried to do too much during her first few days in Europe and her hectic pace had caused the pain in her upper body to flare up.

Although she increased the dosage of Oxycondin she was taking, she still had to slow down considerably and could not accompany Teresa and Carmella and the tour group as they saw the sights of Pisa.

Using her Hometrac Unit helped relieve her pain and Luisa was soon ready for the rest of the Global tour to continue.

The tour moved on to Brussels. The pace of sightseeing slowed down there and Luisa was able to get in some shopping. As a history major she had studied Napoleon and she was captivated when she spotted replicas of the guns used at the battle of Waterloo in a shop window. On a whim, she purchased several to display in her design studio.

Truth be told, she was drawn to the replicas for another reason. When she was a little girl she'd had a fascination with cowboys and Indians and her dad would fashion guns for her out of aluminum foil. The replicas of Napoleon's guns had rekindled her memories of those crinkled aluminum rifles she had so loved as a child.

They journeyed next to Lucerne, Switzerland. By now Luisa knew that she had to seek out medical treatment, for the drugs she was taking had done little to lessen her constant pain. All she was accomplishing was becoming more addicted to the narcotics.

She inquired at the hotel desk and was told there was a drop-in medical facility nearby. She went right over and described her injuries to a doctor. The physician promptly ordered an ultrasound treatment and advised her to slow down her pace.

The ultrasound treatment brought much relief to Luisa. Teresa and Carmella, however, were increasingly concerned that Luisa's medical problems were making her take too many mind-altering drugs. Luisa secretly agreed, but kept her thoughts to herself. She sincerely believed that she needed her various medications to get through the trip, and at the moment that was her most important goal.

When Luisa finished her ultrasound treatment, the three went to lunch at a café to relax. After lunch they shopped for small collectibles. They took their time going from store to store, allowing Luisa to amble along the sparkling clean streets of the beautiful city at a leisurely pace.

The following morning the tour bus headed for a one-day stop in Amsterdam. It was there they hoped to find her dad's relatives. They made several phone calls but were unable to make contact with any members of the family.

Disappointed, they rejoined the tour group for the trip to Cologne, Germany where they took a cruise on the Rhine River. After a brief stay in Cologne, the tour buses headed down the autobahn to the Black Forest. German cuckoo clocks were made there and many on the tour bought clocks with miniature Hummel's and figurines on them.

Luisa drank so much cherry wine that day that she slept through dinner and didn't wake up until the next morning. Since she desperately needed the uninterrupted sleep, she felt that the wine had actually done her more good than her medications.

As the tour traveled through Germany toward France, they saw the haunting WWII concentration camps of Dachau and Auschwitz. Everyone on the tour was deeply affected by seeing the places where so many innocent victims had been put to death.

Luisa told their tour guide Stefan about her physical limitations and he graciously volunteered to massage her shoulders, neck, and back each day during the rest of the tour.

Their bus headed next to Paris where the three decided to explore the City of Light on their own. Luisa flagged down a taxi and used her hand translator to ask the driver to take them around the city, stopping at the sights so they could take pictures.

The driver – whose name was Louis – took them to the Arc de Triomphe, the Bois de Boulogne, and the Champs-Elysees, among other sites. The gardens, cafes, and theater districts were just breathtaking to see and Louis used his broken English to describe the history of each place they visited.

At the end of the tour Louis drove them to the Louvre and Luisa, Carmella and Teresa went in to explore the treasures of the world-famous museum. Inside they were thrilled by the paintings of artists such as deVinci, Delacroix, Chardin, Boucher, Rubens, Rembrandt, Giotto, Raphael, and Titian.

After leaving the Louvre, Luisa, Carmella and Teresa took a bus to the Left Bank and had lunch at Campagne et Provence restaurant. There they had cod, eggplant and fresh French bread. Teresa and Luisa drank Chardonnay with their lunch and Carmella had cherry flavored soda. They had strawberries and crèmes crepes for their dessert.

Then they took a bus back to the Hotel Mecedes where they were staying. They rested for the rest of the afternoon, then, after dinner, they took a taxi to see the night-lights and the city's preparations to celebrate the coming millennium.

The next day they said goodbye to the other members of the tour group and set off for London. As they crossed the English Channel by hovercraft, they stared transfixed at the fabled White Cliffs of Dover.

Finally, they were in London. They were on their own – free at last. Rosanna and Anton joined them the next day and the reunited family spent several joyous days touring England.

Later that week Luisa's best friends Diana, Arnold, Seth, and Lynne joined Luisa. Teresa and Carmella arrived in England for ten days of sightseeing with the Cannolis. The group arranged with Framm's Tours to visit Stonehenge, Oxford and Stratford upon Avon.

It was an all-day tour and very historically enlightening. Another day they traveled to Warwick Castle and to Bath. The Medieval atmosphere of the two sites made Luisa imagine scenes of Knights battling for the honor of their ladies.

In Bath, they enjoyed going to the Roman Baths Museum and immersing themselves in the curative hot springs. The 115-degree temperature of the water did much to soothe Luisa's body pain.

They next traveled to London where they toured Madame Toussaint's Wax Museum, Notting Hill and Kensington Palace. To save money, they all took buses around the city.

That evening they went to the theater in the West End and saw Grease. The next day, they all traveled to Abbey Road, and had a photo taken crossing the road; just like the Beatles did in the cover photo of their Abby Road album. That evening they all went to see the play, Notting Hill at the local theater.

The next day they all took the bus to shop at Harrods and the Chelsea and later went window-shopping. They had lunch at the Chelsea Cheese Restaurant. The waiter sat them at the table where Charles Dickens and Sam Johnson had often dined.

On July 1st, they decided to go on a Royal Tour to Lady Di's estate of Althrop. On the bus ride to Altrop, they were enchanted by the beautiful wildflowers that fringed the country roads.

When the tour bus approached the Spencer estate, goats and sheep were grazing in the rolling green fields. A sweet serenity enveloped all as the bus pulled up the long gravel driveway of the estate. The washed beige brick Spencer homestead was surrounded by huge oak trees and flowerbeds abloom with yellow, pink, red, blue and lavender buds.

The Cannolis and their friends were escorted into the Spencer home and greeted by a personable and friendly Spencer servant who had been with the family for many years. The interior of the mansion was painted a soft green and hung with scores of oil paintings.

The medium oak floors were covered with antique red, green, ivory and blue Persian rugs that blended well with the neutral-colored sofas and chairs. The sophisticated design of the home reflected Lady Di's style and appearance.

Luisa extended her sincerest condolences for Lady's Di's tragic death to one of the servants and mentioned her own close call with death in an automobile accident in 1997. The two exchanged names and Luisa was given a phone number to call to make a donation to Lady' Di's favorite charities.

Seeing the interior of the home allowed Luisa and the others to witness how the Spencers had lived. Their family room was similar to many in the USA. There was even a bottle of Worchestchire steak sauce on an end table, along with a bottle of Vernon's ginger ale.

The tour group next walked outside to the rear of the mansion where a small lake was surrounded by bouquets of flowers. Docked at the shore was a small boat that the Spencers used to row out to Princess Di's grave on a small island in the middle of the lake.

As the tour group slowly walked around the flower-strewn lake, they came upon a memorial wall and bench donated by the Spencer servants in Lady Di's memory. Along the wall were touching notes of love the servants had written to the princess.

They left the lake along a path that led to a group of converted horse stables. In front of the staples a movie screen displayed a film of Lady Di as a child. A room in the stables hosted a display of her toys, as well as mementos collected during her marriage to Prince Charles. In other rooms, many of Lady Di's famous designer gowns were on display. The converted stables also contained a marble wall inscribed with expressions of condolence to the Spencer family from people around the world.

After a box lunch on the estate, the Cannolis and their friends left for London, taking with them the feeling that they had witnessed history.

As the group boarded their plane to fly home the next day, Luisa was heartened by the knowledge that the Cannolis European vacation was an experience none of the family would ever forget.

Chapter 11

Home Again

L uisa really did not want to come home and face the mounting responsibilities and problems that were waiting for her.

One of the first things she had to do was get Rosanna ready for college. Here it was mid-July 1999 and her eldest daughter would be leaving for Master Tech University the following month.

Rosanna had an excellent academic record through high school and had qualified for the Dean's Scholarship from University of Technology School of Engineering because she had decided to major in Bio-Med engineering.

The scholarship was good news for the Cannolis because – although Luisa and Anton had socked away $14,000 for Rosanna's college education – Luisa's medical bills continued to mount and the money was short. In addition to winning a scholarship, Rosanna had worked part-time during high school and saved up money to pay many of her daily colleges expenses.

Although ensuring that Rosanna's college needs were taken care of was not really a burden, other problems loomed over Luisa in particular and the family in general. For one thing, she had gained nearly 60 pounds since the accident and all that extra weight was complicating her medical condition and worsening the constant pain she suffered.

On the morning of August 7 – Luisa and Anton's 23rd wedding anniversary – the couple was sitting at the kitchen table talking and Luisa asked Anton to please pay for a body massage for her anniversary gift. Perhaps that would help with her pain.

He said he would so she left the kitchen and called the masseuse to make the arrangements. When she returned to the kitchen she was astonished to find that the glass tabletop had somehow become cracked while she was gone.

Anton told her that he had done it when he banged his fist down on the glass. He was so frustrated with everything. Luisa didn't know what to say. All she could think of was the scene from the film, *A Beautiful Mind,* in which the wife of the brilliant but mentally disturbed mathematician smashes a mirror in the bath after he turns down her sexual advances because his medications have left him devoid of desire.

Alarmed by Anton's uncharacteristic display of temper, Luisa called Dr. Stuart. The physician told her that he wanted to see Anton and her individually as soon as possible. Anton reluctantly went to see him and afterward Dr. Stuart met with her.

He explained to Luisa that Anton had bottled up everything inside himself. He was the type that could not handle nor express what he was experiencing. His type of personality eventually comes around, but when Luisa needed his support the most he simply couldn't be there for her.

Ominously, Dr. Stuart explained to her that some marriages ended in separation or divorce when faced with all the problems now confronting the Cannolis.

The doctor's words were a revelation to Luisa. For years she had believed that if at times her husband had seemed indifferent toward her, in reality he was simply a quiet man who rarely expressed his inner feelings. Now Dr. Stuart was telling her that the mounting pressures in their life were not something that Anton could easily deal with, and their marriage might be in danger.

Of course, Luisa had long realized that there were differences between them. Anton was analytical and methodical while she was far more of a visionary. He also kept things to himself while she tended to air her concerns and grievances.

She believed in openness and would sometimes tell him, "I should have married Tom Freeby. He was always able to express his feelings to me." She was sorry now that she had said those words.

Their contrasting personalities often brought them into conflict, especially over issues such as Luisa's pending personal injury case. Anton was appalled by the lack of preparedness on the part of their attorney, Michael Wright. He felt that they were losing control of events and needed to spend more time concentrating on the case. Although Luisa was also unhappy with Wright's casual approach, she felt that her focus must remain riveted on her far more important medical problems.

They were also unalike in the ways they viewed leisure activities. While Luisa loved socializing with her friends and going out and meeting people from all walks of life, Anton preferred the peaceful haven of their home. After working long hours at his demanding job, he liked to unwind listening to his daughters play the piano. At other times he would lose himself in the pages of a good book.

Anton understood his energetic wife's outgoing nature, and admired the passion she brought to her work as an interior designer. Yet her way was not his way. Luisa brought her work home and wasn't reticent about discussing the constant challenges she faced in her career. Anton left his workday cares at the office.

Yet as different as Luisa and Anton were in some ways, they were alike in others. They both enjoyed going out to dinner and favored the same restaurants: Sorrento's Inn, Trio's, Applebee's and the Century Inn. They also demonstrated their mutual love of each other with daily expressions of kindness and caring, and started each day with warm hugs and tender kisses.

As Luisa searched for a way out of their ever-deepening dilemma, she wondered, will our love carry us through, or will all the problems we face end up destroying our marriage?

Their financial situation did not improve in the weeks that followed. Anton would not refinance their first mortgage. The interest rate was 6.5% fixed for fifteen years and he didn't want to lose such favorable terms. Unwilling to refinance the mortgage, he was getting more and more frustrated, and tensions between him and Luisa continued to mount.

Meanwhile, Luisa had to fly to Boston to get Rosanna registered for school. Realizing that this would be the last time she would see Rosanna for a while, Luisa chose to stay a few extra days to take Rosanna and her new friends sightseeing in nearby Martha's Vineyard.

The ferry to Martha's Vineyard was a first for Rosanna's new friends. Luisa took the girls to the Brass Crazy Horse Carousel, an attraction the family had last visited when Rosanna was only five. On one of her turns on the carousel, Rosanna had caught the brass ring, entitling her to four extra rides.

On this trip, Rosanna did it again and an excited Luisa snapped a picture for posterity. Before heading back to Boston, Rosanna gave the tickets she'd won to some children waiting in line.

Anton had driven to Boston to pick Luisa up and, after getting Rosanna settled in, they headed home. It was a fretful trip for Luisa because the security locking system kept jamming, and they had no idea why.

Despite Luisa's worries, they made it home without mishap. There another problem awaited them. The clicking sounds on the telephones were becoming more prevalent and Luisa was getting more and more suspicious of a possible tap on their telephone lines.

Anton did not believe someone would do that to them and the couple argued constantly over the matter. Before the stress brought on by Luisa's accident, Anton had rarely argued with her, and Luisa found his newly combative nature upsetting.

On the positive side, Michael Wright finally contacted them about the upcoming trial date, now set for October 1999. It appeared that at last he was getting focused on their case.

Luisa had supplied him with most of the medical records of her injuries after her friend, Carrie, organized her medical files. Carrie had labeled the folders according to doctors, medicines, hospitals, medical equipment, and nursing homecare.

Although legal matters seemed to be moving forward, Anton and Luisa were both concerned that Wright had never given them a contract for the case, even though he'd already met with the opposing defense attorney.

Inexplicably, Wright called them out of the blue and asked that they return the contract to him. Luisa told him adamantly that he had not yet provided them with a contract and that she and Anton were not at all happy with the situation.

Realizing that the Cannolis were angry – and perhaps on the verge of dropping him as their counsel – the attorney finally prepared a contract and began preparation for the trial.

A few days later Wright informed them that Freedom Insurance now wanted to go to mediation. This necessitated cancellation of their October trial date. Luisa thought about the insurance company delay tactics that others had warned her about and wondered if Freedom was now pulling the same underhanded maneuver on them.

Michael Wright called them to ask what demand amount they wished to receive from the insurance company. After much discussion, Luisa and Anton established the figure at $775,000. The trucking company had a $1,000,000 policy on the truck that hit Luisa's car.

After the couple had spoken with Wright, they consulted with another lawyer and with friends who worked in finance. All the financial professionals they talked to were appalled that Wright had not come up with a demand amount himself.

Shortly afterward they went to mediation. The mediator was a well-respected retired judge named Bertman. He explained the relevant judicial codes to the Cannolis and cautioned that there could be delays in the negotiations. He empathized with Luisa, for he too suffered from chronic pain and knew how easily one could become dependent upon medicines.

Michael Wright made their demand to Freedom Insurance Company and its lawyer, Lee Sleazer, one of the most repugnant men Luisa had ever met. Sleazer was in his mid-60's with thinning brown hair, a deeply lined face and a short fat body. His voice squeaked when he spoke, and when he opened his mouth the numerous silver fillings in his teeth glittered like the chrome bumper on a car.

Sleazer tried to infer that the back surgery Luisa had undergone in 1983 – 14 years before the accident – was causing her lower back pain. Wright countered that Luisa had fully recovered from that surgery long ago, as evidenced by the fact that she had a second child in 1986.

Luisa was forced to meet with Sleazer and talk to him on the phone several times and, on each occasion, his snide accusations and overly personal questions so upset her that she experienced bouts of vomiting and sudden diarrhea.

During one mediation meeting with two young Freedom Insurance Company adjusters working with Sleazer, Luisa asked the adjusters to get a letter of apology to her from the driver, Frank Walker. They said they would. Judge Bernard told them they had two weeks to respond to the Cannolis request.

While Luisa waited for a response for the insurance company adjusters, she decided that she'd like to see some of the old friends she had not had a chance to spend time with recently because of her extensive medical treatments.

Her best friend of 30 years, Mary Ellen Porter, welcomed Luisa's call and they arranged to have lunch the next day.

Luisa and Mary Ellen met at Fountain Square. Christmas Holiday decorations were everywhere and the ice skating rink was crammed with ice skaters of all ages.

They decided to have lunch at Pomori's Italian Inn – which had a beautiful view of the square – and ordered Italian wedding soup, Italian bread and tossed salad. While they ate, they chatted about their children and caught up on each other's personal lives.

The two old friends chuckled at some of the experiences they'd shared when they'd taken their children to the Zoo and Kings Island many years before. Carmella – who was only three years old at the time – had loved touring the amusement park on the shoulders of Mary Ellen's husband, Scott, the strings of several colorful balloons clutched in her tiny hand.

As they talked, Luisa suddenly felt a burning sensation in her right nostril and realized that it was being caused by cigarette smoke wafting toward them from the table of a young couple on their right.

She started coughing and sneezing uncontrollably and a moment later she could feel her chest tightening. She knew that the smoke had aggravated the sinus condition caused by her deviated septum, an ailment she had suffered from all her life.

To avoid embarrassing Mary Ellen, Luisa suggested that they end their luncheon immediately. Mary Ellen agreed and they left the table and headed to their cars. As they said goodbye, Mary Ellen expressed her concern to Luisa and wished her well.

Once home, Luisa immediately called Dr. Grizzly who prescribed Erythromycin for her condition. Knowing the effect of this particular antibiotic on her stomach, she decided to take Prevacid instead, a medication she already had. For some time after inhaling the cigarette smoke, she suffered through congested and sleepless nights.

Shortly after her sinus condition flared up, the judge handling her personal injury case decided that the mediation process had failed and reset trial for May 2000. Feeling that her attorney was to blame for the constant delays in her trial, Luisa called Ben Martin, an older attorney who was a friend of her family, to let him know about the lack of preparedness of their case by Michael Wright. All Ben could tell her was that Wright was an excellent trial lawyer. Anton and Luisa doubted that Martin's glowing words about Wright would prove true.

Despite the upcoming trial, Luisa still had a business to run and she consulted with her doctors about going to the Atlanta International Market in January 2000 to purchase rugs for her clients. They advised her that she could go but that it was imperative that she pace herself.

That fall Luisa also took on a kitchen remodel for her neighbor, Oliver. The project was scheduled for October, November and December 1999.

Although she knew that she shouldn't take on new responsibilities in her weakened condition, a business opportunity arose during this time that was too good for Luisa to resist. Her two friends, Meredith and Rebecca, the owners of Total Design, were retiring, and Luisa decided to try to buy their business.

She contacted a local bank and applied for financing. The loan officer explained all the documents needed for a commercial loan. The building and inventory together would cost $139,000.

Luisa also wanted to renovate the building housing Total Design. As she worked on the architectural plans for the changes she envisioned, she found that her time was becoming more precious than ever and that she would need others to help with her professional responsibilities. Her good friends, Anne and Suzanne, were always ready to pitch in and were soon working beside Luisa.

The threesome planned on participating in the upcoming Christmas Walk, an annual event that kicked off the holiday shopping season for local merchants. As part of their Christmas preparations, they helped Meredith decorate her shop for the Holidays. They had luminaries in front, lights on the building, and wreaths and bows on the windows. They were proud of the results, and enjoyed a good response from their visitors. It was a fun weekend.

In addition to his duties at the studio, the ever-reliable William ordered supplies, cleaned the Cannoli home and yard, and drove Luisa around. Anne was made office manager and supervisor, while Suzanne became Luisa's right arm in Design World, specializing in color and fabrics.

Her upcoming trip to Atlanta also weighed heavily on her mind. She would have to make several critical decisions about what rugs to buy for her perspective clients. The purchases – most speculative – would stretch her financial resources even further.

Fortunately for Luisa's mental equilibrium, her mother, Teresa, would be flying down with her. Teresa had been saving her money to buy a rug for her home, and she was elated to be accompanying her daughter to the show in Atlanta. They also planned a brief visit with Luisa's sister, Alexia, who lived in nearby Macon.

Luisa hoped the trip would divert her mind from the pain and stress plaguing her. Emotionally, physically and financially, she was nearing the breaking point, and there was still no end to her ordeal in sight.

By permission of John L. Hart FLP, and Creative Syndicate, Inc.

Chapter 12

Strange Events in Atlanta

Although it was snowing when Luisa and her mother flew out of Clarksville – and both women needed wheelchair assistance to pass through the airport – they boarded their flight on Great Wings Airlines with only minor inconveniences and enjoyed a pleasant flight to Atlanta.

The airport personnel in Atlanta were courteous and helpful, and Luisa and Teresa were soon on their way via taxi to the Grand Tower Golden Palace on Peachtree Street. Almost from the moment they arrived at the hotel front desk to check in, events started to take a strange turn downward.

When Luisa presented her bank charge card in payment for their room, the clerk attempted to process the card, only to find that the transaction had been denied. Luisa was flabbergasted, as she knew she had a zero balance on that card and a $25,000 credit line.

She asked the desk clerk to call the 800 number on the back of the credit card and find out what the problem was. The clerk complied, then turned to Luisa and told her that the issuing bank had refused to give her any credit.

Luisa began hyperventilating. How could a $25,000 credit line vanish into thin air? She'd had the card and paid her bills on time for over 20 years. She'd used it during her entire European vacation. What was happening?

Now agitated to the point of near-hysteria, Luisa took the phone from the desk clerk and shouted into the receiver, demanding the name of the girl at the credit card company. The girl refused to give it. Luisa next insisted that she be allowed to talk to the supervisor on duty. Once more the young woman refused. By now Luisa was gasping for breath. Unable to continue, she handed the phone back to the desk clerk and sagged in disbelief and defeat.

Her mother came to the rescue, giving Luisa her own credit card. That took care of the check-in problem, but another frightening situation had already arisen. Alarmed by the scene that the over-medicated and distraught Luisa was causing, the hotel management had called security.

Unbelievably, Luisa and Teresa found themselves surrounded by three tough-looking security guards. Although Luisa had by now calmed down and her mother was clearly no threat, the unsmiling guards insisted on escorting the two innocent women to their room.

Their accommodations were as disturbing as their welcome – a 12'X12' room with a single king-size bed and one twin-size rollaway. Their three pieces of luggage took up much of the open space.

While Teresa lay down to rest, Luisa left the room to talk to the concierge in person about her rental car reservation, only to be told that her reservation had been cancelled. The rental agency insisted that she had called and cancelled herself, although Luisa had done no such thing. She was beginning to feel like she had dropped down the rabbit hole in Alice in Wonderland.

Deciding that she was up against sinister forces that she neither understood nor could fight against in her weakened condition, Luisa returned to their room and scheduled a therapeutic body massage. She hoped the massage would ease her tensions and allow her to think more clearly.

After making her appointment, Luisa made sure her mother was resting comfortably, then left the room and headed for the hotel exercise area. As she neared the workout facilities, she heard voices behind her.

A woman said, "She is with me now," followed by a male voice replying, "Okay."

Luisa turned and found a casually dressed couple in their early thirties following her up the hall. It was obvious to Luisa that they had been talking about her, as there was no one else around.

As Luisa watched over her shoulder, the man turned into a side corridor while the woman continued to follow close behind her, quickly cutting the distance between them.

When the woman caught up to Luisa she said, "Where are you going?"

Luisa thought the woman's question was strange – after all, they had never even met – but wanting to be pleasant she replied, "I'm going to the exercise area to get a body massage. I was injured in a severe automobile accident and I find that exercise and massages helps ease my pain."

The woman looked at Luisa strangely and said, "Funny, you're not dressed for exercise."

Taken aback, Luisa replied, "Perhaps that's because I'm going for a massage. I'll exercise another day."

The woman shrugged. "Whatever. What kind of work do you do?"

Luisa was getting uncomfortable with the woman's familiarity. Nevertheless – wanting to be civil – she said, "I'm an interior designer."

"What a coincidence, I'm a designer, too," the woman exclaimed. She reached into her purse and took out a business card. "Here, take my card. Maybe we can work together some day."

Luisa glanced at the card. It read:

Descriptive Designs
Graphics and Desktop Publishing
Denise S. Olsen, Owner

"Thank you," Luisa said. "Now I really must be off to my massage appointment."

Without another word, Luisa turned away and hurried ahead toward the hotel gym. As Luisa was crossing the exercise area toward the massage room, she noticed the mystery woman had followed her in and was getting on an exercise bike.

Is that woman following me, watching me? She wondered.

A skilled massage therapist named Michelle worked on Luisa for over an hour and a half, massaging her whole body. She told Luisa that she could feel the torn muscles and scar tissue that had so tortured her.

"The deep muscle spasms are still painful," Luisa responded.

Luisa felt her pain magically vanish as Michelle expertly massaged her tired body. As Michelle's hands worked their wonders, she told Luisa about the twelve meridian lines that cross the body from head to toe. The therapist then proceeded to massage each toe on both of Luisa's feet. As she did so Luisa felt the severe pain in her cervical area lessen.

When Michelle completed the message, she took Luisa into her office and showed her a chart of the meridian lines in the human body. She then recommended that when Luisa went home to be sure to find an experienced masseuse who knew about the entire body – including the muscle and nerve systems.

She told Luisa that she needed a masseuse with at least ten years experience to work on all of her injured areas. Michelle added that she shouldn't lift anything heavy, as her upper torso injuries were serious. Luisa left Michelle's office with a deep sense of gratitude to the caring masseuse.

The massage loosened up Luisa's torn muscles and she felt

much better. As she crossed the exercise area, she noticed that the woman who had followed her down the hall was still on the exercise bike.

The woman looked at Luisa and said, "I find that exercise helps relieve the constant pain I have following my accident."

The woman then hopped off the bike and began to walk beside Luisa, making Luisa feel very uneasy. The woman was simply too pushy.

As they walked down the hall outside the exercise area, the woman kept up a nonstop monologue about her talents as a designer. She then began asking Luisa about her plan to create a brochure featuring her design company. Luisa was shocked. How did the woman know that she was planning to put a brochure together?

The woman then proceeded to pump Luisa for information about her injuries. Luisa grew increasingly uncomfortable and wary, and finally came to a stop in the middle of the corridor, hoping the woman would walk on. But the woman stopped too, and continued asking Luisa questions.

Luisa felt like she was on one of those investigative shows she had seen on Television – 60 Minutes or Dateline. The woman was obviously an investigator, not for a television network but – Luisa suspected – for Freedom Insurance.

Luisa decided to take the offensive, and began asking the woman questions about herself: What was her line of business, who did she work for, how would Luisa get in touch with her?

Clearly nonplussed, the woman tossed her long dark hair and said, "I work for the government."

Luisa gave the woman a look of disbelief and disgust, then stalked away. The woman didn't follow. Still, the strange encounter had unnerved Luisa, for it was part of a pattern of unsettling events that had plagued her since she had arrived in Atlanta.

First her perfectly good credit card had been denied when

she'd tried to check in. Then her conversations with several representatives of Bell Tower – who were holding meetings at the hotel – convinced her that her fears about her phones being tapped were real. And now she'd been approached by a strange woman who somehow knew that Luisa was planning to have business brochures printed up.

By the time Luisa reached her room she was hyperventilating.

The next day Luisa and her mom drove to Macon to visit Alexia, who had the flu. Soon after they arrived, Luisa felt her pain level increasing. Much to her chagrin, when she reached into her purse for her bottle of Tylenol with codeine she discovered that she was out of the medication.

She asked Alexia where the nearest pharmacy was and her sister gave her directions to a CareMed Pharmacy just a quarter of a mile down the road. Luisa found the pharmacy with no trouble and got her prescription for Tylenol filled.

As she went to the front of the store to pay her bill, a woman in her sixties with stringy gray-blond hair approached her at the counter. She was poorly dressed and carried an old purse.

As Luisa was paying her bill, the woman started talking to Luisa about batteries. Luisa innocently listened as the woman explained that she had a pedometer to keep track of how far she walked and that the pedometer – which she didn't have with her – needed a battery.

"Which battery should I buy?" she asked Luisa.

"Without the pedometer, I can't help you," Luisa said. "You should talk to the store personnel."

The woman ignored Luisa's advice and picked out a package of batteries from a display. She then returned to the counter and told the salesgirl that she would buy the package, but if the battery did not work she would return it.

The clerk cautioned her that CareMed Pharmacy did not accept opened packages for return. Luisa advised the woman to find out what battery her pedometer took, then buy it. In reply the woman said that she lived by Bally-Mart down the street and she would go there. She then left the store.

Luisa paid for her medication and went outside in time to see the woman get into a white Chrysler that was parked facing Luisa's car. As Luisa started her car and left the parking lot, she noticed that the woman was still sitting behind the wheel of her parked Chrysler.

Pulling away from the shopping center, Luisa wondered whether the strange-acting woman was another snake from Freedom Insurance. Turning into her sister's neighborhood, Luisa looked into her rearview mirror and was not surprised to see that the woman in the white Chrysler was right behind her.

Now Luisa was certain the woman was a snake for she had told the pharmacy sales clerk that she lived near Bally-Mart and there was no Bally-Mart within miles of her sister's neighborhood.

As she was nearing her sister's house, the woman in the Chrysler turned left and simultaneously a blue Toyota came up behind Luisa's car. There was no longer a question in Luisa's mind that she was being followed – not by a single snake but by a team working together.

When Luisa turned onto her sister's street, the blue Toyota continued on past the intersection. Not wanting to worry Alexia and the others, Luisa kept the latest snake incident to herself. She would wait until she got home so that she could get to the root of the inexplicable events she was experiencing.

The following day Luisa experienced two other strange incidents. While riding the Grand Tower Golden Palace elevator down to the lobby that morning, a couple got on at a lower floor. Luisa was carrying a camera and they asked her what she was going to take pictures of.

By now leery of strangers asking her unusual questions, she told them that she intended to take pictures of the Atlanta skyline from the glass elevator on the outside of the building. She said goodbye to the couple in the lobby and walked to the elevators.

As she waited for one of the glass cars to arrive, a second couple approached Luisa and asked her where she was going. Now why would they want to know where I'm going, she thought to herself. This is really strange.

Luisa felt her breathing becoming more rapid as her tension rose. Forcing herself to be calm, she told the couple the same thing she had told the first couple – she was going to take pictures of Atlanta from the glass elevator.

Inexplicably switching the subject, the man told Luisa that his wife was from Columbia and spoke no English. Unsure who the couple was and not wanting to be rude, Luisa replied that she had a brother-in-law who had married a beautiful Colombian girl who spoke no English.

Even as she spoke Luisa was wondering, who are these people? Are they simply innocent hotel guests wanting to make friendly conversation – or are they Freedom Insurance Company investigators?

Luisa said goodbye to the couple and rode up in the elevator. Although she was still having trouble breathing, she wanted to make lunch reservations at the Top of the Sky restaurant for her Mom and herself. When she arrived at the restaurant she noticed that it was revolving.

Luisa asked the Maitre de if there were a handicap entrance. Assured that there was, she made a lunch reservation for later that week and then returned to her hotel room. Teresa was waiting for her and the two women left to go to the dealer showrooms in the Merchandise Mart.

Luisa and her mom visited the design showrooms of Persia Imports, Custom Rugs and the Braided Rug Company, as well as several floral showrooms. While they were there at the Mart, Luisa purchased a Murano rose-colored crystal vase for the design store she planned to open in her hometown of East Hill Valley. The vase had raised relief and painted flowers in varying shades of green, white and yellow. The elegant 18-inch tall vase also had a rim and base trimmed in 24-K gold.

After spending several hours at the Mart, the women returned to their hotel. Luisa was experiencing breathing problems and tried to relax that evening. She and Teresa had a delicious dinner at The Rib's restaurant near the hotel then returned to their room and went to bed early.

The following morning Luisa gave some hard thought to the three strange encounters she'd had with suspected snakes from Freedom Insurance. The very idea that an unscrupulous corporate entity could be invading her privacy was both repugnant and frightening to her.

Deciding that there wasn't much she could do about the machinations of Freedom Insurance until she got home, Luisa went into the bathroom to take a warm bath. Not really focusing on what she was doing, she reached for a sharp new razor and began to shave her legs.

Suddenly the bathtub was filled with bloody water. It looked like the Red Sea. She had somehow sliced open her entire left shin. As she climbed out of the tub, blood ran down her left leg and pooled on the tile floor.

She grabbed towels to stop the bleeding but to no avail. Beginning to panic now, she let out a shriek, bringing Teresa rushing into the bathroom. Her mother took one look at Luisa's bloody leg and called the front desk for help. Two paramedics came rushing up and bandaged the wound but the experience left Luisa drained.

What else can happen to me? She thought despondently.

The next morning Luisa and her mother prepared to go to the exhibition hall again. Luisa knew that she had to focus – for she would have to make several work-related decisions at the show – but her normal concentration was hindered by her mounting anxiety over the bizarre events that had plagued her stay at the hotel.

She had been uncharacteristically rattled by the denial of her credit card, the mysterious cancellation of her rental car and her repeated encounters with overly inquisitive strangers.

Yet, by the time they arrived at the show Luisa was feeling almost euphoric, a radical mood change that she attributed to the numerous and strong medications she was taking.

In fact, at the Art & Mirror displays in the Looking Glass showroom, a sales representative asked Luisa why she was so "jubilant."

Luisa told the woman how she had survived a major automobile accident on the interstate in July 1997 during which her car had been crushed between two tractor-trailers.

She described how – as she sat trapped in her car – *she had beseeched the Lord to help her, and was suddenly enveloped in a brilliant white glow. She told the woman that the faces of her two beautiful daughters had appeared within the light and that at that moment she knew that God would not let her die.*

Luisa went on to relate how her love of design and helping others had inspired and motivated her throughout the ordeal of her long and painful rehabilitation. When Luisa finished, the woman told her that the story of her miraculous survival had given her goosebumps.

Luisa thanked the sales representative for her understanding and awareness. She and Teresa then moved on to choose some artwork and mirrors for the design shop Luisa planned to open. They also visited the rug showrooms and purchased several rugs, including a rug that Teresa had long wanted for her family room.

After a busy afternoon visiting the many exhibits at the show, the two women headed back to their hotel. When they reached their room, Luisa lay down to rest, only to be seized by multiple spasms. Teresa hovered over her daughter, her face a mask of shock and worry.

Although Luisa had lost control of her flailing body, her mind remained clear. She was all but certain that the spasms were being caused by a reaction to the many drugs coursing through her body.

By now, she was simultaneously taking Darvon, Methocarbamol, Relafen, Tylenol #4, Zantax, Oxycondin, Sulfameth, Buspar, Ranitidine, Trazodone, Promethazine, Roxicet, Hydrocodone, Cipro, Guaifenesen, Paxil, Prevacid, Lorazepam, Neurontin, Lipitor, Dulcolax, Lotrel, Ativan, Hydrocholorothiazide, Restoril, and Zyprexa.

It was a potent chemical cocktail that virtually guaranteed that Luisa would suffer serious side effects.

She began to have difficulty breathing and decided to call her doctor in Clarksville. Teresa put the call through. When Luisa described her symptoms to the physician, he advised her to go the ER.

Luisa hung up and thought over what the doctor had said. She felt uncomfortable at the thought of being treated by physicians she didn't know and trust. She would be returning home the next day, and decided to wait 24 hours before seeking medical help. Meanwhile, she would try to relax.

Yet how could she escape the intense pain she was suffering and the constant mental stress of flashbacks, an inexplicable credit card denial, and encounters with strangers she was certain worked for Freedom Insurance? On top of everything else, she had to struggle to conceal her pain and stress from her mother so as not to upset her.

Luisa decided that the best thing to do was to get out of their hotel room for a while, and she rose wearily from the bed.

Pretending to be fully recovered, she told Teresa, "Let's go out for dinner."

Teresa agreed and they had dinner in one of the restaurants on the lobby level. Sitting through the meal was an ordeal for Luisa, but she somehow managed not to reveal the turmoil broiling within her to her mother and after dinner they returned to their room and retired early.

The next morning they arose early and packed for their flight home, then went to the top of the Sky Restaurant for an early lunch. The Maitre de accommodated them by pointing out a wheelchair ramp leading up to the restaurant floor.

They both ordered spaghetti and meatballs but Luisa had absolutely no appetite. Teresa told her that her face was pale and Luisa felt cold and clammy. Her breathing was slow and drawn, and she was so weak she could hardly lift her fork.

The two women had an abbreviated lunch and then returned to their room. Luisa called the front desk and ordered a taxi. The desk clerk that she spoke to told Luisa that she did not sound right. Luisa told her that she was experiencing difficulty breathing. The clerk advised her to lie down, and told Luisa that she would send someone up to their room to help her.

A few minutes later a hotel staffer trained in emergency medical care arrived. He immediately administered oxygen to Luisa and told her that she looked very sick. After breathing in the oxygen for a short time, Luisa's breathing returned to normal. She told the staffer that she felt better and that it would be best if she went home to see her own doctors.

Reluctantly, the staffer called a taxi. As they checked out of the hotel, all Luisa could think about was that the insurance investigators knew right where she was. If they staged another stressful encounter, she wasn't sure what she would do.

Luisa could not tell her mother about her concerns because she knew Teresa would immediately think that she was having another medication-caused hallucination. The only people who would believe her were Caroline and Suzanne. They had been privy to many of the strange events that had plagued Luisa, and were as convinced as she was that the insurance company was responsible for all the terrible things that had been happening to her.

Luisa and her mother finally arrived at the airport and approached the Great Wings Airlines ticket counter. Still feeling weak, Luisa asked the clerk behind the counter if there was oxygen on the plane if she should need it.

The clerk regarded her coldly, and then said, "If you have a breathing problem, you can't get on the plane for 48 hours. You will have to get a doctor's permission before you can board."

Luisa and her mother sat in their wheelchairs in front of the Great Wings counter stunned at the clerk's words. What would they do now? Luisa reached for her cell phone and called her sister in Macon to explain what had happened.

Alexia advised her to go to the nearest hospital and get checked out. Luisa was doubtful. There was a flu epidemic raging in the southeast and with her weakened immune system she didn't want to risk exposure.

But then, after a moment's reflection, Luisa realized that she had little choice, and asked the Great Wings clerk to recommend a hospital where she could be treated. The clerk advised Luisa to go to Wayward Hospital, located in downtown Atlanta.

By now resigned to the unfortunate situation, Luisa and her mother wheeled themselves to the terminal front entrance and hailed a cab. Teresa was beside herself, for she had had her suitcase checked into the Great Wings luggage system at the hotel and her bags would shortly be on the way to Clarksville.

"I have to get home and pay my bills," Teresa kept saying.

Her mother's worried words only put more stress on Luisa.

After a tension-filled cab ride, they arrived at Wayward Hospital. The emergency room was packed with flu victims. However, Teresa spoke to the head nurse and managed to get Luisa seen by a doctor after only a short wait.

The physician verified that Luisa's breathing was constricted and diagnosed her condition as flu-related. He advised her to get home as soon as possible to be treated by her own doctors.

The doctor signed a note to Great Wings Airlines so they could get on the return flight. Before they could leave for the airport, however, Alexia arrived at the emergency room. A heated argument between the two sisters followed.

Alexia wanted Luisa to go to the airport immediately and get a flight home, insisting that their mother needed rest. Luisa countered that she might need oxygen again soon, and wanted to stay in Atlanta that night.

Exasperated, Alexia told Luisa that she was not going to allow their mother to go through any more stressful events, and announced that she was taking Teresa to her home in Macon.

Luisa watched her sister and mother leave, then called Gerald — one of the security guards at the Grand Tower Golden Palace who had helped her – and explained her predicament. Gerald sympathized with Luisa's plight, and arrived at the hospital within a half-hour.

He told Luisa that the Grand Tower Golden Palace would help her as much as they could. She told him that she appreciated the hotel coming to her aid, but that she would check into the Best Rest Hotel for cost reasons.

Gerald rode with her in a cab to the Best Rest Hotel, then wished Luisa well and said goodbye.

When Luisa checked into the hotel, she told the receptionist of the difficulty she'd had with her charge card. She asked to use a check for her deposit, and to make the amount out for an additional $150 she would need for expenses. After a few cursory questions, the desk clerk agreed.

When Luisa got to her room, she called Anton and told him of her problems at the airport. She also reminded him that her credit card had been declined when she'd tried to check into the Grand Tower Golden Palace several days before, and told him she was running short on cash. He coldly told her to calm down and wait it out.

After Luisa hung up with Anton, she called Suzanne and told her of her predicament. Suzanne said that Luisa's experience in Atlanta sounded like the movie *Trains, Planes, and Automobiles* starring John Candy and Steve Martin.

When she finished her conversation with Suzanne, Luisa

stretched out on the bed. She knew she needed sleep, but sleep wouldn't come. The late night talk shows didn't help. By now she had gone for three full days without any real rest.

After a fitful night spent tossing and turning, she struggled out of bed the next morning and called Great Wings Airlines to arrange to have the tickets for herself and her mom upgraded to first class.

The reservation clerk told Luisa he could accommodate her upgrade request but that switching to first class would cost an additional $600 for the two tickets. Luisa explained that she had been having problems with her personal charge card, and that she would call her husband and have him put the additional charge on one of his cards.

After speaking to Anton, Luisa called Alexia, who agreed to arrange for a limo to take their mother to the airport. Relieved that she and Teresa would finally be going home, Luisa checked out of the hotel and took a taxi to the airport.

Luisa met her mother at the Great Wings Airlines counter and an hour later they boarded their flight for Clarksville. They were seated up front near the bathroom. A husky man in an ill-fitting suit sat next to them and began casting furtive glances toward the two women. After Luisa caught him at it the second time, she became suspicious.

A moment later the man asked her if she had any gum. What a weird request, Luisa thought, her apprehension rising. Who asks for gum on an airplane?

"I don't have any gum," she replied stiffly, then buried her face in a magazine.

The strange man persisted in his all-too-obvious attempt to engage Luisa in conversation, asking her if she knew anything about airplanes.

"Do you mean toy airplanes?" she said coldly. "The kind made out of balsa wood and rubber bands?"

The man's jaw dropped and he turned away, apparently aware

that his cover had been blown.

No sooner had Luisa put the man beside her in his place than she noticed another man two rows back staring at her. She began to think that the whole plane had strange people on it – half of them busy watching her and her mother.

Following a stressful flight for Luisa, the Great Wings jet finally landed in Clarksville. After taxiing to the terminal, the stewardess unexpectedly announced that the passengers would disembark from the rear of the plane, instead of the front as usual. First-class passengers would have to remain seated until last. Luisa was dumbfounded. She had flown dozens of times, and on every occasion first-class passengers had disembarked before coach.

Why pay the extra money for first class if you have to go through this? She thought.

She watched as the pilot passed down the aisle and positioned himself near the rear exit. As the passengers left, each and every one complimented the pilot on a safe and comfortable flight. On every flight before this one, Luisa had seen the occasional passenger praise the pilot – but today everyone on the plane went out of their way to give the pilot a pat on the back. Strange!

In the terminal Luisa and her mother were met by porters with wheelchairs who wheeled them into the main terminal where Anton waited for them. Luisa told the porter pushing her wheelchair about her strange flight from Atlanta. She added that her request for onboard oxygen the day before had possibly triggered a flight delay. She also reminded him that a plane had blown up over the Everglades a few months before because the oxygen canisters had been improperly stored in the luggage compartment.

She went on to tell the porter of her pending personal lawsuit against Freedom Insurance. She then asked him what he knew about her and the present situation and whether the Great Wings flight had been a security plane.

The porter responded that the airline did not know who she was and that only normal security precautions had been taken.

The strange events surrounding the flight continued when Anton told Luisa that when he got to the airport the parking lot attendant ordered him to re-park the car a quarter of a mile away from the terminal.

Then Anton told Luisa that they had had no mail for two days. Luisa shook her head silently to herself. What was going on? Were the unexplainable events of the past few days connected to her suit against the insurance company?

What other explanation was there? After dropping Teresa off at her home, Anton drove Luisa to the hospital in Clarksville for a check-up. The doctor who saw her told them that Luisa was suffering from a severe flu-related sinus infection, compounded by stress and sleep deprivation. He advised Luisa to go home and get as much rest as possible.

As Anton drove away from the hospital, Luisa sank into the seat beside him and numbly watched the highway signs go by. She felt under siege, and wondered if she could survive her constant confrontations with insurance company stooges.

When they got home, Carmella showed her mother an email message addressed to her. The message said that Luisa Cannoli would be arrested for fraud for using bank charge card number 45781920698347.

Luisa knew at that moment that her identity had been stolen sometime before she arrived in Atlanta and checked into the Grand Tower Palace Hotel.

Carmella asked her mother what "fraud" meant. Luisa told her young 14-year old that fraud meant dishonesty. She went on to tell Carmella that someone had stolen her identity by using her charge card number.

Trying to remain calm, Luisa called B.A.N.K. charge card services. The supervisor listened patiently as Luisa read her the email message and explained that that her card had been denied when she tried to check into the hotel in Atlanta.

The supervisor checked her data system and found that there was no fraudulent notice attached to Luisa's account. She advised Luisa to call her internet service provider and ask them to trace the origin of the message.

Luisa hung up slowly, dazed by this latest inexplicable event. ***Where does it all end, she thought? When do I get my life back?***

Chapter 13

No End in Sight

The strange and threatening events that had happened during Luisa's trip to Atlanta had taken an emotional and physical toll on her, worsening her existing medical problems. She was now nearing a total collapse.

Despite the emergency room doctor's diagnosis that Luisa was suffering from a severe flu-related sinus infection, Luisa did not believe that his prescription for getting as much rest as possible was the answer.

Recalling that her own doctor had advised her to seek medical attention at a hospital, Luisa called her cousin Angela – with whom she had always been very close – and asked Angela to drive her to the North Lakeland Hospital Emergency Room. Luisa explained that she had called her doctor from Atlanta and he'd advised her to be checked out at the hospital when she got home.

When they arrived at the hospital, a triage nurse checked Luisa's blood pressure and found that it was elevated. Angela sat with Luisa as she told the nurse of her concern that her sinus infection might be spreading.

The nurse arranged for a doctor to examine Luisa. He then listened to her lungs and did not detect any abnormalities. He told Luisa that she was under stress. Luisa informed him of the many medicines she was then taking, including the antibiotic Ceclor for her sinus infection. He advised her to continue taking her medications, and go home to rest. Luisa complied with his advice.

Angela drove Luisa home. Around 7:00 Anton arrived from work looking very tired and drained. It had been a long day for him, and Luisa decided not to add to his worries by telling about her visit to the emergency room that day.

Knowing that Luisa was spent from her Atlanta trip, Anton volunteered to cook a spaghetti dinner. Carmella pitched in and prepared a salad. Luisa tried to be enthusiastic about the dinner Anton and Carmella were putting together, but she was not at all hungry.

She felt weak and wanted to just sleep, but could not. Her nerves were frayed, perhaps, she thought, from the 80-mg Oxiconotid pill she had taken that afternoon. Her body pain had decreased greatly but even this brief respite was little relief because she felt so hyper from the drugs she was taking.

She had been taking antibiotics for two months to fight her rapidly spreading sinus infection, which she was convinced had been caused by cigarette smoke. Her doctors had first prescribed Erythromycin, and then Ceclor. Luisa wondered if her immune system was in such a weakened state that it could not fight the infection.

She was confused, frustrated and in shock from the frightening events that had taken place in Atlanta. Part of her frustration was that Anton just did not want to hear any more about her strange encounters, believing that Luisa was imagining things.

As the evening came to a close, Luisa prayed, read Simple Abundance and listened to music in an attempt to fight off flashbacks about her horrific experiences in Atlanta. Yet – try as she might – she simply could not avoid the terrifying feeling that the recent strange events and her suspicion that her phones had been tapped were somehow linked, and the handiwork of insurance company agents. Unscrupulous people were violating her life, and there seemed nothing she could do about it.

Plagued by fear, Luisa went to bed alone. Anton had moved into their guest bedroom to get the much-needed sleep he couldn't get laying beside the continuously tossing and turning Luisa.

That January night was very cold and snowy, with four inches of snow covering the ground within a few hours. About 2:00 AM, Luisa awoke abruptly. She was gasping for air and extremely cold, despite the heavy comforter and blankets covering her. Her chest felt tight, and body pain had become severe.

She wondered if her shallow breathing was a repeat of her breathing attack at the hotel in Atlanta when Leon and Gerald had had to administer oxygen to her. Weak and wobbly, she arose from her bed and went in to seek help from Anton.

Luisa quietly entered the guest bedroom and gently shook Anton awake. "What's the matter?" he asked sleepily.

"I can't breathe normally," she said. "What do you think I should do?"

Anton sighed in frustration. "You're just imagining things again," he said. "Go back to bed and get some sleep."

Anton's dismissal of her breathing problem left Luisa feeling alone and abandoned. Nevertheless, she knew how drained her husband was by all that had happened, and decided not to get into a verbal confrontation with him at that hour.

Resigned to handling the problem by herself, she went downstairs to call 911. She told the operator who answered that she was having severe breathing problems, and ran down the list of strong medications she was taking. The operator said that they would send an ambulance. Luisa asked that no sirens be used, as the noise would awaken her family and the neighbors.

When Luisa got off the phone, she went back upstairs and changed from her flannel pajamas to black slacks and a beige sweater. She put on her winter jacket and boots, and turned the outside lights on.

A few minutes later, the ambulance drove up their snow-covered driveway. An EMS attendant approached Luisa's front door. Luisa met him before he rang the doorbell. He told Luisa that he wanted to check her blood pressure first. It was elevated. Then he walked her to the ambulance where a second EMS attendant sat behind the wheel.

The attendant strapped Luisa to the stretcher-bed inside and gave her oxygen to calm her. About 3 AM, they reached North Lakeland Hospital where the attending emergency room doctor met Luisa. He took her medical history and – after listening to her chest to check for pneumonia – ordered chest x-rays. He then asked her what medications she was taking, and wrote down her long list of prescriptions.

For once a doctor is listening to me, she thought. And he seems so caring and thorough.

Luisa asked him for his name and he told her that he was Dr. Marc Goldenberg. The physician then excused himself to get the results of Luisa's chest x-rays. He returned a few minutes later and told her that her lungs were clear.

He attributed her breathing problems to stress and prescribed Ativan for her to take – one now and a couple more later if needed. Concerned for her transportation home, he asked Luisa if she wanted someone to call her husband.

Although she was concerned about Anton driving the 30 minutes to the hospital when he was so tired and drained; especially with snow still falling. Luisa knew this would be better than a long taxi ride, and agreed to let an attendant call her husband.

Within forty-five minutes, Anton was there, looking like he had just awakened – which he obviously had. Now it was nearing 5:00 AM. The Antivan calmed Luisa down and they were both silent on the ride home. Anton didn't even turn on the radio.

Anton stayed up and got Carmella ready for school.

Exhausted, Luisa went to bed and slept until 8 AM. She did not even hear Anton and Carmella leave that morning.

Although business concerns beckoned Luisa, she decided to stay focused on her health. Suzanne, Anne and William were handling her two design projects competently. The Oliver job was nearing completion, and the new client kitchen job was just getting organized.

She called a medical specialist she knew, Dr. Doede – who had treated her many years before for a serious sinus infection – and arranged an afternoon appointment. She planned to pick up Carmella from school first. With clammy hands, she drove to Carmella's school, collected her daughter, and then headed for the doctor's office. Carmella chose to stay in the car to do homework while Luisa was seeing her physician.

Luisa had no sooner walked in the physician's office than she had to race to the bathroom where she vomited up so much phlegm that she thought her entire insides were going to tear apart. Within minutes, the nurse called her name to be seen by Dr. Doede.

Dr. Doede started his examination by asking Luisa for a list of her medications. She knew her medicine list by heart and promptly wrote down all her many prescriptions. Dr. Doede then checked her sinuses, which were very infected. He told Luisa that she needed medicine sprayed into her nostrils, and brought out a dark brown bottle of liquid.

It was only after he had sprayed the mist into Luisa's nostrils that he told her what it was: Cocaine.

Luisa, in her weakened physical and mental state, thought he was joking. Why would a doctor give any patient cocaine? Cocaine was an illegal drug, and Luisa could not imagine a reputable physician giving it to his patients.

She suddenly felt lightheaded. Doede dismissed her to go home with no follow-up appointments scheduled. He did, however, give her a prescription for a sinus medication called

Rhinemsis.

By now Luisa felt so weak that she dared not attempt to drive. She called her friend, Kate to take her and Carmella home, knowing that she could return for her car later.

They arrived home about 3:00 PM and Carmella finished her homework. Luisa went upstairs to take a bath, but felt suddenly weak. She put on her flannel pajamas and collapsed on her bed for ten minutes. As she was recovering her strength, William knocked on the bedroom door and told Luisa that he would be downstairs in her office.

Luisa decided to go down and talk to William about the Oliver job, which he was then working on, and to give him his wages. Luisa paid William daily for his work and also let him take her Ford Club Wagon home. Oblivious to the fact that she was still wearing her pajamas, Luisa went down to her office and held a brief conversation with William.

When she'd finished talking to William, Luisa decided to call Dr. Doede back and tell him that – despite his unorthodox treatment that afternoon – her sinus condition had not improved. She was told that he was not available, but that one of his many physician assistants would take her call.

Luisa described her symptoms to the physician. He told her that he would call the drugstore immediately and leave a prescription for Bactrin, a potent medicine used to treat sinus infections.

William offered to go to the drugstore and get the prescription for Luisa. It was approaching 4:00 PM when he came back with the prescription.

Luisa had bottled up her Atlanta trip and needed someone to talk to about it. It was so traumatic for her. William had always been a trusted confidant, and Luisa poured out her heart to him.

When she had finished telling William about the strange encounters in Atlanta, he looked at her with deep concern and said that he believed she was having a panic attack.

Luisa nodded her head in agreement, feeling her heart racing and her breathing becoming more labored. Thinking that her sinus condition might be hampering her breathing, Luisa opened the Bactrin bottle and swallowed two pills with a glass of water.

Within minutes, she felt like she was fainting. William sensed something was wrong but Luisa insisted she was okay. Yet inside she was quaking and terrified.

She knew that she should lie down and rest, but first she had to pay William for that day's work. She asked him to follow her upstairs as her checkbook was in her upstairs office. However, when they got there Luisa could not find her checkbook anywhere. She clearly remembered leaving the checkbook on top of her upstairs desk, and its mysterious disappearance further upset her.

Composing herself, Luisa decided to search her downstairs office. Sure enough, she found the checkbook in a desk drawer. She did not remember putting it there.

"How did my checkbook get down here?" she wailed, growing more distraught by the moment.

William had no idea, as he did not handle office paperwork for her at her home.

Luisa was struggling with her breathing again and felt as if she were about to pass out. William offered to stay with her, but Luisa insisted that he leave before the rush hour traffic got too heavy.

After William left, Luisa called Carmella from her room. She held her youngest daughter in her arms, giving her a very tight hug and telling her that she loved her. Although Luisa fought to be strong for Carmella, the sight of her hands and arms turning white – and her increasing sense that she might lose consciousness at any moment – made her feel as if she were dying.

Carmella looked at her mother with fear in her eyes and told Luisa that she loved her very much. Tears rolled down her face as well as Luisa's. Luisa knew that she had to get help for her deteriorating medical condition or their family would be shattered.

Luisa told Carmella that she wanted to speak to grandma, and went into her first floor office to call her mother. Although she felt like she might lose consciousness any moment, she managed to call her mom and tell her that she loved her. Luisa added that her medical condition was deteriorating and that she needed emergency care.

Her mom's voice quivered as she spoke to Luisa, asking her to describe her symptoms. All Luisa could say was that she could not breathe and was losing consciousness as they spoke. Luisa told her mom again that she loved her and hoped to talk to her soon. They said a tearful goodbye.

Luisa then called Suzanne's home. Suzanne's son, Jason, answered the telephone and told her that Suzanne was not home. Luisa told Jason that she loved him and that she'd loved vacationing with him and all the other kids over the past years. She told him that she felt like she was dying.

As Luisa talked to Jason her breathing was becoming ever shallower and she was gasping for air. She said good-bye and hung up.

She called Anne and Caroline, but they were not home either. In the messages she left, she told her friends the same things she had told Jason. Then she thought of Alena – a friend she knew from Lancome products – who lived nearby. However, she could not remember her telephone number. Luisa called 411 for Alena's phone number.

The 411 operator told Luisa that her breathing sounded very labored and that she needed to call 911. At that point, Luisa collapsed into her office chair and her mind went totally blank. She held onto the chair to keep from falling and sank into semi-consciousness.

All of a sudden, her cousin Angela appeared at the door to her office. The look on her cousin's face revealed her shock at seeing

Luisa blurry-eyed and white as a ghost. Angela immediately called an ambulance. Minutes later five EMS attendants arrived and crowded into the house. Outside, the driveway was bumper to bumper with a total of seven ambulances and five police cars with lights and sirens blaring.

They put Luisa into an ambulance as her neighbors crowded their front lawns to see what sort of trouble had befallen the normally quiet and peaceful Cannoli home.

On the way to the hospital, Luisa started screaming about the audacity of the insurance company to send operatives to follow and harass her in Atlanta, and to eavesdrop on her private conversations.

"Look at my shoulder scar!" she cried out from her stretcher. "Is that fake? Look at the MRI and Sony pictures of my displaced ovary! Look at my adhesions from major surgery! Read the letter from my surgeon!"

The ambulance arrived at the hospital and Luisa was hurriedly wheeled into the emergency room. Several minutes later Luisa regained consciousness as the nurse pulled her flannel pajama bottoms off to inject her left thigh with medicine in a large needle.

To her horror, she discovered that her hands, arms, legs and angles were strapped to the bedsides. A blue uniformed officer stood over her.

"Why am I being restrained?" Luisa cried out.

"To prevent you from injuring yourself," the policeman replied.

Standing around her were her husband Anton, her sister Anna, her cousin Angela, and three nurses. The nurse who had given her the shot asked Luisa why she did not have underwear on.

"I was going to take a Jacuzzi bath when I finished making phone calls," Luisa replied in a groggy voice.

The rest of that first day in the hospital was a blur to Luisa. The next afternoon – 18 hours after being rescued by the Life Squad – Luisa awoke to find that she was wearing a hospital gown. There were wires protruding from her head and chest, and she was still strapped to the bed.

A nurse was standing at her bedside and Luisa asked what had happened to her. The nurse replied that the doctor would tell her. She added that Luisa's family was waiting to visit her after the doctor had seen her.

"The doctor will be in soon," the nurse assured her.

Luisa was beside herself. She had never been treated like this in a hospital before. She knew that she was totally exhausted. Did she have a nervous breakdown due to extreme stress and severe chemical imbalance caused by drugs? This was a major concern to Luisa.

A few minutes later the nurse un-strapped Luisa's arms and legs and told her to get into a wheelchair beside the bed. Luisa complied, noting the kindness and concern in the nurse's soft voice, and her gentle touch. The nurse's caring demeanor did much to ease Luisa's apprehension.

A few minutes later the physician arrived. Dr. Anderson was in his sixties and had brown hair with grey highlights. He told Luisa that he was there to help her. His words gave Luisa a sense that she was in good hands.

Dr. Anderson looked at Luisa's file – which obviously contained a transcript of her panicked outbursts the day before – and asked Luisa what had happened to her in Atlanta. Luisa related her strange encounters with individuals she was convinced were insurance company investigators, as well as her suspicion that her phones were tapped. She also told the doctor that her house had been broken into, and several items stolen.

The physician listened carefully, and then told Luisa that he had heard of insurance companies using invasive tactics to investigate fraud during the course of lawsuits against them. He added that Luisa's account was the most extreme example of underhanded insurance company tactics he had ever encountered.

He told Luisa that she was over-medicated, and that her panic attacks were most likely caused by the mental torment that she endured in Atlanta, as well as the invasion of her privacy through phone taps. He explained that she was suffering from a severe chemical imbalance brought on by the interaction of the many medications she was taking, and recommended hospitalization in a psychiatric ward to wean her off the medicines.

Dr Anderson emphasized that panic attacks could happen to anyone under so much stress. He went on to say that, unfortunately, there were doctors who over-prescribe medicines, thinking they were helping their patients.

"I'm convinced that a period spent in detox will do wonders toward restoring your good health and mental equilibrium," the physician added. "Do I have your word that you'll check into Good Heart Hospital for evaluation and detox?"

Luisa agreed and Dr. Anderson clasped her hands with a smile, and then called in her family.

Anton entered the room first, a very worried look on his drawn face. He appeared helpless, as if he was at a complete loss as to how he could comfort his wife during her latest medical ordeal.

Accompanying Anton were Luisa's sister Alexia, who had flown in from Georgia to support Luisa, her other sisters Sophia and Anna, and her cousin Angela. The family all hugged Luisa and assured her that they were there to get her though this medical mess caused by doctors. They gathered Luisa's personal items to take her home.

Anton helped Luisa to the car and opened the door for her, a courtesy he rarely performed. Other than Anton telling her that he had taken the week off to be with her, they did not talk at all on the car ride home.

When they arrived home, Luisa called Suzanne and Anne. They arrived at the house an hour later. She explained that she would be checking into the hospital the next day and asked them to take charge of her two ongoing design projects. She also asked them not to tell her clients of her medical problems. They assured

Luisa that they would keep her hospitalization to themselves.

When Carmella got home, Luisa held her daughter tightly as they both cried. When the tears stopped, Luisa told Carmella that she was okay, and that her condition was due to the many strong drugs she was taking. She asked Carmella to talk to her about her feelings.

Carmella told her that seeing her mother's medical problems steadily worsen had upset her so much that she would never talk about it. This devastated Luisa. How much pain was little Carmella in?

Luisa recalled when Carmella, at age 10, had asked her if she wanted to be buried in her 1989 Toyota Cressida because she lavished so much attention on the car. Now – almost three years later – Luisa wondered what else has Carmella kept inside her? How could Luisa make this up to her child and heal her mental anguish?

Carmella gave her mom a hug and headed for her room to do homework. Shortly afterward, Luisa got a call from her sister, Anna telling her that the family wanted to have her evaluated by a Good Heart psychiatrist because they no longer trusted the doctors who had over-medicated her. Luisa agreed, and Anna said she would make the appointment.

The next morning, Luisa, Anton and Luisa's family members went to the office of Dr. Stephen Young, a psychiatrist at Good Heart. Dr. Young had agreed to meet with the family on short notice, and when everyone was seated he conducted a family-counseling meeting.

Dr. Young told the family that he would prescribe appropriate medicines for Luisa. This upset Luisa and Anton. Why more medicine? Didn't prescription drugs cause Luisa's recent medical meltdown? They took the prescriptions, thanked the doctor for his time and left.

The family was dumbfounded that – like the psychiatrists before him – Dr. Young had prescribed medication as the solution to Lusia's condition. Luisa's sisters insisted that they were only trying to help. Anton thanked them for being there for Luisa, and told them not to worry about what had happened. They all then said goodbye and headed home.

Again, Anton and Luisa did not talk on the way home. Once home, Luisa began experiencing slight breathing problems. By nightfall, her breathing difficulties had increased significantly and Luisa asked Anton to take her to Good Heart. She had agreed to go to detox. She wanted to be admitted. What she didn't want were any more new doctor evaluations.

Anton took her to the Good Heart emergency room. It was not crowded and a nurse saw her immediately. After hearing Luisa's explanation of why she had come in, the nurse summoned a physician, Dr. Silverson, who called Dr. Stuart, the physician who had been treating Luisa.

Good Heart had a policy that only doctors who were on the hospital's staff could admit patients, and Dr. Silverson discovered that Dr. Stuart was on staff at another facility. Despite Silverson's best efforts, he could not get around the hospital rules, and he finally had to tell Luisa that he simply could not get her admitted.

Luisa felt like the medical profession had let her down severely. Here she was ready and willing to be treated for her addiction to prescription medications, and the bureaucratic rules of Good Heart Hospital were preventing her admission.

Anton took Luisa home. The next day, she called Suzanne and Anne and asked them to take her to the hospital again. Despite the admission policy at Good Heart, Luisa was determined to try once more to be admitted and treated for her deteriorating condition.

Suzanne and Anne arrived at 10 AM to take Luisa to the hospital. Despite Anton's skepticism about his wife's medical condition – and his disbelief that insurance company operatives were harassing her – he agreed to accompany them to Good Heart.

They arrived in the emergency room and were met by a nurse. She took Luisa's blood pressure and found that it was 180 over 70. The nurse also noted symptoms of possible stress. Concerned with Luisa's condition, the nurse admitted her to the emergency room to have her stress level evaluated by a doctor.

How different this caring nurse is from the arrogant doctor, I saw here yesterday, Luisa thought to herself.

Unfortunately, the male emergency room doctor that saw Luisa shortly afterward was a far cry from the nurse. In his mid-thirties and cocksure of himself, the physician was arrogant and demanding. When Luisa told him about her personal injury case against Oceanic Land Transportation, he snidely asked her how many other lawsuits she was involved in. Luisa told him just suits over business disputes; at least she thought that was the case. Anton told her to be quiet.

Luisa was seen next by a Dr. Arrogen, who told her that it was possible she'd had a stroke. He ordered a brain Catscan, as well as blood work.

During her treatment in the emergency room, Luisa started talking to the nurses, asking them what they thought about her condition. She felt that nurses in general were more perceptive and sympathetic than physicians, and more likely to recognize the seriousness of her condition and recommend that she be treated by a physician. Luisa was catching on to the ways of the medical system.

Her family was busy making hospital arrangements. Luisa got a call from Anna before checking in the family decided to get an opinion from Good Heart psychiatrists. They wanted Luisa not to be treated by the doctors who overmedicated her. Luisa complied with the genuine wish. So the next morning the family, all of Luisa's sisters and Anton went to see psychiatrist, Dr. Stephen Young. It was a brief family-counseling meeting. Dr. Young met with family on short notice – one day. He told the family that he would prescribe the medicine for Luisa. This upset

Luisa and Anton. Why more medicine? Did not the medicine cause this recent medical explosion for Luisa? They took the prescriptions and thanked him for his time.

The family said that they were only trying to help. Anton thanked them for their genuine help. They all headed to their homes.

Again, Anton and Luisa did not talk on the way home. Once home, Luisa kept having slight breathing problems. She did not want it to get out of hand. Dr. Anderson had taken her off Bactrim, as that contributed to her near death. So they made another trip back to the hospital.

She told one nurse that she wanted her examination to be very thorough, and asked that the doctor do a urine test to determine whether she had too many drugs in her system. The urine test was conducted, and Luisa was found to have an extremely high level of Oxicordin and cocaine. Given the possible side effect of the powerful drug, the doctor decided that Luisa should be admitted to the hospital and kept under observation.

Luisa felt vindicated after her shabby treatment at the hands of the emergency room doctor the day before. She wanted answers to her medical problems – as did Anton and her family – and now perhaps those answers would be found.

Luisa had prepared her overnight bag for Good Heart Hospital for that day.

Suzanne and Anne came to Luisa's rescue regarding the cocaine. They knew of her emergency visit to Dr. Doede.

Proactively they called him and demanded that he write a letter to Luisa's doctor, Dr. Chuck Stuart and lawyer, Michael Wright within that hour. They were headed to his office immediately to get it and on the way to the right people.

They received the letter. It read as follows:

Dear Dr. Stuart and Mr. Wright:
I am the ENT Doctor treating Mrs. Cannoli.
She is suffering from a major respiratory infection and
has not responded to the basic antibiotics. Her health
condition suffers from sleep deprivation, which has
severely weakened her immune system.

I sprayed three doses of medically approved
cocaine into her right nostril.

I observed her health condition before allowing
her to go home.

She had driver assistance to my office with her
daughter with her. With her weakened condition, I
advised her to contact someone to drive her home. She
did so.

If you need further information, feel free to call
me at 465-672-7123.
Sincerely,
Dr. Doede

Suzanne and Anne, as true friends for life, finished their task, decided to make brownies and take them to Luisa. However, Luisa did not know the double doors were locked coming into the Psych ward. Anne and Suzanne could not get in to see her nor was able to give her the brownies. Luisa did not get to see her friends. They sat outside the locked door and ate the freshly baked brownies! They were still warm and delectable. Then Anne and Suzanne headed home on that cold January 2000 night.

Luisa called her husband Anton and told him about the hospital conditions. She requested a down comforter and her toiletries. The hospital bed mattress was only two inches thick and most uncomfortable. There was no TV, no radio, and the room was cold. The shower curtains were only four feet in length; the water went all over the floor. The water came on hot for ten seconds only! Luisa counted this. She thought the temperature gauge was broken.

With her company background, Luisa went to the front desk and offered suggestions to fix the short curtains and defective water gauge. Nurse Donna looked Luisa straight in her face and said – "That is the way things are to be."

Luisa was stunned by her comment. Luisa asked her who ran this institution. It appeared like a prison to Luisa. Nurse Donna looked up from the file drawer she had opened and told Luisa – it is run by charity. Luisa just shook her head in dismay and returned to her room. *ADJUST, ADJUST, ADJUST. Mama Mia!*

This place was getting to her on day two. Luisa then called her Godmother, Aunt Tureda to tell her of her plight. Then, the desk nurse, Marsha, monitoring the telephone cut into the phone conversation to say "no more calls for you; you are only supposed to use the telephone for five minutes." Luisa could not take it anymore! She asked Aunt Tureda to pray for her and hung up the telephone.

As the second day progressed, she kept thinking of the project she was doing. She knew the client would not understand what was going on. Luisa relied on Anne, Suzanne and William to keep her happy and content. Luisa also realized that her presence and responsibility of the project was really hers. Luisa knew she was not a drug addict. She knew her patient rights needed to be addressed. Nurse Rachel was on duty. Luisa felt her to be a 'friend'. Nurse Rachel called for the Patient Rights Representative to see Luisa. PRR came immediately. Luisa told her she wanted to go home immediately. PRR said, "you are on 72-hour hold that is not up yet." This upset Luisa so much that she threatened to call her attorney to get her out of that hospital. PRR said she would call Anton and request that he pursue the discharge from the hospital.

Luisa called Anton to come immediately and poor Anton was called from work and was faced with another situation in this whole ordeal. Anton arrived and Luisa was discharged. During her 48-hour stay she had been probed with wires and examined by MD Katz, an elderly man in his 70's who appeared to understand Luisa's situation. He knew Dr. Stuart who enlightened him of the PI, lawsuit, and the magnitude of injuries sustained. His medical report cites the complexity of the situation. Unbeknown to Luisa at that time, the paths of Dr. Katz and Luisa will cross once again, a few years later.

After 48 hours of treatment, Luisa was released from Good Heart feeling much better. Her intake of drugs had been strictly regulated during her hospital stay, and she felt that this regimen had helped her immeasurably.

Feeling renewed, she was now ready to rally her resources and get back on her feet.

Chapter 14

Back to Work

Following her release from Good Heart Hospital, Luisa's first order of business for early February 2000 was to prepare for an important Designer Show to be held at the Village of Woods Convention Center on April 1, 2000. She started by planning an open house exhibit for her design company.

The drug withdrawal symptoms were hitting Luisa hard by her checking out of the hospital within 48 hours. The severe sweats and body vibrations along with severe coldness running throughout her body was no picnic.

Her baby sister, Sofia, was at her side to help through this Oxycondin withdrawal. For three years, Luisa was on that very strong narcotic. Sofia drove Luisa to their Dad's grave to pray together and to show Luisa how close she came to joining their beloved Dad. Luisa had her last bottle of Oxycondin with her.

As they both cleaned around his headstone praying the Lord's prayer, Luisa took that prescription bottle from her coat jacket as it was snowing lightly. She lifted the perpetual candle vase from the ground. She placed the prescription bottle in the bottle of the vase pledging to Sofia and the Lord to get through this terrific withdrawal stage. She knew that it would take time.

Sofia and Luisa held each other tightly and started deep loving tears of extreme closeness. This one step to drug recovery was the step that Luisa needed. Without Sofia's direct hit at this reality in the cemetery, Luisa did not know if she could have made alone. So many very close friends and family helped her so much that Luisa did not want to let them down. Her thoughts went to the religious song, Amazing Grace, the words Lord, *save this wrecked wretch* kept ringing in Luisa's mind as they walked back to the snow-covered car. They drove safely home.

Sofia made warm vegetable soup and hot brewing Earl Grey tea for Luisa. They ate lunch together and chatted that her family means so much to her. Sofia words of looking to the future gave the motivational thoughts for Luisa to reflect on as she went to her bedroom for an afternoon nap. Sofia straightened up Luisa's home a bit.

She went to Luisa' room to see her finally sleeping soundly. She kissed her forehead and left to tend to her young girls coming home from preschool.

Upon wakening an hour later, Luisa called Anne and Suzanne to see how that small kitchen job was going they were handling. All was well they reported not to worry Luisa. This was good news to hear.

Then Luisa received a call from Rebecca, the designer, from Total Designs wanting to find out why Luisa needed all the tax returns for 10 years for the purchase of their building and inventory. Luisa told her that the bank needed it. In a hot-headed voice, Rebecca said "What do they think this transaction between us is? Business fraud?" Luisa told her "No, they just cannot determine the value of the inventory for the $36,000 loan needed to finalize the sale. Sam and George, the realtors, have received earnest rent money from me for 5 months of $5,000."

Rebecca told Luisa that the purchase was off that moment. She needed to move to the South in thirty days. Since the bank will not get our tax returns, the deal is off. Luisa had enough on her mind without telling Rebecca the details of her situation. Luisa agreed to cancel the purchase. They hung up the telephone as friends.

Luisa called the realtors to cancel and receive her rent deposit back. They knew all of the designers in this deal as friends for twenty years. They told Luisa that they had her check in their office vault. It was mailed that day to Luisa. Luisa's focus returned to getting stronger mentally and physically.

The next morning feeling somewhat refreshed Luisa went to Lock Bank in Rockport, Ohio to talk with the branch manager about her charge card incident in Atlanta, Georgia. Luisa met with Amy, the bank manager. All was explained to Amy.

She explained that charge card identify theft was growing by the thousands in today's world. Luisa asked her to call the B.A.N.K. to get her a lower charge card interest rate for her upcoming show. The girl on the B.A.N.K. line told Amy that there was over a hundred Cannoli's in her system. It was going to take at least 45 minutes to get to her account. Luisa asked Amy to hang up.

She did. Luisa explained to Amy about the recent events in her life, and that once you find one snake, there will be one hundred more to find.

Further more, Luisa explained to Amy her theory about an illegal portable computer system tracking her movements. Amy listened most attentively to Luisa's story. Amy suggested that they should look up Freedom Insurance on the computer to see their assets and other information as Luisa thought that to be beneficial to her attorney.

Surprisingly, the web site was shut down. Amy printed this paper up and wrote a note on it for Luisa along what transpired in her telephone conversation with the girl from B.A.N.K.

Just then, a tall, slender 50'ish lady wearing black horn rimmed eyeglasses and wearing a gray polyester pant suit with a white ruffled blouse buttoned all the way up to her long neckline came rushing into the bank manger's office shouting I want an I.R.A. right now.

Luisa stood from the chair and excused herself. Amy asked Luisa to have a seat right outside her office. Luisa did so.

The lady spoke loudly. Luisa decided to make a phone call to a lawyer's office. He had sent to her a letter requesting if she had any player pianos for sale. This letter raised some questions in Luisa's mind. She had a player piano that was being restored. This was a two-year plan with the piano specialist.

He had come to Luisa's home in fall of 1998 to pick up the piano internal parts to rebuild. The restoration job would be completed late 2000.

When Luisa dialed the telephone number, this young guy asked of Luisa "Are you working at the bank today, Mrs. Cannoli?" Luisa was so shocked that he knew she was calling from a bank telephone. Was this telephone and mail fraud Luisa wondered?

Luisa answered his question "NO! Who are you? And how did you know where I was?"

He said, "My name is Nielson." Luisa said "Oh, just like Nielson Rating Company? He said, "Yes, I am Carl Nielson." Luisa thought quickly about the year 1997 when she was called on her unlisted home number about what television shows does she watched? She was asked "Don't you watch soap operas all day?" Her reply was "No, I watch 60 minutes, 20/20 and Dateline." They told her information would be sent to her in the mail in two days. Magazine stamps came but no television survey.

Luisa called Nielson Rating that day. They told her that they do not solicit homes that way. They appreciated Luisa's information. Luisa's theory was that this was another way of Sleazer's snakes was investigating her.

Then, the rude lady told Amy in a loud voice that she did not want an I.R.A. after all and just as she abruptly entered Amy's office she left it.

Amy asked Luisa to come back into her office. She was still shaking from this lady's rudeness. As she told Luisa that she would not even give her name.

That ended the meeting with Amy, they shook hands and Amy wished Luisa well. She told Luisa that she would pray for her. Luisa thanked her.

Luisa was finding it hard to concentrate on the show because of the increasingly threatening tactics of the insurance company snakes. The clicking sounds on her phones were becoming ever more frequent, as were hang-ups during the night. In addition, the fax machine was still not working properly. Every day Luisa woke up thinking that she simply couldn't handle any more stress, and every day more problems would be piled upon her plate. With spring approaching, Luisa arranged to leave her design company in the hands of Suzanne and Anne and take Carmella and William to their condo in Florida for a week's vacation. William traveled with them, as Luisa was still experiencing withdrawal systems from the drugs. He assisted her with carrying the groceries. She desperately needed a vacation with her youngest daughter, and, in fact, her doctors had recommended that she get away for a while. Anton took their dog, Princess, to his Mom's for the week.

Luisa, Carmella and William soaked up the sun, then visited Disney World and spent time reestablishing their mother – daughter bond. That week in Orlando was relaxing and well spent.

Luisa returned home rejuvenated and ready to resume her struggle against the injustices of Freedom Insurance. So far the insurance company snakes had won all the battles, but she was determined that they would not win the war.

That evening Luisa was reading the paper to relax and get caught up with the current news locally and worldwide. She flipped through the work ads and to her surprise saw a 3" X 5" ad that read:

Freedom Insurance
Needs private investigators
Come to be interviewed – no job experience
Needed Wednesday February 5th 9:00 a.m.
Village of Woods Convention Center

When Luisa saw the ad in the paper she called Marshall. He had seen it earlier that day. He told Luisa that it was probably her case as the word was her case was high profile in the North County courthouse. Now that she saw it, he told her to do as he advised her a while ago which was to document car description, license plate numbers, driver and passenger descriptions along with anything else they may say or do to you. She listened so carefully to his direct words to her. She hung up the telephone and cried out "loudly how could a DUI driver have wrecked my life before only to now have complete strangers violate my life some more?"

It was a restless night for her and she did not get any sleep at all. Noises from her attic kept her up. It did not sound like birds or woodpeckers but it began to concern her. She just did not know if she was getting paranoid or educated in this other side of life. She just wanted her world of naivety to return, as she was basically a private person who just loved her passions of raising a family and having her design business to keep her world balanced.

Suzanne and Anne volunteered to run the design studio to allow Luisa to put her energies into planning for the upcoming Show. One of the first things she did was gather pictures of her projects over the years to put in a brochure to showcase the many services her company provided.

Yet as her plans for the show were progressing well, other problems continued to surface. A week before the show was to begin; she received a call from a woman official at a local bank,

B.A.N.K., which had issued Luisa a credit card 13 years before. The woman introduced herself as Linda, and told Luisa that her account was seriously in arrears.

Luisa felt humiliated. For all those years she had never made even a single payment late. Then the terrible automobile accident in July 1997 had sent her spiraling down into a quagmire of medical, emotional and financial problems and she'd fallen behind in some of her creditor payments.

Linda asked Luisa what the problem was, and Luisa began telling her about all the medical and emotional anguish she had endured since the accident. She also detailed the suspicious noises on her telephone, and the sudden disappearances of her camcorder, checkbook, charge card folder and company invoices.

She spoke of how all the problems flowing from her accident had adversely affected her family. Linda listened sympathetically, then promised that someone from the bank would call the Luisa sometime in the next few days to discuss ways in which the bank could help Luisa.

The following Sunday newspaper ran that same Freedom Insurance ad, Luisa read it and called Marshall and reported all the additional snakes entering her life and the same ones showing up from prior strange encounters. She recognized them. Marshall told that probably that Freedom Insurance was running that ad periodically to hire for a low fee some more snakes to intimidate and harass her. Luisa wanted them to let her alone. Marshal reminded her to just keep documenting everything and give it to her attorney. She assured him that she would. **WOULD ANTON BELIEVE HER NOW?**

That following Saturday, a supervisor named Jim called from B.A.N.K. He told her that they valued her all her years as a client. He offered to settle her account. He would give her 90 days to pay half of the bill, and the bank would waive the balance.

This most compassionate offer brought tears to Luisa's eyes. Here, at last, were business people who understood all that she had endured. She told Jim that she would gladly accept the bank's generous terms.

Meanwhile Suzanne and Anne organized the studio and tastefully arranged samplings of tile, wallpaper and furniture in the large display window.

Although the upcoming design show was taking most of Luisa's time, she still had to undergo medical treatments for her injuries. Twice she had to go to Tri-Health Pavilion to have physical therapy for her upper torso injuries. She also went to Complete Health Care in Leland Community Center for her head, neck and jaw problems, and while there, also received Electro-stimulation, ultrasound and heat to those areas.

The stress Luisa was under was compounded by the $5,000 cost of her company's participation in the upcoming show. As the date of the show approached, Luisa decided to withdraw the money from her dwindling savings.

Now she was faced with the question of what in the world was happening to the financial investment account faxes from Lock Investment Company? A representative from Lock Investments told her over the phone that the company had faxed Luisa 36 pages, yet she had only received 30 pages. Where did those missing six pages of financial information go?

As if the missing fax pages weren't enough of a worry, Luisa's personal investment checkbook had been stolen. It was not in her office desk drawer, and she was certain that someone had access to her account number. She called the Lock Bank to report that she had not received several pages from the last fax they had sent her.

She added that she suspected someone was illegally monitoring her account. A Lock branch manager told Luisa that the bank would keep its eyes open for any suspicious activity on Luisa's account. Luisa reluctantly trusted the manager's assurance.

Anne and Luisa decided to see if the installation of a home security system would prevent the break-ins to her home. They went to the All Security Systems Company on the east side of the city. They met with the office supervisor, Mark Woodall. Explaining to him the pattern of noises on her telephone lines and the robberies to her home, he listened but told them that his company could not install a security system to Luisa's home. He told his concern would be that if word got out of the installation on your home to the police and telephone companies while this personal injury case is still pending. He believed that in this corrupt world that the security system could be tampered with and catching that perpetrator would be difficult.

Luisa remembered a story that someone had told her recently. This lady, Bethany Jones, was involved in a personal injury case with another large insurance company, Lockwood Worldwide. Their case involved a tractor-trailer, also on the interstate, and resulting in similar injuries to Luisa's.

She went on to telling Anne and Mark that this lady's garage door was opening and closing at all hours even though she has a home security system. Luisa added that her telephone was ringing all hours of the night with no one on the other line. But one night, the man told her that I thought that you were not going to be home. She also had a strange clicking sound on her telephone lines.

Mark, being honest with them, told Luisa to save her money as he would not take it from her, considering the circumstances.

He told them that his brother retired many years ago from the FBI. After his retirement, stories were told of similar incidents of invasion with large insurance companies. He further explained that the government has sophisticated surveillance equipment that got into the wrong hands. They often mimicked the government in order to obtain this equipment to monitor their subjects.

Luisa and Anne thanked him for his direct honesty and left with a better understanding of this horrific mess.

Anne and Luisa then traveled to the city's newspaper headquarters to trace the newspaper ad for those two Sundays. To their shock, they could not find the ads, and there was a spliced section in the microfilm. With that, Luisa went to call Marshall Kent on a pay telephone. He explained to her that whoever ran the ad wanted to cover his tracks, and probably did the splicing of the microfilm. Marshall went on to say that he probably used gloves as to not leave any fingerprints. She hung up with him. Now she felt like Charlie's Angels and a level up from the Nancy Drew stories after hearing more about the world of insurance espionage. Luisa told Anne Marshall's theory, with out telling her his role in this matter. They drove back to Luisa's to tell Suzanne of the new event. Suzanne questioned, "How can they ever be stopped?"

Luisa told them that she must go to the police soon.

They left Luisa's home. Luisa pondered that same question repeatedly in her mind.

She tried to put these troublesome problems, and the problems with Lock Bank out of her mind, and went back to work. With the show now organized, she asked Anne to go to the Print Shop with her and help her with photo selections and layout for the company brochure. Despite the past three months of almost constant violations at the hands of Freedom Insurance, Luisa was determined to stay focused on the upcoming exhibit.

Concentrating on her work wasn't always easy for Luisa because she often had to switch her attention to her medical treatments. On the evening of March 25, 2000, she had an appointment with Dr. Chuck Stuart, her pain psychologist, and had much to discuss with him.

At the Print Shop, Luisa and Anne chose a large round table to layout the photos for the brochure. There were many photos to choose from and the women spent several minutes discussing which ones would work best.

Luisa wanted to show varied design work : four kitchens, external work, lower levels, bedrooms, and baths. She also decided to highlight specialized window treatments and various furniture styles ranging from traditional to transitional to contemporary, as well as all styles in between. The color spread showed myriad shades of peach, rose, green, blue, and yellow.

As they were discussing the layout, a woman in her sixties showed up at their table and said abruptly, "My name is Luisa."

Anne and Luisa looked up from the photos they were poring over. The woman was about five feet three inches tall and had short gray-blond hair. She looked vaguely familiar to Luisa, and she wondered if this was the same woman who had followed her to Alexia's house from the Med Mart pharmacy in Macon several weeks before.

Luisa said to the woman, "Luisa is also my name."

Without being invited to join them, the sixtyish lady sat down. She was holding a folder with an outdoor scene on the cover. In her other hand was a dry paintbrush. Luisa felt instinctively that she was a snake for Freedom Insurance and tapped Anne's foot with her own to alert her friend to her suspicions.

Luisa then asked the woman what sort of work she did and the woman replied that she painted houses for local Homeramas. The woman, in turn, asked what Luisa and Anne were doing. Luisa explained they were putting together a brochure for her company. She then told the woman that she often used painting companies in her design work and asked her for a business card.

The mysterious woman replied, "I am not allowed to give you one."

Taken aback by the woman's response, Luisa decided not to ask her any more questions.

Anne, however, refused to be dissuaded. Using the forceful Texas manner she reserved for difficult people, she asked the woman again for her business card. Rattled by Anne's unblinking 'I'm-going-keep-asking-until-you-give-me-a-card' attitude, the woman gave in and handed Anne her card. It read:

HOMES by ELLEN
426898 River Ridge
East Hill Valley, Oh 53788
(888) 591-6677

The woman's card was for a different company than the woman had mentioned, and Luisa and Anne knew immediately that she'd been lying. They suspected that she was probably a snake from Freedom Insurance. Obviously rattled by the openly skeptical looks on the faces of Luisa and Anne, the woman rose from her chair and hurried away without saying another word.

Luisa looked over the woman from head to toe. She resembled the lady who confronted her in Med Mart Pharmacy in Macon, Georgia that past mid January. Her grayish-blond hair cut straight to just below her ears and parted to the right with bangs. Her weight of 5'4" and weight of 125 lbs along with her blue jeans and beige sweater look the same.

This time Luisa tapped Anne's foot a few times just to let her know like the how old fashion telephone used to work – tapping messages away.

Luisa and Anne could hardly believe that the snakes knew where they were. It was becoming more and more evident that Freedom Insurance was determined to keep violating Luisa's life.

They finalized their selection of photos and placed an order with the Print Shop for the business brochures to be printed that week so they would be ready for the show on Saturday. On the ride, they discussed the upcoming show and what else had to be done. Anne had contacted the two local newspapers and reserved space for a full-page ad for the studio. Anne and Suzanne had also had invitations to the open house printed and mailed to Luisa's clients.

By now, Luisa had also received the Murano crystal from Venice, the cuckoo clock from the Black Forest and artwork and rugs from suppliers she contracted with at the Atlanta show. All of the displays were ready to be set up for the important April 1 show.

But in the middle of her preparations for the design show, Luisa had a sudden attack of strong emotional anxiety. The attack reminded her of how vulnerable she was to psychological flare-ups. As her doctors had told her, the horrific memories of her accident and all the pain she had suffered would last her entire lifetime. She had to learn to adjust, adjust, adjust, adjust!

To help her deal with her psychological problems, Luisa and Anton started collecting books by experts on Post Traumatic Stress Disorder, anxiety and the side effects of all the medicines she was taking.

Since the accident, Luisa had been having repeated "floating" sensations which came on suddenly. She spoke to her doctors about this sensation and they told her that several neurological tests they'd performed on her had confirmed damage to her brain. The books she and Anton read made them both more aware that PTSD as well as anxiety attacks and panic attacks are very real psychological reactions to trauma.

The books she read on trauma dealt with medications, biofeedback, and support groups. One book that impressed her was Beyond the Light by P.M.Y. Atwater. She could relate to many of the testimonials Atwater presented in his book describing the symptoms and suffering of those afflicted like her. She was especially relieved that others also described the "floating" sensation, for it meant that she was not imagining the feeling she had so often experienced.

Atwater wrote that it took time to recover from traumatic events, and reading his words Luisa realized that neither she nor anyone else could predict how long her healing process would take. Her recovery was something she would simply have to work on each day.

It would not be easy accepting the hard fact that she wasn't going to recover from the traumatic events of July 22, 1997 in the next few weeks or months. Indeed, she might well be facing years of continuing pain and psychological problems.

She also knew from what she had been taught in rehabilitation programs that most people who had not experienced trauma in their lives had no concept of how to deal with it. It was a learning process, a long road that took time to travel and courage to complete.

It was also hard for Luisa to accept that her medical problems – and the psychological side effects – had resulted in her losing several friends she'd had for many years. Though she has gained many more, she often prayed for those lost friends.

As Luisa recovered from her attack of anxiety and panic, her thoughts turned to her upcoming June 2000 jury trial. She prayed for God's guidance, and for Him to open the eyes of the jury to the physical pain and mental anguish she had suffered.

On the outside, her body appeared normal, and she wondered if the jury members would look at her and assume that her injuries had healed. Hopefully the jury would ignore her appearance and instead focus on the X-rays, MRIs, Biofeedback, CAT Scans, blood tests and photographs that all verified her internal injuries.

While she awaited her trial date, Luisa continued to plan for the design show she would be participating in the following month. Anne and Suzanne helped coordinate all the items for the exhibit and contacted the convention center to nail down the costs Luisa would incur.

The day of the design show finally rolled around. Luisa reminded herself to memorize the names and faces of everyone who came to their booth, in the case that one of her visitors could be an insurance company snake.

Her booth attracted approximately fifty people, and sure enough at 10:45 AM Luisa spotted a possible snake. The suspect was a tall, plain-looking woman with sable brown hair. She was wearing glasses and looked to be in her early fifties.

She had on a gray polyester pantsuit with faux jewels pinned to the jacket. For several minutes she sat on a bench across from the entry to Luisa's showroom. Then promptly at 11:00 she got up and walked straight to the entrance table.

Luisa just knew that face and lady was the same one who wanted the IRA at Lock Bank last January. She told Anne and Suzanne to keep an eye on her, as she was the same one from the early encounter.

Anne ask the lady if she help her with any questions that she might have about Luisa's interior business. The lady said a blunt "No, I am here to just walk through." Anne asked her to sign up on the appointment sheet. The lady refused.

However, she did take a brochure and headed into the display area. She never spoke a word to Luisa, or to Anne, as they stood there ready to greet their visitors, nor did she respond to their 'Hellos.' Luisa watched as the woman walked in the front door of the display area and straight out the rear door. She then exited the Convention Center. Luisa was convinced that such strange behavior could only mean the woman was a snake and she was the same one from Lock Bank.

At the entrance, they had a signup sheet for visitors. The show only lasted four hours and when it was over, there were twenty-six names on their list.

As the last visitors left the exhibition hall, Luisa and Anne began to dismantle the display. They finished the teardown the next day and by Monday they had trucked everything away, returning some items to vendors and storing others in Luisa's garage.

After the hospital ordeal, Luisa was not sure of how to care for her children when she could not even take care of herself, or even her business. She phoned Michael Wright to inform him of what was happening. He had started putting his office recording on when Luisa called him.

One night she even called him at 3:00 a.m. and told him that

Anton was furious with him. Anton was sounding off about Wright's ineptness and lack of interest in the case.

Luisa told Wright's answering machine that she had enough of these verbal attacks from Anton, especially at night. She told Wright to meet her at the Cool Comfort and Relaxing Inn in Village of the Woods the next day, as she was checking into it. With Anton's loud words in the background, Luisa was certain that the loud words from Anton were also recorded on his home's answering machine.

The next morning, Luisa packed an over night bag just in case she would have to do what she said she would do. By that morning, Anton was telling Luisa that so many frustrations were building up in him the night before. He said that he was sorry for waking her and sounding off.

Luisa told him to comfort him that her thoughts were the same about Wright. They both knew that his legal representation of them was coming to an end. Anton kissed Luisa and left for work.

After that morning makeup with Anton, Luisa thought against staying at the hotel. But if there were anymore strange encounters with the swarm of insurance snakes, she would end up at the hotel to escape the harassment at her home.

That day, she decided to have her LS400 Lexus serviced by the dealership for normal maintenance, but also to check it for any surveillance bugs on it, as Luisa was still perplexed as to how the insurance company seemed to know where she was at all times. She had also gathered up her fax carbon that showed 6 pages missing from her investments and the answering machine tapes that had spun out in front of her from the answering machine. She was going to go to Wright's downtown office without an appointment later that day. After placing 15 calls to him during 6 weeks and receiving no return calls, Luisa felt that this was the only thing to do.

When she brought the car to the dealership, she told the service attendant that she wanted the normal maintenance along with this $39.00 charge for checking her car for any bugs on it. But if a device was found, she simply wanted it removed – she did not want to know about it. Her growing anger towards the whole defense team would probably force her not to get into her car ever again, if this was the case. Anton and Anne differed on this with Luisa. Anne's dog, Skipper, was given a small electric jolt through his dog collar when standing by Luisa's car in Anne's driveway while the car was off, and this raised more suspicion of foul play.

The underlying question of what set off the dog's collar went unanswered, as Luisa insisted that she could not handle any more confirmed violations in her life. Her home, family, friends and company had already been so violated that she could not bear to think her LS400 Lexus had also been invaded.

The dealership provided her with a rental car, a white Camry Toyota while the worked on the car. So she proceeded to head to the lawyer's office downtown.

Parking in the lawyer buildings' parking garage, Luisa headed into the office front door, registered at the security station, and took the elevator to the 6th floor.

Approaching the front secretary, Luisa asked for Wright. She responded that his was at the dentist. Since it was 4:30 P.M., and she had come unscheduled, Luisa thought this was the truth, and was ready to leave. Just then, Mark Kinship, Wright's lawyer partner, walked in. Luisa knew and liked him from his prior handling her father's estate when he died many years before.

Luisa asked if he had any time to look over these evidence items. He had the time and walked Luisa to his office. He looked at them. As she explained all her telephone problems since July 1997, he told Luisa that her concerns about the insurance company's possible involvement in these tactics were very valid. But, unfortunately, he was not assigned to her case.

He commented that Wright is known for not always communicating with his clients, but he has won millions of dollars against Freedom Insurance in the past years. However, he admitted that they were not represented by Lee Sleazer back then.

Kinship walked Luisa to the elevator and told her to keep her chin up. She would manage to get through this mess.

Luisa thanked him for his time and descended to the lobby to go and get her car. When she got to the car, she could not find the key for it. Looking into the driver's window, she noticed that the key was on the seat. It had fallen off the bag that she had the evidence in.

Taken back with that, she returned to the security desk in the lobby and called the car rental store. They told Luisa that they had a second key but they were closing for the day. It was 5:30 p.m.

With that, Luisa knew she had to call a cab. The security girl called one for her. She knew the downtown companies. The city is not like New York or Chicago. Luisa explained that she had a 7:00 p.m. doctors' appointment that evening. The girl said the cab would be there in fifteen minutes.

45 minutes later and no cab, she called again. Within 10 minutes one arrived.

The taxi driver walked into the lobby to get Luisa. He was most heavyset about 350lbs. His age was mid 30's and wearing dirty blue jeans and torn tee shirt.

He took Luisa's bag on rollers to put in the trunk but then he opened up her bag and asked Luisa why the fax carbon was in her bag. This certainly rattled Luisa. She told him to just put that bag into the back seat with her. He reluctantly did so.

Luisa asked him to take her to the eastern city of Rockport for her appointment, so he called his dispatcher in order to get directions. He did not seem very talkative, but out of the clear blue after 10 minutes of driving, Luisa noticed that he was heading in the wrong way, based on the direction the dispatch had given him.

Rudely and in a gruff voice, he told Luisa, "Lady, don't you dare tell me where to drive to. I am bankrupt from a car accident as an insurance company refused to pay me a dime. Now, I'll get you to Rockport my way. I drive a taxi to pay my bills. Now tell me why you are going to see this doctor?"

Luisa felt unsafe with this fierce sounding man. Briefly, she said that the doctor was a pain psychologist. The driver responded, that he was in so much pain that he just drank beer to help him cope.

Luisa decided to change the conversation after he finally drove 15 minutes in the opposite direction to where he told her he lived in the city. He told Luisa that he lived in the suburbs of the city. The town is called Highridge as that part of the city has 4 towers visible from downtown westside. Luisa knew the area. She asked him what street that he lived on. He responded Sacramento Road. It was at that point that Luisa knew that he was another snake. It all added up in her mind: very late coming to pick her up as his taxi was only around the block from the lawyers' office, getting "lost" after the dispatcher told him the directions, claiming to live on Sacramento Road which does not exist in that small sector of the city, and succeeding in making her miss her medical appointment with Doctor Stuart at 7:00 p.m.

Luisa told this driver that she had only $20.00 for her fare. With him getting lost, Luisa told him that she would not pay for the additional time on the meter. He grunted that she would. Her safety was becoming an issue. He would now know where she lived. As he pulled into her driveway, the meter read $24.00. She told him that she would write a check for the difference. He told her roughly to pay him cash, or he would call the police.

Anton's car was in their driveway, so Luisa told the driver that she would get her husband to settle up with him. Anton heard Luisa's short story and walked to the cab. Politely, Anton asked him for his operator's license, the man showed Anton it. Anton paid him $8.00 told him his that was his payment. The man took the money and then pulled away from the driveway.

Luisa explained to Anton all that occurred that afternoon with

Kinship and his verbal support of her theory. Anton just took it all in as he carried Luisa's bags into the garage. The garage was full of the show's display. He asked Luisa when she would be putting it all away. She told him after Easter week.

This happened on Thursday of Easter week. On Good Friday, Luisa rescheduled her medical appointment for noon later that day. It was sunny that early morning, and Luisa picked up her Lexus by having William drive her to the   dealership. The dealership kept their word not to tell Luisa about any bugs per her wish even though Anton differed with her on its conclusion. She then returned to the car rental store to get the other key for the Camry. She returned downtown and picked up the rental car downtown. She returned home to see Carmella for a quick visit, and decided to drive the Nissan Quest to her doctors' appointment.

By noon the skies were still clear, but after her two-hour doctor appointment, it had rained. She, unfortunately, had left the sunroof open and could not get the security system to work. Panicky, Luisa called William to help her. He came quickly, but also could not get the security system to work. The rain continued to pour down, and there was nothing to do. William and Luisa went home to wait for Anton to get home and to solve this problem.

He did get home and drove to the medical parking lot and worked on the car for twenty minutes before he could get it to work, and finally shut the window. So they finally returned home with the car, albeit a little soggy.

That weekend, Anton said that he was tired of manually opening the garage door. He reconnected the old garage door opener. This was against the advice of the garage technician who had just been at their home two weeks ago.

That weekend, their home was robbed again. This time, the cell phones, and fax evidence from the bag was missing.

To their surprise and disappointment, their brochures and

their new client list also had disappeared from Luisa's garage. It had cost Luisa $1,500 for the double-sided colored brochures, so replacing the brochures was out of the question. Even worse, the disappearance of the visitor's list meant a loss of business that could amount to thousands of dollars.

The time and money they had poured into the show were now wasted. Luisa was devastated. Mentally and physically, the show had been draining on her. Worse, she had counted on a new client list to boost her spirits and help rebuild her ailing company. One client was even a neighbor of hers.

She had thought that after the show she would be sipping the sweet wine of success. Instead, all she could taste were the bitter ashes of yet another defeat.

A month later, as if the disappearance of the new client list were not misery enough, when Luisa came home from another medical treatment on her neck and jaw, she discovered that their house had been broken into again. This time, the charge card folder, and the company checkbook were missing.

This was not the first time things had mysteriously disappeared from their home. Before her trip to Atlanta, the camcorder had vanished from the dining room table.

The continued invasion of her home – her sacrosanct English Tudor fortress – left Luisa feeling violated. The very thought that strangers had sullied her home with their sordid presence made her want to scrub the house from basement to attic. In a moment of near panic, she imagined she could smell the stench they had left behind.

Forcing herself to be calm, Luisa started going through the mail. Strangely, there were acknowledgements from furniture and flooring vendors for orders she had never placed.

As Luisa looked more closely at the orders, she discovered that the furniture was coming to her home, not the receiving warehouse where it was usually shipped. Someone named Becky had placed the order. There was no one named Becky working at her studio. Equally puzzling, the furniture was tagged for a hospital and Luisa had never done any design work for a hospital.

During this time, the noises on their phone and fax lines increased. The clicking sounds became more frequent and the fax machine started making clicking noises without a fax transmission coming through. In addition, the answering machine cassette tapes would spin forward for no reason and the machine would click on and off.

Luisa contacted the answering machine manufacturer and the Cannolis were sent a total of three new machines to try. No matter which machine they connected, the clicking continued. Finally, Luisa took the answering machines to be examined at a local repair telephone shop.

The electronics repairman told her that he hated to charge her the $26.00 because there was nothing wrong with their telephones or fax machines.

Luisa finally decided to go to the East Hill Valley police for help. She spoke to a detective Mark Crosswell. She told him of her motor vehicle accident, thefts, and noises on her phone. His attitude was arrogant.

"What medications are you taking?" he asked.

"Paxil and Oxycondin," she replied. "Why?"

"Because you're acting like you're over-medicated," he answered. "I suggest that you keep track of further phone problems on a calendar. Here's my cell phone number. Call me if you have any more trouble. By the way, you should turn off your cell phone numbers, because your cell phone numbers can be easily be stolen or plucked from the airways."

Luisa could not believe her ears. But she took some reassurance from receiving Crosswell's cell number, that he was there to help her.

He then called her husband at work to express his concern about Luisa driving in her present state. His demeanor was chauvinistic, demeaning, and uncaring.

As Luisa headed home, her head spun. Between someone obviously tapping her phone lines, her home being broken into and fake orders being given to her vendors, she felt like she was under siege. Throw in all the snakes, she kept encountering, the denial of her charge card at the Grand Golden Tower Palace Hotel and the strange events on the flight home from Atlanta and it all added up to an insurance company conspiracy.

Over the next few days, the noises on her phone and fax lines continued to get worse and Luisa finally put a call through to Detective Crosswell. He wasn't available. Although she tried to reach him several times that day, he did not return her calls. Once again Luisa felt violated – this time by a public servant.

Giving up on Crosswell, Luisa called her private investigator, Marshall Kent. After discussing her case for several minutes, they agreed to meet in the Grocery Mart's parking lot to exchange information.

Luisa decided that it was time she brought Anne and Suzanne in on her secret private investigator, so she called and arranged to pick them up on her way to Grocery Mart. In the car, she explained to them who they were meeting and why. Both women were intrigued and watched intently through the windshield as Luisa and Marshall held their whispered meeting.

Luisa had been concerned about how Anne and Suzanne would react to her hiring a private detective. As it turned out, she had no need to worry. Her cherished friends told her that they were there for her, and that they would not have missed her cloak and dagger rendezvous for anything!

The next morning, Luisa told Anne and Suzanne that she was going to listen to the company answering machine tapes in her car that day. She was also taking another piece of evidence with her in the Lexus.

The week before, she had also discovered that the painted air vent in the master bedroom had been removed. The paint on the screw heads and around the vent was chipped. She put the tapes and the screws in her purse, along with the security key to her Lexus.

After Luisa had taken Carmella to school, she pulled into the USA Quik gas station in Village of Woods and used a pay phone to call Detective Crosswell's cell phone. She was using a public phone because the police had told her that there were illegal ways to pick up cell phone calls.

Luisa discovered that she didn't have enough change and went into the USA Quik gas station to call the detective. She got in line at the counter behind four other people. At the head of the line was a tall husky man who looked like Nick Nolte with his thin blond shoulder length hair and wearing tan dockers and soft yellow polo shirt. His weight about 180 lbs. And his height was 5'10".

As Luisa waited impatiently, she heard the man say to the clerk in a loud voice, "I went through her windshield last night. My head hurts but I didn't go to the hospital."

Wanting to be helpful, Luisa stepped forward and told the man that she had also suffered severe head pain from a car accident, and that he ought to go to the hospital.

The man didn't reply, and shouldered his way out through the station's glass doors muttering to himself. Luisa shrugged off the slight, and decided to call her unlisted home number from the store telephone rather than wait in line any longer for change to go back to the pay telephone.

When she called her unlisted phone number, a man answered and said, "They are already here."

Stunned, Luisa stammered, "Who are you?"

The man immediately hung up on her. She knew she had dialed the correct phone number, as the phone's digital readout showed her unlisted home number. Her heart sank. She could feel her blood pressure rise. She was more convinced than ever that someone was tapping both her home and cell phone transmissions.

She quickly went to her car and discovered to her horror that she had not locked the doors. Her purse was clearly visible on the front seat. When she looked inside, she discovered that the plastic bag that held the paint-chipped screw and the cassette tape – her only hard evidence of the insurance company's violation of her life – was missing, along with the security key for her Lexus and her house key.

Instinctively, she whirled around and looked toward the suspicious man who had been in line in front of her in the USA Quik gas station. The man was just opening the passenger side door of a car. He caught Luisa staring at him, and hurriedly hopped into the maroon Toyota. The driver began backing up.

Luisa memorized the license number and got a good look at the driver's face. He appeared to be in his mid-twenties and had dark hair and eyes. As the car swept past her, Luisa noticed the Nick Nolte lookalike had a black laptop computer on his lap. When he saw Luisa looking into his car, he quickly covered the laptop with a jacket.

As the car sped away, Luisa decided to go to the Station down the street to report this upsetting incident to the Village of the Woods Police. When she arrived, she met with Police Chief, Steve Stone. She knew him from church. He listened carefully to her story, and jotted down the man's license plate number.

When Luisa had finished recounting the incident, she told Stone that she had a medical appointment to keep. He asked her to come back when she could to talk to a detective about the incident. She told him that she would do so.

Luisa drove to her medical appointment Community Center, thirty minutes away, to receive treatment for her injured jaw. The physical therapist noted that she was shaking. She took Luisa's blood pressure and found that it was very high.

When Luisa told the therapist that she had an ultrasound treatment scheduled for later that day, the therapist told her that the treatment would be too risky with her blood pressure so high, and volunteered to call Luisa's doctor and cancel the appointment. Luisa accepted her offer.

After her therapy session, Luisa called home from the therapist's office. When her call was answered, she heard a recorded message come on. The message said, "This is a non-working number."

Luisa was taken aback. Her phone had been working perfectly that morning. There could only be one explanation for the recording: the insurance company was hacking into her phone line again.

Knowing that her blood pressure was undoubtedly going through the roof, she drove back to the police station and met with Detective Dave Gant. He took her report and then accompanied Luisa outside to look over her car. When they checked the trunk, Luisa discovered that someone had hurriedly gone through her medical files, leaving the files in disarray.

The detective wrote up a report and gave a copy to Luisa. He also suggested that she watch the movie, ***Enemy of the State***. It might help her better understand the world of espionage. He shared with her that his Mom was a school teacher like Luisa was many years prior. He told Luisa to hang in there, as he did not doubt her at all about this terrifying situation.

Before Luisa drove away, she called Anne and Suzanne and told them what had happened. Anne said she had purchased the movie that the detective had recommended and would lend it to Luisa.

By the time she reached home, Luisa was thoroughly stressed out. Her anxiety increased when she checked her business file box and discovered that the charge card folder was not there. Several business records were also missing. Luisa felt like screaming.

When Anton got home, she told him about the missing charge card folder and records, but he seemed unconcerned.

"If you ask me, it's unlikely that these things have been stolen," he said. "I'm sure that you've merely misplaced them."

"It's certainly possible that I could have misplaced a single item," Luisa said, her frustration mounting. "But you can't convince me that I could keep continuously losing things. I'm telling you, Anton, someone is burglarizing our home."

Luisa stormed away from her skeptical husband and started going through her records again. She kept all her business files in a single 18 X 18-inch container. If the charge card folder and business records hadn't been stolen, they could only be in that box. But they were still missing.

As she sat on the living room floor looking at the box in utter despair, she suddenly yelled, "I can't believe this is happening to me!"

Anton came into the living room to calm her. He asked, "Do you want to go back to the hospital?"

This was too much for Luisa. She began crying and couldn't stop for almost an hour.

The next day she regained her composure and sat down alone at the kitchen table to do some hard thinking. She relied heavily on Suzanne and Anne to help her run her design business. Yet she hadn't signed up any new clients lately and there was not enough money coming in to pay them. Sadly, she would have to lay them off.

Luisa and Anton decided to have their Nissan Quest serviced for this security problem after the drenching of their car on Good Friday. The dealership provided her with a new beige Nissan Altima, while they found and fixed the security system issue.

She had other financial worries as well. The stock market had started to drop just as she and Anton had been forced to withdraw funds from their investments to pay Luisa's ongoing medical expenses. They had lost a considerable amount of money by having to sell stocks that had declined in value.

The automobile accident that had caused her so many debilitating medical problems had also wreaked havoc on both her design business and their family finances. The strange and sinister events that had followed her accident – especially being under constant surveillance by insurance company snakes, and having her phone tapped – had also taken a terrible toll on both her and her family.

Luisa already had her bags packed and decided to go to the Comforts of Home Hotel. After the USA Quik gas station strange encounter, Luisa knew that in order to convince Anton and Wright of what was happening, she needed evidence from outside people. She went into the hotel to check in.

Upon checking in she specifically told the grandmotherly lady at the front deck that no calls were to be placed to her room. She asked for the lobby attendant to help her carry her bags and boxes of medical files to her room. She settled in and decided to go swimming in their heated pool. She called Anton, and told him that she would fax to him 8 pages about their relationship and how this accident had affected them, for the attorney to have on record. Anton supported her decision to clear her mind and refocus with a change of scenery. She told Anton that she would stay at least 2 nights. Then she called Anne, Suzanne and William to meet her there for breakfast.

She had dinner and went to sleep after reading her Simple Abundance Book for at least an hour being dosing off for the night for once.

The nest morning, Anne, Suzanne and William met Luisa for a very early breakfast. Luisa thanked them all for their support and for believing her about the snakes. Anne told Luisa that she was going to the Radio and Telephone Store to get caller ID units for her telephones, to try to get to the root of the strange clicking sounds. Luisa told that if they handled the home office, that she would organize her medical files. All was set, and off they went to help each other. Anne told Luisa that she would drive her to Target to get a casual jump suit for her.

Luisa needed some casual clothes and for $10.00 Anne knew where to shop for such bargains. They decided to try a telephone there and to hear if any clicking sounds were on their store lines. Sure enough, the pay phone Luisa used to call her mom had the same clicking sounds. Anne tried the store telephone by the front door but it did not work. The clerk told Anne that was unusual to try another telephone. It happened again. Anne tried a third telephone, while Luisa found the clothes needed. Then Luisa explained to store manager her theory that someone with the insurance company was in the parking lot with that black laptop scrambling their telephones as they tried to call her home and family.

The manager's name was Leroy Parker, and in his mid 50's. He asked Luisa how he could help her. Luisa wrote down on a piece of paper Wright's telephone number. She explained to Mr. Parker that Wright was her personal injury attorney. She asked of him to call him 20 minutes after Luisa left the store, to tell him what was happening. She also explained that the Village of Woods police already knew of the situation. He told Luisa that he would make the call. Anne then took Luisa back to the hotel to change, and left her to go buy the caller id units.

As Luisa walked up to the front desk to get the fax that was sent to Anton, the grandmotherly clerk was on the telephone, Luisa heard her say, "Oh, this is the government, I'll put the call right through for you." She hung up the call.

Luisa asked her for her fax papers. The lady only gave Luisa 6 pages of the 8 pages back. Luisa questioned her for the other two. She responded very weakly and would not look at Luisa, and said that " you only gave 6 to me." Luisa knew she was lying to her face. How did the snakes of Sleazer get to this weak personality, and whose room did that call go through to? Luisa asked to talk to the manager. Edmound Randoph, the manager met with Luisa immediately. She told him about the faxes and her telephone problems. He told her to use his company's private line from here on out. He had the U.S. Today newspaper in his hand, the front page had an article about a young computer hacker just arrested.

He told Luisa that in this world of computers that cyber-terrorism was a growing threat. Luisa shared with him that her knowledge was growing in her readings of these new crimes and she had watched 20/20, 60 Minutes, and Dateline feature stories on the subject. He told Luisa that he would talk to her attorney about any strange incidents that happening while she was at his hotel.

She thanked him and returned to her room. She saw the red flashing light on her telephone message button. Playing it, she heard "Luisa, this is Anne. Let's meet for Lunch."

This was also very strange - that message was on the stolen answering machine cassette tape from two weeks prior – how did the tape and message get replaced two weeks after it had been missing?

With that, Luisa went back to the manger and told him what the grandmotherly lady did. He told Luisa her name as Gladis Harper, and to tell her attorney to be easy on her because of her age. He tried to assure Luisa that Gladis did not want to harm her, but in her ignorance and naiveté, she simply was a victim to a fraudulent claim of impersonation.

Luisa had another jaw and head treatment at Complete Care in Leland Community Center to go to that later that morning. As she was leaving the front entrance to the lobby, she took notice of a newer royal Blue Toyota sitting next to her car. The dark skinned 30'ish lady with braided hair took a quick glimpse at Luisa, as Luisa did the same.

Wondering if this was another snake, Luisa decided to drive around the parking lot a few times. This lady did the same thing. Luisa just confirmed that the woman was following her.

Then Luisa drove to Leland Community Center, checking her mirrors enroute. Sure enough, the snake was behind her. As Luisa parked her car, the rented Nissan Altima, the lady pulled her car next to Luisa's and parked.

Luisa knew what Marshall Kent had told her to do. No conversations, but write down their names, description, card description and license plate number and anything they may say to her. This is what Luisa did as she walked behind her car.

Noticing that the lady was watching Luisa in her mirrors, Luisa went to her own trunk and opened it to get something from it. Perhaps this would erase the woman's concerns.

Luisa went to her medical appointment for about one hour. Upon returning her car had been keyed on the driver's side. Luisa suspected that lady had done it, but to prove it was another thing. Luisa saw a security guard in the booth on the right side of the parking lot. He had a surveillance camera, and sure enough this lady was spotted doing the vandalism on her car.

Luisa called Marshall Kent to meet her to show him the keyed car on her way to return the rental car. He met her at the baseball field, McKinley Run, at the corner of Rapid View and Groundrun Roads. He was there by the time Luisa arrived. Marshall, in his straightforward way of talking, told Luisa that the keyed mark two inches in length was fresh. He took photos of the vandalized car. He told Luisa that he was there for her at any time. She thanked him.

Off to the dealership Luisa went. The service manager, Skip, saw the car and heard Luisa's story. He told her that there would be no cost to her. He confirmed that a screwdriver put into the ignition, which damaged the security system, had vandalized her Nissan Quest. The repair bill was $800.00.

Skip told Luisa to call her auto insurance company, as vandalism was covered. She did call Savings for All Insurance to report this vandalism claim. Her deductible was $500. The claims adjuster came to her home and took the damaged part. He wrote the $300 check on the spot. Luisa asked if this would raise her premium for three years. He told her yes, unfortunately.

Luisa was upset with insurance tactics once again. They will get their $300 back in three years. Why file this claim? It seems very unfair to lose needed funds to simply recover from the "covered" vandalism – what was the point of paying the insurance in the first place?

Then the carriers drop you if you file a small claim of $400, or accuse you of insurance fraud because you do not know an answer to a question. Then the new insurance company charges you higher premiums because you are a new customer. There has to be a better way, she thought. This has been going on for decades.

With her cell phone missing, Luisa now had to deal with the cell phone bills from three companies. When her cellular bills arrived, showing a combined balance of $2500, she was shocked. She checked the calls that were placed, and the telephone numbers did not match up to the calls that she made.

Luisa placed calls to all three providers and spoke to the supervisors from each one. She told them about the thefts and the fact that the calls were not placed by her, but may be in fact have been placed by the insurance carriers as yet another form of harassment. The carriers gave her credit immediately, and advised her to make proper payment on the corrected balances. She told them that she would tomorrow. They also advised her to call the Federal Trade Commission to report the thefts. Luisa looked up the FTC phone number and reported it. The agent gave Luisa a claim number and to contact them with any names and additional information if she could.

That Friday evening, Carmella and Anton were in Luisa's office by the answering machine. She heard them say "Hello, Mr. Gary Landman, CEO of Freedom Insurance, this is the Cannoli's. It is Friday night; we need a large pizza with mushroom and pepperoni on it. Please deliver it to us." Luisa, feeling drained mentally and hurting physically, asked what are you two doing? Anton, sheepishly, told Luisa "You need a to have some humor – we just thought it would give you a laugh – maybe cheer you up."

Luisa told them "Thanks for this fine effort, but what we are going through is no joke to me at all. In fact, it reminds me of when I taught grade school. A boy named Chris Youngman, spit paper spitballs on to the classroom walls. I turned around and saw him do it but chose to see if he would admit to doing it. He did not.

So I had the class write a 1050 word essay on honesty instead. As they starting writing the essay, others in the class started demanding that he to own up to it. Finally, he confessed and the essay writing was halted. Then, on another incident, the desk brass bell was taken off the teacher's desk and flushed down the school toilet as a joke. The written lesson on responsibility and honesty in life brought out the culprit in that situation as well."

" Perhaps those boys are now the culprits running these corrupt companies," he said. " Anton and Carmella, this is not a joke at all."

That evening, that Cannoli's actually ordered their favorite pizza from the Pizza Parlor up the street from their home. Anton and Luisa sipped wine as Carmella drank her soda eating the pizza. They watched Seinfeld for the rest of the evening to have some laughs.

The next morning Luisa received a telephone call from Teresa about receiving a pizza at midnight for some person named Morris who did not live in her neighborhood. Teresa went on to tell Luisa that there was a car parked across the street from her home and stayed parked there with the bright headlights aiming at her home until 4:00 a.m. Her dog, Chow, barked all night and she could not sleep at all. Luisa did not dare tell her about Anton and Carmella's inside joke. She told her mom it was just a mistake and to make light of it. And they hung up the telephone. Luisa knew that Morris was a friend and client of hers.

Luisa called the Valley of Greenville, Kentucky police to report this incident at her elderly mom's home. The police chief knew her family well. Her parents were quite active in the city's political scene for many years. He assured Luisa that his team of officers would look after her mom with this personal lawsuit still pending.

Then, Luisa told Anton and Carmella how their sense of

humor was not funny as it backfired and kept mom up all night wondering who would do that to her.

Anton called his mother–in–law to reassure her that it was probably a computer mistake and to not think of it.

As Luisa decided to pay the cell phone bills at the Kentucky stores on the next day, she called her own mother 40 miles away in the Valley of Greenville, Kentucky. She spoke to her about the spring updating of their yards. Luisa told her that William was helping her mulch the flowerbeds. Teresa asked to have William help her. Luisa told her he was available the beginning of that week. She would see her tomorrow after she paid her cell phone bills. The clicking sounds were still evident on the telephone call as always.

Teresa told Luisa that she sounded like her calls were from a garbage can. She also told Luisa that Suzanne's telephone lines were coming through to her telephone lines. She further told Luisa that she heard Suzanne's kids talking in their family room. She told Luisa that she reported this to Mid West Telephone Company. Luisa told Teresa that she would tell Suzanne about this strange incident.

That next morning at noon, Luisa drove to the World Wide Cell Company's store, listening to WSAI am with Dusty Rhodes playing some old Beatle hits. "Can't Buy Me Love" and the entire "Meet the Beatles Album" played for the long ride to the mall. She pulled into the store's parking lot.

Just then an older green wood-paneled Ford station wagon pulled into the parking spot next to Luisa's.

That car looked identical to the one the young obnoxious guy parked at the North Lakeland Hospital Parking lot earlier in the prior month. But this time a young 30'ish girl with long blond hair was driving the car.

Luisa noticed that the front license plate was missing from the car, as she walked to pay her bill - but the store was closed because it was Sunday. The lady called out to Luisa, "Is the store closed?"

Luisa said, "Yes." The lady said " I drove all the way from East Hill Valley to pay this bill."

With that comment, Luisa knew this was a snake - possibly the wife of the obnoxious guy. Luisa said, without, thinking, "Don't tell me that you are from Freedom Insurance and one of Lee Sleazer's snakes." The lady told Luisa that you got it right and pulled her car abruptly from the parking lot screeching tires out of that parking lot.

From there, Luisa went into the mall to pay the Mid West bill, but was on her guard this time. As she entered the store, a young 20'ish stocking 5'5" young guy wearing torn worn out jeans and torn tee shirt approached Luisa. He said, " My name is William. I do landscaping and I understand that you need landscaping. Here is my telephone number." Luisa knew again that he was a snake and an amateur at that. After seeing that ad in the local newspaper months ago of Freedom Insurance needing people off the street to become private investigators, this pattern of people was the same. Strange people knowing facts about her life, and offering services to her to learn more – would they ever learn?

She took his telephone number, but did not give her information to him. She told him that she would think about it. She paid her bill and left. She decided to mail her third cell phone bill as she had had enough for one afternoon.

She and Teresa then went to dinner at the Pizza Parlor close to Teresa's home.

At dinner, Luisa told her all about the days' events.

Teresa agreed with Luisa to have this 'William' come to her home with Marshall Kent to find out who he really was. She told Luisa to schedule it for that Tuesday about 11:00 a.m.

Determined to fight back, Luisa called Marshall Kent, and filled him in on what had been happening. They arranged to meet at DeAngelo's Pizza to discuss recent events and today's meeting.

As they shared a pizza, Luisa told Marshall about the harassing

calls she was receiving at home. She explained that the phone
would ring at all hours of the day and night, and when she picked
up the receiver there would not be anyone on the other end, and
what had happened to her mother. She also explained her plan
of setting up a sting operation to identify the young landscaper,
William.

Marshall told Luisa to call him from the pay phone from where
they were. William answered the call and agreed to meet her at
her mom's at 11:00 p.m. that Tuesday.

Marshall nodded that would be fine for the meeting. She
hung up the phone with the understanding that William, the
landscaper would meet her the next day. Marshall then told Luisa
that he often heard strange clicks on the phone when he called
her home. He reminded her that during their first meeting he
had suggested that he look into the possibility that her phone was
bugged.

"I think we need to pursue our investigation immediately. First
we will go to your mom's then to your home." he said.

Luisa agreed, and Marshall scheduled his inspection for the
next day.

As Luisa drove away from the pizzeria, she prayed silently
that Marshall would be able to uncover the phone bug that had
been causing her such anguish. It wouldn't solve all her many
problems, but it would be a positive start.

Luisa drove to the Futishi Client kitchen job in the Leland
Community where Nicholas DeVinci, Anne and Suzanne were
handling this small job for Luisa since her trip to Florida. They
told her that they could not use their cell phone that day. They
also told Luisa that Futishi's home phone was not working. Mr.
Futishi had left them a note to call him about the project. Luisa
told them that she would call him from a pay phone on her way
home that hour.

She left them at the home finishing the project up.

Seeing a pay phone, she called Mr. Futishi. He told Luisa that he was pleased with the work but he had problems with his phone for about 3 weeks since she started the job.

Understanding that there was a significant language barrier between them, (he had only been in the USA for 1 year from his home in Spain), Luisa carefully told him that she also had problems with the cell and home phone lines. But she was checking into that the next day. She hoped that comment would ease the matter with him.

That next morning Marshall met Luisa at the Jackson Exit in the Valley of Greenville, Kentucky at 10:30 a.m. There, in the USA Quik gas station parking lot, Marshall told Luisa his plan of action, just like a general would prepare his army of soldiers just before the battle. He would meet her mom and introduce himself, as he would do the same to the young landscaper. He told Luisa to ask him for his driver's license and work references. Then they left for the confrontation.

Marshall, a true gentleman with his salt and pepper hair, well-trimmed physique, in his 60's greeted her mom by shaking her hand at her front door.   He wore a navy blue lightweight sports jacket, crisp white tie of maroon and beige, freshly pressed dockers, and dark brown dress shoes.

Promptly at 11:00 a.m., two newer red Ford pickups pulled up with two young guys in each vehicle. But neither truck had any tools or mulch in it.

Marshall and Luisa approached the four young men and requested their driver's licenses and references. Luisa wrote them down as Marshall wrote down the license plate numbers off the trucks. They were from the western north side of the city, about 45 miles from the city.

Marshall inquired about their references that they had promised to provide. He asked them where their tools and mulch was to do the work needed. They continued to stutter as Marshall continued to verbally hammer at them.

With that, they told Marshall and Luisa that they had to go see their boss. Marshall told them good riddance and to come better prepared next time.

They left the neighborhood and did not come back. Marshall ran the plates and they belonged to Dwight Browne. He was not a landscaper nor professional landscaper.

Marshall told Luisa that he probably saw that ad a while ago ran by Freedom Insurance in the city's newspaper and hired these rascals to harass her and her family. He complimented Luisa on catching them red handed. Then they headed to her home.

Marshall and Luisa arrived at her home, and he swept the house with electronic devices designed to detect listening devices. Although he didn't find any bugs in the home itself, he did monitor strange noises on Luisa's telephone lines. He advised Luisa that the chipped paint vents indicated the possibility of an illegally placed camera system throughout her home. From the initial placement of the missing items in her master bedroom, offices and great room, she just knew that there had to be cameras. The strange clicking sounds in the attic above her master bedroom periodically through the night, had been waking her from some time now.

Marshall advised her that probably was the relay station for the camera system possibly resetting itself or reloading the digital film cartridges. This infuriated Luisa to hear how violated she and her family was.

And with her recent trip to Florida in March, it was highly likely that they removed the sophisticated set up from her home in her absence. Luisa's neighborhood is rather secluded and most private, and they would have not be interrupted.

Marshall also reminded her that the prior snakes that she saw in her driveway did not have a visible car. So her neighbors would not have detected anything unusual.

"It's illegal for me to open the telephone box outside," he told Luisa. "I suggest that you use a pay phone to call Mid West Telephone Company security. Ask for a supervisor and tell the supervisor that you think your phone line may be tapped and you want them to come out and investigate."

"Thank you, Marshall, I'm going to do just that," Luisa said.

She drove immediately to a local deli and put through a call to Mid West Telephone Company which took her 45 minutes to get through to a supervisor, and explaining the situation. The supervisor she spoke to asked Luisa to describe the noises on the telephone. Luisa told her they were clicking sounds and that she had been hearing them on her phone line for over two and one half years.

"I've tried three separate answering machines and I've heard the same noises on each one," Luisa added.

"Perhaps it's the telephone itself," the supervisor suggested.

"No, I've had both my phone and fax machines tested by a technician at an electronics store," Luisa said. "There's nothing wrong with either one."

"This does sound suspicious," this supervisor said. "I'm going to send a security technician to your home tomorrow morning."

Luisa thanked the supervisor, and called her friend Anne, and told her that a telephone company technician would be coming to her home the next morning to check her phone lines for bugs.

"I have to go in for a jaw treatment tomorrow morning," Luisa said. "Could you come over to my house and be there when the technician shows up?"

"Sure, I'd be happy to," Anne said.

"Why don't you bring William over to keep you company," Luisa suggested.

"Good idea," Anne said. "We can go over what needs doing this week while we're waiting."

"Thanks, Anne," Luisa said, then hung up and headed home.

The next morning Luisa left for her medical appointment, then returned home in late morning. As soon as she saw Anne and Will's faces, she knew something had happened.

Anne had tried the 3 caller ID units that she had bought a few days ago and they did not work.

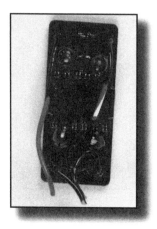

"Luisa, your suspicions were right all along," Anne blurted out the moment Luisa walked in. "The telephone company technician found a bug in the phone box outside. My God, this is like a spy movie."

"I knew it, I just knew it," Luisa said. "Tell me what happened."

Bursting to tell his version, Will said excitedly, "The technician found a sophisticated high-tech computer chip attached to the telephone lines entering your house. He told us that the type of bugging devise he'd uncovered would definitely interfere with your telephone line and fax machine."

"Whoever put it there committed a felony," Anne added. "They could go to jail for a long time."

"Where's the computer chip now?" Luisa asked.

Anne walked over to the kitchen countertop and held up a small baggy. "Right here. The technician said you should keep it for evidence, and report this to the police as soon as possible. The technician told us that there is a recording device within 300' of this illegally placed computer chip of your home in the yard somewhere about 3'4" into the dirt right under the grass roots. All telephone calls placed to and from your home went to it. Luisa, the most shocking news is that all these people that you spoke to or called your home are now in this huge computer data base."

Luisa was totally shocked by this bizarre knowledge now surfacing. Luisa repeated to Anne her mother's comments earlier about her sounding like she was talking from inside a hollow garbage can. The events now started to make sense.

Luisa reached for the baggy, and for a long moment stared at the computer chip inside. Here at last was hard evidence that she had not been hallucinating, that someone was listening in to her phone calls. She said a silent prayer of thanks.

Luisa called Marshall Kent and told him the news. She asked if he could meet her at the Futishi's home to explain what had happened with the telephones. Within an hour, they met at the Futishi home. Luisa saw Mr. Futishi on his sofa, but he would not open the door. Then Luisa remembered that the doorbell did not work. So Marshall knocked on the door.

Mr. Futishi, then opened up the door. Marshall explained the telephone problem to him as best as he could with the language barrier between the two. Mr. Futishi appeared to understand and thanked them. He then told Luisa that their project was so near to completion, but he did not need her workers to complete the little task of filing the nail holes; that he could do that. He paid Luisa the remaining balance that night and shook both Marshal and Luisa's hands for coming over to explain the problem.

When Carmella and Anton returned home later that day, Luisa showed them the bug with a triumphant flare. Both looked sheepish that they had doubted her, and not just a little worried. The Cannolis got very little sleep that night.

Chapter 15

Despair and Disillusionment

As a young girl, Luisa had read every Nancy Drew mystery novel she could get her hands on and had also loved Huck Finn and Tom Sawyer. But no work of fiction could match the real life intrigue and cast of nefarious characters that now swirled around her.

At one point she became so desperate for help in dealing with the terrible events overtaking her that she had even called the local Women's Shelter for support. The Shelter traditionally helped women in crisis, but unfortunately they weren't equipped to handle a complicated case like Luisa's.

She desperately wanted her family to believe her when she told them that there had been at least one and probably multiple illegal entries into their home resulting in the theft of property and phone eavesdropping. Yet, try as Luisa did, Anton and the girls simply couldn't believe that their home and privacy had been violated.

Instead they kept asking her why Freedom Insurance would hire operatives to commit these horrific and unlawful acts. They also reminded Luisa that there had been no forced entry to their home.

"You sometimes misplace things only to find them later," Anton insisted during one of their arguments on the subject.

"Yes, it's true that I tend to misplace things and then find them once I retrace my steps," Luisa conceded. "But this is different. I'm talking about items that suddenly disappear right after I have mentioned them to someone on the phone. It's happened too often to be a coincidence."

"Give me an example," Anton said.

"Okay. Earlier this month I was talking to my accountant about filing my business tax return and I mentioned that I would bring my company charge card folder to our next meeting to verify expenses. The very next time I went to get the folder, it was missing from the desk where I always leave it. Now I'm going to have to file for an extension on my tax return."

Tears came into Luisa's eyes. "In all my years in business, this is the first time I've ever had to file for an extension with the IRS. I tell you, Anton, I can't take much more of this."

"I'm sorry you're going through this," Anton said. "But a missing folder doesn't prove that insurance company operatives have been sneaking into our home."

"Don't you ever watch the news?" Luisa countered. "Both the national media and news shows like 60 Minutes and Dateline routinely carry stories about underhanded and illegal insurance company tactics."

"But why would Freedom Insurance be doing all this to us?" Anton asked.

"Because the damn company is desperate to win the personal injury lawsuit we've filed against them. Whether you believe it or not, Anton, there is corruption, fraud and deceit in this world. You need to take your head out of the sand and see things as they really are."

Despite Luisa's fervent appeal to be believed, her family continued to be highly skeptical of her suspicions. As a result, tensions heightened between her and Anton. Never had their marriage been under so much strain. Their normally calm and peaceful home had been turned into a living hell in the wake of her terrible car accident.

Luisa received a call for a small kitchen remodeling job near her home to do. This would be two week job with materials and stock cabinets. She scheduled the appointment for that evening with the Hazelwoods, a young couple with 4 boys, 2,4,6, and 8 years of age.

That evening the call went smoothly. All selections were made for the cabinets, flooring, wall paint color, and flooring along with family room carpet and wall color.

The Hazelwoods paid their deposit and Luisa left with them understanding that all would be ordered that next morning and the project to start in two weeks. It would only take two weeks to finish up this project. They were quite happy with spring approaching and outdoor grilling to take place.

The next day, Luisa placed all the orders and the venders confirmed the materials would be ready for pick up in two weeks. The Hazelwoods were contacted of this start of the project to begin as planned.

Soon after her unsuccessful attempt to convince her family of the machinations of Freedom Insurance, Luisa encountered yet another example of the underhanded tactics of the company's lead attorney Lee Sleazer.

She went to a local Print shop to copy additional medical records for Michael Wright. She also needed to copy a follow-up claim form with UPS for a cracked glass flower vase she had purchased on her European trip in 1999.

As she spoke with the store's supervisor, Brad, about her claim, a woman in her thirties with long dark hair appeared to Luisa's right. Luisa glanced at her and was startled to discover it was the same woman who had approached her at the Grand Tower Palace Hotel in Atlanta the previous January.

Now Luisa knew for certain that snakes working for Sleazer were following her. As if on cue, the obnoxious woman interrupted the conversation between Luisa and Brad with a loud declaration that she had a prior claim for damaged goods shipped to her home from London.

Rather than risk an argument with the woman, Luisa simply told Brad that she had copies to make and for him to go ahead and wait on the woman first.

Within twenty minutes the woman had left the print shop and Luisa had finished making copies. She returned to the counter, only to be told by Brad that the woman seemed to know all about Luisa's claim for reimbursement for her broken vase.

Since Luisa had spoken to no one other than Brad about her claim – except on the telephone from her home – the woman's knowledge of the event verified to both Brad and Luisa that the Cannoli phone line had indeed been tapped.

Luisa shuddered involuntarily. Now the insurance company snakes were in her hometown of East Hill Valley! Saying a worried goodbye to Brad, Luisa went home and noted today's unsettling encounter in the journal she had started to record all the strange events that had taken place in her life since the accident.

A few days later Suzanne, Anne, Caroline, and Luisa had lunch at a restaurant called Country Morning and Lunch Restaurant. Luisa's appetite was quickly ruined, however, when she glanced over at a nearby table and spotted the same longhaired woman she had encountered in both Atlanta and in the Print and Mail Shop.

The woman was staring at her, and her intrusion didn't stop there. When Luisa went to the front of the restaurant to make a call on the pay phone, the woman followed her and abruptly snatched the receiver out of her hand. Luisa was convinced that the woman wanted to provoke her into a fight.

Fortunately, the restaurant manager, Mick, was standing nearby and saw what happened. He came over and said in a calm voice, "Is there a problem here?"

The strange woman remained silent, but Luisa vented her

frustration and anger. "You saw what happened, Mick," she said heatedly. "I want you to ask this woman for her driver's license. This isn't the first time she's harassed me and I want to know who she is."

"That sounds like a reasonable request," Mick said, turning to the woman. "May I see your driver's license please."

"No, you may not," the woman spat, and turned on her heel and stalked out of the restaurant.

"I'm sorry about this," Mick said to Luisa.

Luisa managed a weak smile. "It's not your fault, Mick," she said, then went on to tell the restaurant manager about her personal injury lawsuit against Oceanic Land Transportation and how the insurance company investigators were tormenting her.

Mick shook his head sadly and told Luisa he would pray for her. He added that if she needed his help she had but to ask.

Luisa expressed her gratitude to Mick and made her phone call, then returned to her table. Shortly afterward she and her friends left the restaurant to continue their day.

The next day Luisa had to fax some material related to her case to her attorney, Michael Wright. Since she was certain that her phone and fax lines had been tapped, she decided to ask to use the fax in her realtor's office in a local business mall.

At the realtor's office, a staff member named Marianna greeted Luisa warmly and asked how she could help her. Luisa told Marianna about her personal injury lawsuit and that she believed that – in an effort to win the lawsuit by underhanded means – the insurance company and the trucking company she was suing had tapped her phone lines.

"May I use your fax to send some pages to my attorney?" Luisa asked.

"Of course," Marianna replied warmly.

Marianna not only faxed off Luisa's material, she added a personal note telling the attorney that Luisa's phone line had been tapped and that was the reason they were sending the pages from the realty office.

Marianna also told Luisa that she was there to help at any time, and Luisa sent her faxes from the realty office all the rest of that week.

The following Monday Luisa received notice that one of her her clients, a Mrs. Baxter, had not received her furniture order. Luisa contacted Brown Freight Lines, which had shipped the furniture, and was told that the shipment had apparently been stolen from the company's loading dock. Luisa called Anne and asked her to file a claim for the missing furniture.

Although the stolen furniture upset Luisa, it didn't surprise her. She was convinced that it was another dirty trick committed by the Freedom Insurance Company snakes. They were obviously trying to ruin her business. In addition to the robbery, Luisa strongly suspected they were responsible for sending a string of unauthorized vendor orders to her office.

As if the attacks on her design business weren't enough, the insurance company continued to harass her at home. The family had recently begun to notice problems with their automatic garage door opener – the red light on the opener was continuously on – and Luisa was forced to call the company that had installed the device. They told her they would send someone over, and to disconnect the opener in the meantime.

On May 2, 2000, Luisa received a letter from Carol Baxter. The letter read:

Dear Luisa:
There seems to be a problem with your answering service or your phone in general. I left two messages on your answering machine over three weeks ago and have not heard from you. Now when I try to call you, there is no answer or a pick up by a machine.
My concern is about the furniture we ordered last fall. When I last spoke with you, you said it was on its

way but that has been almost two months ago. Is there a problem with the order?

Please call me as soon as possible regarding this matter. We are very anxious about getting the furniture down to the lake.

My phone number is 356-567-2512. Please leave a message on my machine if there is no answer.

Thank you,

Carole Baxter

That same week, Luisa and Anton were shocked to receive a letter from Michael Wright stating that he wished to withdraw from their personal injury case. He claimed that Luisa had done some things, which he and his firm did not approve.

Luisa promptly sat down at the kitchen table with a pen and legal pad and began listing all the critical mistakes Wright had made in his handling of their case.

1. Michael Wright failed to communicate with them regarding their concerns.

2. Michael Wright took their case in July 1997 and filed suit in December 1997. However, he did not have them sign a contract until November 1999.

3. Michael Wright did not focus on their case.

4. Michael Wright did not return calls made to him regarding thefts from the Cannoli home, the illegal computer chip put on their telephones, and the vandalism of the family's Nissan Quest automobile.

Michael Wright failed to address the continuous harassment of Luisa by Freedom Insurance Company snakes, even though an attorney from his own firm had told Luisa that he believed that someone working for the insurance company could have tapped her phones.

Luisa got the nerve after sustaining all these violations to call the head office in the East coast in New York City of Freedom Insurance to speak to CEO Gary Landman. She called in on the 800 number, but the young girl would not transfer the call to Mr. Landman when Luisa requested that she do so. She, adamantly, told Luisa that her case was in Cleveland. Luisa asked that girl for her name, she refused and transferred the call to Cleveland.

The young man that answered the call refused to provide Luisa with his name. He asked Luisa why she wanted to talk to Mr. Landman. Luisa simply told him that she had evidence of illegal tactics by their defense lawyer and his team of investigators, and that she wanted him to know about it, and put a stop to it. He told that he would convey the message for her. Luisa asked him for his name, he refused again and hung up the telephone.

Not long after receiving the withdrawal letter from Michael Wright, Luisa and Anton met with the attorney outside in the local courthouse to sign a release. Luisa asked Wright what they owed him in legal fees. The attorney responded, "My fees and expenses amount to approximately $1,900, but don't worry about the money. It is not that much. This was a contingency case; with my withdrawal there is no bill due."

Wright also told them that he would provide them with the names of several good local attorneys who might be willing to take their case. He added that their new attorney would undoubtedly need three to four months to familiarize him or herself with their legal and medical files, and get ready for trial.

Following their meeting with Michael Wright, Luisa and Anton discussed several unsettling facts about the involvement of the attorney and his office in their case.

"Did you ever meet Wright's secretary Marie Sue?" Luisa asked. Anton shook his head no.

Luisa said, "She's a busty woman who usually wears frilly low-cut blouses and high heels. She prefers red nail polish and heavy make-up and with her long blond hair, I'm sure a lot of men would consider her pretty."

"Could you get to the point?" Anton said.

Luisa made a face. "I'm trying to! Since we gave the case to Wright, I've gotten to know her fairly well, and she's told me several things about her boss' conduct of our case."

Anton sighed impatiently. "Such as?"

"Marie Sue once heard Wright yelling into the phone at a Freedom Company adjuster named Melanie McGill, that she and he would both be better off, if Freedom just settled the case and stopped all the legal maneuvers."

"I don't see what that proves."

"Let me finish. Marie Sue also said that Lee Sleazer told her that the insurance company gets all their information relating to a case from their own sources, and they don't rely on the plaintiff's attorney to supply materials like medical files. If that's true, why did Wright need my medical files?"

Anton shook his head in bewilderment. "Doesn't make any sense."

"Exactly," Luisa said.

"Look," Anton said, "You tried calling Wright in his office at every hour of the day, and he was always 'out of the office' or 'in a meeting' or some other damn thing. Didn't you even try reaching him at home."

Luisa nodded. "Yes. I was irate that he hadn't responded to my message that I had information on the insurance company snakes that were harassing me. I hope his wife got my message, and now has some idea of what a miserable lawyer her husband is."

Anton said, "The man was obviously avoiding you, and he sure didn't do much to serve our interests as far as our suit against Freedom Insurance is concerned. The bastard was inept. We're better off without him."

"His whole rationale for taking our case was money, not what was morally right," Luisa said.

"What goes around comes around," Anton said. "The guy will get his eventually. What should concern us now, is that we have thirty days to get a new attorney. That needs to be our focus."

On the day that the Cannolis were scheduled to sign the withdrawal papers that would separate Michael Wright from their case, Luisa appeared before the judge who was handling the proceedings. He asked her if she had a problem with Michael Wright. She told him that she had nothing to say about Michael Wright personally or professionally. The judge granted the withdrawal.

During the next thirty days, Luisa got a first hand description in how the power structure within North County's judicial system actually functioned. Several City Hall employees told her stories about how judges favored certain attorneys, and were able to sway juries. The objectivity she was expecting from the judicial system now seemed an unrealistic dream.

Mulling over what the City Hall employees had told her, Luisa recalled a chilling conversation she'd had with Michael Wright. He told her, "Law suits are part of the business of making money. Don't take anything personally. You are too ethical."

Luisa was still appalled at Wright's words. He knew full well that money was not the motive for her suit. She simply wanted justice. After that conversation with the attorney, she lost all trust in his ethics.

As a history major, she had studied the Bill of Rights and fervently believed in the principles the founding fathers had put forward. Now she was faced with a judicial system that obviously strayed from the centuries-old precept of Justice for All.

Luisa's faith in the American way of life was being sorely tested, and she could only pray that in the end Right and not the Might of a multi-billion dollar insurance company would prevail.

The next day, the Hazelwoods stock items arrived and the project began. Unfortunately, Anne, Suzanne, Nicholas, and

Luisa's cell phone would not work at all. As Niclolas Devinci moved quickly with Luisa marking the walls for the cabinets, they all decided not to talk but to write down on a piece of drywall the conversation as they highly suspected the snakes were eavesdropping on their cell phones. They had to keep their phone on for personal reasons in case any calls came in.

When they had finished for the day and hanging the last of the cabinets, Nicholas picked up the small 14" X 14" drywall piece with all the scribbled notes of conversations on it. He held it up and showed all of them.

All of them were laughing internally and covering up their laughs, as Nicholas nailed that drywall piece above the refrigerator and hung the refrigerator wall cabinet.

It was a day to remember on how they wanted to remain normal in their course of day and stomp on the snakes invading their life.

Chapter 16

Searching for a New Attorney

During the month following Michael Wright's withdrawal from her case, Luisa met with several attorneys in an effort to find a lawyer to represent her in her bitter battle with Freedom Insurance.

One of the attorneys she interviewed was Ernest Gaits, an African American man who had been a well-known lawyer and then judge for many years before retiring from the bench three years before. He had recently started practicing law again.

Gaits had a deep forceful voice. When Luisa spoke to him on the phone he told her that – in addition to being an attorney – he was also a Minister of the Lord. Being quite religious herself, Gaits' words impressed Luisa. He advised her to put her trust in the Lord, as He would protect her.

She thanked him for his kindness and encouraging words, and told him that she was in the process of interviewing attorneys and would get back to him.

Anton contacted Bill Hamm, a local attorney and conservative radio commentator, and scheduled a meeting for the following Sunday at one of the two pubs that Hamm owned locally.

While waiting the confirmation of the appointment with Hamm, Luisa called Marshall Kent from a pay phone at the pub. She heard clicking sounds on the phone as she spoke to Marshall about meeting Hamm's lawyer-partner, Willard Moore. She even had the bar attendant listen to the noises. He described the noises in writing on a small piece of paper for Luisa and wrote down his name and telephone number. He also asked Luisa to call the telephone company to report the noises.

To her surprise, the phone company representative told Luisa that he could not provide any assistance as they were closed on Sunday. With that Luisa knew that the laptop computer that scrambles telephone messages had to be in the shopping plaza parking lot outside.

As she opened the pub door, she noticed a red corvette parked nearby with a man who resembled the Nick Nolte look-a-like character she had spotted before sitting behind the wheel. As Luisa walked toward the Corvette, she could see that the man was holding a laptop.

The man saw her coming and hurriedly started his car, threw it into reverse and sped out of the parking lot. It all happened so fast that Luisa was unable to get his license number, although she did notice that he had North County, Tennessee plates.

Later that next day, Anton received a phone call from Hamm saying that he was tied up in his office and asking the Cannolis to drive downtown to meet him at his office at the corner of Fourth Street and Broadway instead of the pub that next morning.

With Anton driving Luisa's Lexus, they headed for Hamm's office. When they reached the address they parked in a nearby underground garage. However, before they could open the doors, Anton hit the locking button, which turned on the security system. Luisa's door would not open nor Anton's.

Neither one of them knew how to disengage the car's security system. Sweat quickly began to pour down their faces in the closed up car. Luisa saw an attendant and yelled for him to call a Lexus dealership. He called 911 instead. While the attendant was still on the phone, Anton finally found the button to shut off the security system and they jumped out of the car and hurried up the ramp to the outside sidewalk.

As they reached the street, two police cars and a fire truck screeched to a halt in front of the garage and emergency personnel began racing down the ramp.

"Where's the car with the people trapped in it?" one of the fireman yelled at the attendant.

"Just keep on walking," Anton whispered hoarsely to Luisa.

Luisa said, "I have my camera. Should I take a picture?"

"Don't you dare!" Anton snapped. "Keep walking straight ahead and don't look back."

When they reached Fourth and Broadway, they could not find Bill Hamm's office despite going into each corner building and checking every floor of each building. This up and down endless search was draining the Cannolis. Luisa restrained herself from saying anything to Anton. Anton called Hamm's office telephone but only got his answering machine.

They finally decided to leave a message for Hamm to contact them ASAP and went home. When they arrived home they discovered that Hamm had already called to reschedule their meeting, explaining that he was leaving town on Monday. His partner Willard Moore would call Luisa the next morning to set up an appointment for the next day or so.

Willard Moore called Luisa the next morning. He explained that they needed $10,000 up front as a retainer. They would use the retainer to cover the expenses of taking depositions from her doctors.

Before agreeing to sign a contract with Hamm and Moore, Luisa insisted on taking Moore to meet her OBGYN, Dr. David Joseph, who had already written a notarized letter stating that her displaced ovary was due to the traumatic impact she had suffered during her car accident on July 22, 1997.

Significantly, Dr. Joseph served on the American GYN/OB and Internal Medicine Board committee that reviewed injuries suffered by women who had been wearing seatbelts when they were involved in automobile accidents.

Despite Luisa's documented injuries and the prominence of her OBGYN, Willard Moore seemed reluctant to accept her doctor's assessment of her medical condition and used such terms as "probability" and "possibility" when referring to the medical problems she now suffered as a result of her accident.

After hearing Moore express his uncertainty about her condition, Luisa decided that the attorney could not possibly relate to the serious injuries she had sustained.

She was so incensed by his skepticism that she finally told Moore, "The only way you could possibly understand the pain my injured ovaries have caused me is if you pulled your testicles out four inches and held them there. There's no way I'm going to hire you as my attorney."

Several days after telling off Moore, Luisa met with "Junkyard Joe" Willard, another well-known attorney in the city. Most of his cases were high profile. He represented professional athletes and had handled several prominent cases against the police department.

After Luisa gave Willard the details of her accident and the medical injuries she had suffered, he told her that her case was very complex and that he didn't presently have the time to take it on. She thanked him for meeting with her, and left his office wondering if she'd ever find a competent attorney.

Then, driving home, she suddenly remembered Tom Freeby, the law student she had dated in college at the same time she was seeing Anton. She had seen Tom at a high school graduation ceremony in May 1998 and learned that he was now a successful attorney with a thriving law practice.

She had had major surgery on her groin several weeks before and was still recovering. Although the tall and handsome Tom was most appealing in his dark suit and tie with the scales of justice woven into the fabric, Luisa was in considerable pain and not really up for a conversation with anyone. Still, she had managed to tell him, "I like your tie. Most appropriate for a lawyer." Tom had smiled and they exchanged a few brief friendly words.

As Luisa walked away, she had flashbacks about the warm relationship they'd once shared. They sat at separate tables during the reception following the graduation. When the luncheon was ending, they had run into each other again on the sidewalk and Tom had reached for her arm to have her join him but Luisa had felt embarrassed and gently moved away.

Their chance meeting at the graduation came to mind as she decided to call him and tell him about her horrific accident on July 22, 1997. Since she knew her phone was tapped, Luisa decided to make the call from the nearby Lock Bank where she was a valued customer of long standing.

Luisa told the Branch Manager Brenda that she wished to phone an attorney from the bank because her home phone had been tapped. Brenda was aghast that criminal eavesdroppers had violated Luisa's home and assured her that if there was any phone interference at the bank it was a felony and that the FBI would be notified.

Luisa was able to put her call through with no problem and Tom came on the line. His voice was pleasant. He said he had time to see her that Friday. That was only three days away. They scheduled a meeting at 10:00 a.m. at his office.

Luisa planned carefully for her meeting with Tom. She gathered all her notes on the case and chose a nice Susan Bristol pastel blue print skirt with a blue sweater to wear.

When she arrived at Tom's office he greeted her warmly. He looked especially handsome in a lightweight medium green suit and matching tie. She noted that his suit complimented her pastel blue and green skirt.

Luisa thanked him for meeting with her as they shook hands. Their hands remained joined for quite awhile. When their fingers finally slipped apart a slightly flustered Luisa told Tom that she had always retained warm feelings for him. She added that Anton knew of their meeting.

Tom motioned Luisa to a chair and sat wearily down behind his desk. "I didn't sleep at all last night," he said, stifling a yawn.

Although curious about why Tom hadn't been able to sleep, Luisa resisted the temptation to ask him.

Tom sat forward and rested his elbows on his desktop. "Well, why don't you fill me in on your case, Luisa."

Luisa took a deep breath and began, telling him about the injuries she had suffered during her accident and the medical treatments she had undergone to date. She then detailed the thefts at her home, the planting of an eavesdropping computer chip on her phone line and the insurance company snakes that had plagued her.

They spoke for nearly three hours. Tom told her they had a solid case and would ask for at least $550,000. He would begin preparing the case immediately. He presented a contract and scheduled a time for him to meet Anton. He explained he would hire a co-attorney to assist in the case.

Luisa's thoughts recalled the Italian verse - Non e possible nascodere 'amore ogli occhi de chi ama - One cannot love from lover's eyes - as Tom accepted her case. His warm reception of their meeting and the sharing of their thoughts touched Luisa's heart.

As Luisa was preparing to leave, Tom told her to go back to Judge Perrino as scheduled but ask for a two-week extension. He also told her to let the Judge know that she was looking for a new attorney, but to leave his name out of it for now. Luisa agreed.

When Luisa met with Judge Perrino and Lee Sleazer several days later, the insurance company attorney voiced his frustration that this meeting was wasting his time. He insisted that Luisa could have called the information in. Luisa maintained her composure; although she was truly disgusted that Sleazer's only concern was the use of his time and not a just resolution of her case. Two weeks later, when Tom was up to speed on her case, Luisa informed the Judge that she had hired him as her new attorney.

A week later, Tom met Luisa at the North County courthouse for an appearance before Judge Perrino. The 6'10" Tom looked every inch a prestigious lawyer in his dark suit and tie and his bifocal glasses. The glasses reminded Luisa that he was now in his 50's.

Tom was surprised at the sheer volume of records Luisa had brought along. "You sure have a lot of documents for me to go over," he grinned. "I can see that I've got my work cut out for me."

Luisa responded, "The rest are in my car."

Tom just looked at her and shook his head in wonderment.

Tom displayed a direct and professional approach in his interaction with the court clerk and judge, and Luisa's confidence in his legal abilities soared. Lee Sleazer had never met Tom before, and Luisa took a great deal of satisfaction in knowing that the insurance company lawyer would soon learn how tough Tom was.

Tom looked over the trial schedule the clerk had given him, and then turned to Luisa. "The trial date has been changed from June 2000 to March 2001," he said.

"Why?" Luisa asked.

"The court wants to allow time for discovery and trial preparation," Tom explained. "It's normal procedure."

They left the courthouse and Tom walked Luisa to her car to get her medical files. On the way he told her that he intended to interview as many reliable witnesses on her behalf as possible, including her doctors, family and friends. As to her loss of wages, he would talk with her accountant.

When they reached her car, Tom's eyes widened at the sight of the boxes of files in the back seat. He told Luisa that it was going to take considerable time to organize the files and that he would need help.

"Would you mind driving me to my car so that I can transfer all these files?" he asked.

"Not at all," Luisa said.

During the short drive Tom explained that large insurance companies like Freedom Insurance often deny any liability in their personal injury cases but that he believed that Judge Perrino would see right through any motion by Lee Sleazer's to deny liability.

"How could Freedom Insurance deny liability?" Luisa asked.

"As an example, they could contend that you obstructed the truck's right of way or made some other driving error that caused the accident," Tom said.

"But that would be a lie," Luisa said.

Tom grinned wryly. "Welcome to the world of personal injury litigation."

They reached Tom's car and he unloaded the files and thanked Luisa for asking him to take her case. He told her that he would contact her as needed.

"I'm putting my life in your hands, Tom," Luisa said.

"I know that, Luisa," he said. "Rest assured that I will honor your trust and confidence."

Luisa drove off with a feeling of relief that she had finally found someone who cared to take her case.

Although Anton knew that Luisa had decided to hire her old flame, Tom Freeby, as her attorney, during the spring of 2000 he was still wrestling with his wife's selection. Luisa knew he was jealous and rather than being annoyed she was touched by Anton's emotions. Although her husband was not a demonstrative man, he obviously loved her very much.

Dad was right about Anton, she thought. Still waters run deep.

Luisa tried to tell Anton that she chose Tom as her new attorney because Dr. Ba had diagnosed her as bipolar and this disorder would make it difficult for her to relate to a lawyer she had never met before. She had known Tom for many years, and she would be comfortable dealing with him under the trying circumstances.

During this time Luisa's medical appointments took her to many places. She had physical therapy three times a week along with regular massage treatments and doctor visits.

Believing that her phones were tapped, she had decided not to contact her doctors anymore from home and so on May 2, 2000 she drove herself to North Medical Office to schedule her blood pressure check-up in person.

As she pulled out of her driveway, an older light green station wagon with simulated wood panels pulled from the curbside where it was parked and began to follow her. The young man driving the car did not look familiar to her but she took notice as Marshall Kent had instructed her to do.

As Luisa drove she kept looking in her rear-mirror to see if the station wagon was still behind her. It was, following her all the way to North Medical Office. By now totally rattled, she parked in the only spot she could find, which was about four rows from the medical office front entrance door.

The driver of the station wagon parked nearby. Nonchalantly, Luisa walked to his car and wrote down his Kentucky license plate number. Then – without saying a word to the driver – she walked away.

As she did she heard the driver shout out, "Insurance and business fraud. Got you!"

She then heard the car door open and the sound of footsteps rapidly approaching her from behind. A moment later the young man was beside her. He was carrying a red plastic container with no label and ranting at Luisa about insurance fraud.

"Your injuries are fake!" he shouted.

Luisa kept her mouth shut as Marshall Kent had cautioned her to do in such a situation.

Once inside the medical building lobby, Luisa entered the first available elevator hoping the door would close and the young guy could not get in with her. Unfortunately, the doors remained open long enough for him to enter.

Luisa exited quickly before the door closed, grateful that she had not pushed the floor button before the strange young man got on the elevator.

Fortunately, the elevator doors on the left opened as the other doors closed. Luisa got on the second elevator and rode up to Dr. Morrow's office on the fourth floor. Dr. Morrow saw her immediately. As Luisa had expected, her blood pressure was elevated and Dr. Morrow told her to return in a week for another check-up. Luisa left his office.

As the elevator doors opened on the fourth floor, she discovered to her horror that the young man who had been harassing her was already onboard.

"I did not know where you went," he said with a leer. "How did your medical appointment go?"

Luisa said nothing and as soon as that elevator door opened on the first floor she hurried away from the man.

As she reached the parking lot, she spotted a gentleman walking to his car. He looked like a pro football star and Luisa asked him to walk her to her car as the man behind her was harassing her.

The gentleman gave the young man a hard stare – which caused him to back off – then escorted Luisa to her car. Luisa thanked him, got in her car and quickly drove out of the parking lot before the young man had time to reach his car and follow her.

When Luisa reached home, she jotted down the details of her bizarre encounter in her journal. After that, exhaustion set in and she lay down on her bed and slept for four straight hours.

Luisa's company, Interior Designs by Luisa, was destroyed by the events that followed her terrible accident on July 22, 1997. The combination of her frequent absences due to medical treatments, the cost of her care, her distraction and emotional trauma, and machinations of insurance company snakes led to an inevitable decline in sales. Sadly, Luisa had no choice but to lay off many of her employers, who were family to her.

In August 2000, Luisa applied for a part-time job at L&M Department Store. She had worked there 19 years before. At the time she was faced with large co-pays for her medical treatments and she asked the manager, Arthur, if she could be paid $10.00 an hour in consideration of her experience. Arthur agreed.

Luisa had gained 70 pounds in the two and one-half years since her accident and her weight was now approaching 240 pounds. None of her clothes fit anymore. Fortunately, her earnings – along with her employee discount – allowed her to buy some new outfits at L&M.

Luisa stayed with L&M until October 2000. She was finally forced to quit because her persistent neck and shoulder injures – her pain level was a ten – prevented her from lifting anything, which was a serious drawback for anyone with her job. Her doctors put her back into physical therapy, which only deepened her frustration.

Shortly after leaving L&M Luisa decided to try to find a position with an interior design firm. She chose Miller/Taylor, which was owned by two businesswomen Luisa respected, Phyllis and Jeanne. They knew and admired her design work and promptly provided her with a position. They even ordered a special new desk/hutch for her.

Because of her ongoing and time-consuming medical treatments, Luisa could only work part-time. The firm agreed to pay Luisa $300.00 for 10-15 hours a week of work.

Despite the generous employment terms Phyllis and Jeanne extended to Luisa, it soon became apparent that her full-time co-designers did not like the hours she worked. She told her colleagues about her accident and the ordeal she had been through, but they were unsympathetic. She couldn't understand how people could be so cold.

The attitude of her colleagues was not the only thing wrong with her new job. The store had very few new clients. Her co-designers had time to dust and rearrange the furniture on a weekly basis. The owners seemed to be the only ones bringing in sales.

Luisa soon realized that she was working in a cut-throat and jealous atmosphere. Obviously, the other designers felt very threatened by her unusual employment deal with the owners. They failed to grasp the fact that she had been given special consideration because she had twenty years experience in interior design and had won top awards for home shows.

Phyllis and Jeanne had even put an ad in The Post, a local newspaper, highlighting the design honors bestowed on Luisa.

Luisa was embarrassed by the ad. She'd always believed that it was her duty to use her God-given talents to live up to her credo that Excellence is Worth the Effort.

In late November 2000, the Cannolis had a peaceful family Thanksgiving meal. The next day, Rosanna and Carmella were eager to get their Christmas ornaments and decorations from the attic.

To their surprise, they couldn't find all the ornament boxes. The main two boxes with the girls' baby ornaments and collectable ornaments were missing. Anton checked the attic. The tree was up there, but there were no more ornaments, nor could he find their stockings for the mantel.

The Cannolis had little cash available for gifts that year. The girls and Luisa cried together. They were all devastated by the living hell that had enveloped the family in the two and a half years since Luisa's accident.

After discovering the missing ornaments, Luisa became more and more suspicious of violations in her life. Both personal and professional items were missing from her home, Marshall Kent had discovered an illegal eavesdropping device on the family's phone lines and she was being followed and harassed by insurance company snakes.

Feeling overwhelmed, Luisa decided to tell Tom Freeby of her additional concerns. He listened attentively, and then told Luisa to make careful notes about any further invasions of her privacy.

Luisa and her family tried hard to make the best of Christmas 2000, but the onslaught mounted against them by Freedom Insurance made the holidays a time of stress and uncertainty for everyone.

One of the tools Luisa used to cope with the disintegration of her life was to take comfort from the scriptures. A reading from Isaiah in the Old Testament – "***It comes like a gentle dew***" – reminded her that when grace comes you stop being preoccupied and abandon believing that your own meddling, managing and manufacturing can create inner peace.

We're trained to be managers, to organize life, to make things happen, she thought. That's what's shaped our Western culture, and it's not all bad. But if you transfer that to the spiritual life, it's pure heresy. It doesn't work.

It's a matter of letting go, Luisa realized. It's a matter of getting the self out of the way and becoming smaller. Spirituality requires great kenosis. As Paul talks about in Philippians 2:6-11, ***it involves the emptying of the self so that there's room for another.***

Over the holidays, Carmella had to finish a newsletter for a school project. She wrote about the strain on Luisa and her design business, and her hope that the coming trial would end her mother's stress. Carmella's caring words touched Luisa deeply, and made her wonder anew how much her car accident had affected her daughter.

January 1, 2001 arrived and with it new problems for Luisa. During her time at Miller/Taylor, she had made many sales and received a fair commission. However, her co-designers kept telling the owners untruths about her performance. The workplace strain had a negative effect on Luisa's health, and also undermined her position with the owners. Things finally became intolerable and she was terminated on January 17, 2001.

Yet leaving Miller/Taylor also had a positive side for Luisa. Carmella was having health problems and needed her mother at home to take care of her. Luisa decided to leave the cutthroat world of design work behind for now and prioritize her family.

Yet she also needed at least a part-time income and she tried to find a new job. She accepted a position with a carpet store, but their workers smoked and she was allergic to tobacco smoke. She could not work there and soon left. She next got a job at a furniture store, but the owner would only give her a three percent commission on sales. She could not exist on such a small income, and quit after only two days.

On the positive side, Tom was moving steadily ahead in his preparations for trial. He hired a hard-driving attorney named Rocko Marcine to assist him. Rocko had a sharp tongue and gruff demeanor, and looked a lot like Larry King.

Luisa began meeting regularly with the two attorneys to map out their strategy for the upcoming trial. She soon learned that Rocko was not only an attorney but had also been an insurance adjuster.

"I've assisted Tom with many insurance cases over the years," Rocko told her. "Hopefully my experience with insurance companies will be an asset to our legal team in your case as well."

The two lawyers had reviewed Luisa's medical records and were aware that Dr. Ba had diagnosed her bipolar the year before. They also knew that Luisa's internist and pain psychologist differed with this diagnosis.

Looking over the contrasting physicians' opinions, Tom told Luisa, "You know, we were quite close once and we've known each other for many years now, and I have to say that I agree with your internist and pain psychologist. I just don't believe you're bipolar."

Luisa felt comforted by Tom's words.

Anton attended one of their meetings and told the two lawyers about his research into the many strong medications Luisa was on. Anton said that he was convinced many of his wife's emotional problems – perhaps some of her symptoms as well – could be traced directly to her being overmedicated.

Tom and Rocko took notes as Anton spoke, occasioally nodding in agreement with his observations. Finally Tom said, "Luisa has been very clear-headed and focused during our meetings. This is not what I'd expect from someone who was being overmedicated."

"She's able to focus now because she's finally off most of the heavy drugs she was taking," Anton explained.

"I see," Tom said.

During their next meeting, Rocko grilled Luisa as a defense attorney would. He questioned her sharply about her injuries and how they had affected her life. Luisa carefully explained her physical limitations and the adjustments she'd had to make to her life style.

Knowing that the insurance company lawyers would go over Luisa's tax returns with a fine tooth comb, Rocko zeroed in on the losses of $21,000 and $37,000 she'd reported in the years since the accident had destroyed her ability to run her business.

"Why did you continue to run a company that was not profitable?" he shot at her.

Luisa explained that she'd had contracts with clients for several large projects and that she couldn't just shut down her company without risking ruinous lawsuits. She'd had no choice but to continue to run her business and pay her employees despite the fact that she was losing money.

Using shock tactics to prepare Luisa for the treatment she was sure to receive from the defense, Tom threw insults at Luisa. "Hell, you could have made more money slinging hamburgers at McDonald's than running your design company," he said.

Although Luisa knew full well that both attorneys were only trying to help her get ready for the trial, still she felt wounded at Tom's harsh words.

You ought to know about money, she thought bitterly. You were so cheap when we dated that you've probably still got the first dollar you ever earned.

As Tom and Rocko buffeted Luisa with tough questions, she ached to explain that money was not her motivation. What inspired her was the opportunity to use her design skills to help her clients create their dream homes at a reasonable cost. The professional recognition represented by the many awards she had received was also far more important to her than the money she earned.

Tom told her that they were now going to talk about how the accident had affected her teenage daughters. He told Luisa that he knew she had not been able to give as much time to Rosanna and Carmella as she had prior to her horrific car crash.

"The law clearly states that damages can be recovered if an   action by a defendant results in the interruption or loss of parental consortium," Tom said.

"What does 'consortium' mean?" Luisa asked.

Tom tented his fingers under his chin. "Simply put, consortium means the legal right of a child to the company, affection and service of a parent."

Luisa nodded. "Well, there's no question that my medical problems have prevented me from doing as much for the girls as I used to before the accident. And, truth be told, I know the medications I've been taking have made me less affectionate toward Rosanna and Carmella."

Tom said, "What about spousal consortium? Did the accident affect the marital relations you and Anton normally enjoy?"

Luisa blushed. "Yes, very much so."

Toward the end of their meeting, Luisa asked Tom how he determined the dollar value of the damages she had suffered.

"I normally demand five to seven times the amount of the bills incurred by my client," he said. "In your case, that would put the figure at roughly seven hundred and seventy-five thousand dollars."

Before Luisa left, Tom told her that he had hired a graduate law student named Annette Brock to help organize Luisa's legal files, which had grown voluminous. He added that Annette would undoubtedly be contacting Luisa with questions about various documents.

Although Luisa felt that her legal preparations were going well that January, her medical problems continued to mount. Her jaw had been misaligned since the accident and her doctors now told her that they needed to operate on her jaw before the end of the month.

Both Dr. Grizzly and Dr. Fritz cautioned Luisa that full recovery from her surgery and her other injuries would take time. The body heals from the inside out. Luisa was reminded of the words of Dr. Chuck Stuart who had said that healing takes place layer by layer like an onionskin.

Before undergoing her jaw surgery, Luisa had several meetings with Annette Brock. Together the two women tackled the enormous task of organizing Luisa's ten-foot tall stack of legal and medical records.

There were legal depositions, motions, medical bills, medical records, and doctors' files documenting her numerous injuries.

There were also countless articles on anxiety, panic attacks, posttraumatic stress, and computer hacking. Lastly, there were Marshall Kent's files on truck driver Frank T. Walker and Oceanic Long Run Transportation.

During the days that Luisa and Annette worked together on the complex files, Luisa became quite familiar with the layout of Tom's cherry wood paneled offices and the impressive parade of well-dressed clients going in and out all day.

Tom Freeby was obviously a most successful attorney with a

thriving law business. This realization reassured Luisa that her case was in good hands.

After her disastrous experience with Michael Wright and her disappointing interviews with other potential attorneys, perhaps she had finally found her legal knight in shining armor.

Chapter 17

Preparing for Trial

Tom called Luisa to have her meet his new legal assistant from law school who was also a registered nurse. He explained to Luisa that her understanding of medical terms would help relate to the medical files. He arranged the meeting for the first Saturday in January, 2001 at 9:00 A.M.

He greeted Luisa at the front oak door and as he led her up, he told Luisa that he was still a straight-line personality as he was many years ago in their relationship.

Then he brought Luisa a fresh glass of water and told her that he would be downstairs in anything comes up regarding the files. He left the two alone to continue with his request.

As Luisa and Annette Brock labored to put all the case-related documents Tom Freeby had assembled on computer disks, Luisa discovered that she and Annette had the same organizational skills and worked well together. Luisa also would be sitting in on trial preparations with Tom and Rocko within the few hours.

Luisa thoughts of seeing Tom again in this working atmosphere would help resolve some internal romance issues that intertwined in her relationship with Anton.

Tom and the Cannoli's had similar friendships and would sometimes occasionally meet at the social affairs quite unexpectedly.

As a teenager, her grandmother Nonni and mother enlightened Luisa to the world of love and romance through Italian proverbs, poems and thoughts. On this particular day this poem came to her memory, as it seemed fitting to this renewed friendly encounter with her former passionate lover and friend from 27 years ago.

> *Ore che sei venuta*
> *Ore che sei venuta,*
> *che con passo di danza sei entrata*
> *nella mia vita*
> *come folata una stanza chiusa-*
> *a festeggiarti, bene tanto atteso*
> *le parole mi mancano e la voce*
> *e tacerti vicino giá mi basta.*

> *Now That You Have Come*
> *Now that you have come,*
> *Dancing into my life*
> *a guest in a closed room-*
> *to welcome you, love longed for so long,*
> *I lack the words, the voice,*
> *And I am happy just in silence by your side.*

Annette told Luisa that Tom wanted to do his best for her and her family. Her doctors were also impressed with Tom and his approach, and several of them remarked on Tom's compassionate nature.

Her physicians' positive assessment of Tom put Luisa's mind at ease. Her growing confidence in Tom was further heightened when he told her that he believed her regarding all that she and her family had been through.

He added that unfortunately – although the insurance company investigators had understandably upset her – they had a legal right to follow her. She told him that in addition to the two snakes who had shadowed her during her European trip many other strangers had approached her and asked very personal questions.

"I suspect there may be ten or even as many as twenty-five insurance snakes involved in this," she said.

Rocko Marciene arrived at 2:00 P.M. Tom and Luisa met with him in the outer conference room while Annette continued with the organization of the files.

Rocko told Luisa that the main concern of insurance companies was insurance fraud. He added that it was not unusual for insurance companies to turn plaintiffs' lives inside out in a dogged effort to prove fraud.

Rocko told Luisa that eventually he wanted to inform Lee Sleazer about the illegal computer chip that had been placed on her phone lines. However, without solid proof, they would only be able to allege that the multiple robberies of her home had been the work of insurance company operatives.

Luisa continuously sent Tom new documents as her mountain of records grew. Their debt – due almost entirely to medical expenses and lost income – was mounting steadily. She'd had jaw surgery on both jaw joints and was getting treatments to prepare her for surgery again. The stress on Luisa was almost unbearable.

During the intensive trial preparations both Dr. Grizzly, and Dr. Stuart counseled Luisa about the importance of maintaining a normal lifestyle.

She told them both, "That's easy advice to give but living a normal life in the midst of all this turmoil is all but impossible to do."

On a Saturday morning in mid-January, Luisa met with Tom at

his office. They warmly shook hands. Luisa felt her heart skip a beat as they shook hands. After some small talk, Tom led her up the old creaking staircase to a back office to meet with Annette.

Annette was organizing some medical files. Tom explained to Luisa how he wanted the files – doctors' names, treatments, and medical bills separated from the documents relating to pharmacists and hospitals.

Tom told Luisa that he would enlarge certain records to present to the jury in June. He showed her an example and made sure Luisa knew his procedure. Luisa felt an ever-growing confidence in Tom as his long strong hands went through the files to show her how he wanted them organized. He then told the two women that he would be in his office if they needed anything, and left them to their filing.

Through the rest of the morning, Luisa and Annette worked on different sections of the case files. While Annette worked with doctors' files, Luisa concentrated on the hospitals and pharmaceutical bills. After a few hours of this filing routine, Tom came upstairs and told them it was time for lunch.

Tom took Luisa and Annette to a small Italian restaurant down the street named Gino's Pizzeria. Sitting down at a table with bar stools, they looked over the menu and ordered. Tom chose a small pizza and Annette had the same. Luisa ordered a tuna salad sandwich and a small green salad. With her jaw problems, Luisa knew she could only eat a little at a time.

During lunch Luisa asked Tom about his two sons.

"My oldest son Joey just graduated from college with a degree in architecture," Tom said proudly. "He's in London now doing graduate work."

"The family and I were in London not long ago," Luisa said. "The architecture in the city is fascinating. You can see the way building styles have evolved over the centuries."

Tom nodded in agreement. "Joey's learning a lot over there."

"How's your younger son doing?" Luisa asked.

"Jeremy just graduated from high school. He's planning on going to a local college, although I don't think he's settled on a major yet."

Tom took a bite of his pizza. "What about your girls, Luisa? How are they doing?"

Luisa patted a smear of salad dressing from her lips with her napkin. "Rosanna is attending Master Tech University on a scholarship."

Tom said, "Scholarship! I wish my boys would bring one of those home. Save me a ton of money."

Luisa laughed. "We're very proud of her. Hopefully our youngest, Carmella, will follow in her older sister's footsteps. She's just started high school, and, like Rosanna, she's really into sports."

Tom said, "And Anton's doing well?"

"Yes, you know Anton. Solid as a rock. How's your wife been?"

"Gayle's a realtor. You know how the real estate market goes – up one year, down the next. The uncertainty would drive me up a wall but somehow Gayle manages to deal with the swings."

Luisa turned to Annette. "Do you have children?"

Annette swallowed a bite of pizza and nodded. "Three girls, twelve, fourteen and sixteen. Like your two, Luisa, they're doing well in school and love sports."

After a relaxing 45-minute lunch, the three left the restaurant.

As they walked back to Tom's office, he spoke of a case he had settled the year before. The client's bills had been $1,500 and Tom had won an award of $15,000.

"Unfortunately, after receiving the settlement my client chose to just sit in his recliner and watch television. He never got back into the rhythm of life. Several months later he had a massive heart attack and died. I don't want that to happen to you, Luisa. When your case is over, I hope you'll pick up your life where you left off."

Luisa was touched by Tom's concern. "You don't have to worry about me, Tom," she said, patting his arm. "I'm a survivor. When this is over I intend to rebuild my life and start smelling the roses again."

"I'm glad to hear that," Tom smiled.

When they reached Tom's office Annette and Luisa headed up the old creaking staircase to resume their work on the medical files. They chatted amicably and Annette told Luisa that she had been a Registered Nurse before going to law school.

"I'm convinced that my nursing experience will allow me to relate tmore closely to the injuries suffered by accident victims," Annette said.

"I think you're right," Luisa agreed, remembering her unhappy experience with Michael Wright. "Before I hired Tom, I was represented by an attorney who couldn't relate to my injuries at all. All he seemed to care about was the money he could earn from a settlement. There was constant friction between us, and – thank God – he finally withdrew from my case."

Annette told Luisa that she had written dozens of letters to local lawyers offering her assistance as a legal student with nursing experience. Tom Freeby had called her right after he'd received her letter.

Luisa thought she knew why Tom had been so anxious to hire Annette: he would be getting an assistant with talents in two fields – medical and legal – and only have to pay her a single modest salary. For the frugal Mr. Freeby, it was undoubtedly a money-saving opportunity he couldn't pass up.

Feeling that she could confide in the friendly and warm Annette, Luisa told her that she and Tom had had romantic relationship years before when she was in college and Tom was studying for his law degree. Annette was intrigued by Luisa's revelation.

After a full day of work, they decided to call it a day around 4:00 PM. They decided to get together again soon and exchanged telephone numbers. Annette said that she was taking files home to create a database compatible with Tom's database.

Luisa explained that she wanted mileage reimbursement and that USA Road Travel Agency provided her with exact mileage to all the medical facilities. Annette told her that she would set up a file for that data. They set up a late afternoon meeting for Friday of that upcoming week.

Tom came upstairs, as they were getting ready to leave. He agreed that they had put in a full day and it was time to go home. Annette gathered her purse, said goodbye to Luisa and Tom, and departed down the creaking old oak staircase. For the next few minutes Tom and Luisa talked about the files.

"I want you to know how pleased I am with all you and Annette are accomplishing," he said. "Your hard work is really helping with the trial preparation."

"I'm glad to do it," Luisa said. "It makes me feel a part of things."

"Good. You look a little parched. Would you like a glass of water?"

Luisa smiled, "Yes, thank you. You're very observant. The medications I'm taking tend to dry out my mouth."

Tom got Luisa a glass of water. When she was finished drinking, they headed for the stairs.

"What are your plans for the office space up here?" Luisa asked as they headed down the complaining steps.

"I'm going to rent it out to other lawyers," Tom said.

"I like your carpet selection, both the color and the quality. You have excellent taste."

"Thank you, Luisa."

When they reached the bottom of the stairs Luisa turned to say goodbye and felt her heart fluttering at the nearness of the tall, strong-featured Tom.

"Thanks again for all your hard work today," Tom said, putting out his hand to shake hers.

Luisa glanced at his hand, and then looked him in the eye. "Would it be all right if I gave you a hug?" she asked.

"Of course," he said without hesitation.

As they held each other, a torrent of thoughts flooded through Luisa's mind. Tom was compassionate, thoughtful, warm, charismatic, and honest. A man to be admired. She could feel his heart beat as they held each other tightly. He was so tall that her head reached only to his shoulder.

Luisa looked into Tom's blue eyes and said, "You are so tall and strong."

Tom smiled and said, "You should see my son, Joey. He's taller than I am."

They slowly released their affectionate hug and shook hands warmly. Tom thanked Luisa again and told her that he would call her if he needed her for anything else.

"Fine," Luisa said. "I'll be happy to help in any way I can."

Tom opened the heavy leaded glass oak front door for Luisa and she went down the steps and headed for her car. As she walked she thought, the friendship we once shared is still there today.

As Luisa drove home she reflected on how good she felt that Tom would be representing her interests – and those of her family – in court. She believed the jury would recognize his integrity, and that he would be able to make them understand the terrible violation that she and her family had endured at the hands of Freedom Insurance. She prayed that the Lord would give Tom and Rocko the strength to win the coming battle with Lee Sleazer and his unscrupulous agents.

When Luisa arrived home, Anton asked her how her day had gone. Luisa explained that she and Annette, Tom's Law Clerk Assistant, had spent most of the day organizing files in preparation for the trial in June.

The Cannolis had a relaxing evening. Luisa sorely needed the tranquility for the upcoming week would be grueling. She had several medical treatments scheduled, and also faced jaw surgery a week from Friday.

At 1:00 PM the following Wednesday Luisa had just gotten off the cell phone in her Lexus when she got a call from Tom. He asked her to come to his office immediately as an urgent matter had come up regarding her files.

She told him that she would have to clear it with Phylis at Miller/Taylor. Luisa already, was well aware of her personality and attitude to work hours at her design furniture store. She told Tom she would call Phylis and call him back. Luisa called Phylis and explained to Phylis that her attorney, Tom Freeby, called her to ask her to come immediately to his office pertaining to her files. Phylis quizzed her on how long would she be gone. Luisa told her that she did not know but there was a good possibility it could go for a few hours. Phylis, most reluctantly, told Luisa to go ahead in her icy knife cutting voice. Luisa knew she could not last at that design furniture store until May. It churned her stomach to go there. The small mindedness of those people added to Luisa's stressor list.

"I'll be there as soon as possible," Luisa told Tom.

"Great," Tom said. "I'll see you soon."

When Luisa arrived at Tom's offices she found him in a foul mood. He had come across a discrepancy in her files and asked her rather abruptly to straighten the matter out. Without another word he turned on his heel and returned to his office, leaving her with a pile of documents.

Luisa had never seen Tom so short-tempered before. For a while his demeanor bothered her, but as she worked on the files she rationalized that this was simply the lawyer side of him surfacing. On the positive side, she knew that Lee Sleazer could not stand up to Tom's aggressive nature for very long in court.

Luisa finished the task Tom had asked her to do and went downstairs to his office. He was sitting behind his desk and she could tell by his expression that that he was still ticked off about the filing mistake she had made.

"I think I've corrected the problem you found with the files," she said. "I'd better be on my way. Carmella's home alone."

Tom's face softened a bit. "Thank you for coming over on such short notice," he said. "I've got some encouraging news to give you before you go."

"What's that?"

"I've talked to the researchers who help me assess the damage values of my cases. They tell me that your case is worth at least $550,000."

"That's good to hear," Luisa said. "My medical bills and business losses are skyrocketing. Anton and I are about at the end of our financial rope."

Tom rose from his chair. "I know it's been hard on you both, Luisa. Just hang in there a little longer and I fully expect that we'll win you a jury award that will ease your financial burden. C'mon, I'll walk you to the door."

Luisa headed home wondering what other instant demands would Tom have. Her jaw surgery was next week and she doubted that she'd be able to help Tom much during her recovery.

She suddenly felt an all-consuming desire to just get on a plane and go live on an island far removed from all the terrible stress that she suffered on a daily basis. Her weight had now topped 240 pounds and none of her clothes fit anymore. She knew she looked terrible, and the realization had eroded her self-esteem and added to her misery.

When Luisa got home she comforted Carmella – who hated being home alone – then went upstairs to her bedroom and sought solace in the pages of Simple Abundance. Slowly she began to experience a sense of tranquility. It also helped when she remembered the words of Dr. Stuart, who had told her that she was experiencing situational anxiety and that the condition would pass as her medical and legal problems were resolved.

The days that followed were like a roller coaster ride for Luisa.

She was constantly juggling medical appointments, family needs, trial preparations and business responsibilities. Lack of sleep added to her fatigue. She could not sleep for more than two hours at a time before the pain of her injuries woke her up.

In an effort to help relieve her constant stress, she began to go to Tri-Health Pavilion every night. There she would spend four to six hours doing aquatic therapy and physical exercises. She also found the steam room relaxing, and regularly went to the sauna to meditate in the soothing heat.

And every night alone in her bedroom she would pray to the Lord:

> *Make me a channel of your peace.*
> *Where there is hatred, let me bring your love.*
> *Where there is darkness only light.*
> *And where there's sadness ever or, Master grant*
> *that I may never seek.*
> *So much to be consoled as to console.*
> *To be understood as to understand.*
> *To be loved, as to love, with all my soul.*
> *Make me a channel of your peace.*
> *It is in pardoning that we are pardoned.*
> *In giving of ourselves that we receive.*
> *And in dying that we're born to eternal life.*

Luisa had now reached the point where she was spending a good portion of every day receiving one medical treatment or another. Unable to either serve her clients or solicit new ones, her design business hit rock bottom and her income dried up.

With the theft of the list of new clients from the Village of Woods Show in April 2000, she had no way of bringing in new business. Luisa had to let Suzanne, Anne, and William go. They told her that they did not want her to spend any more money paying them. They knew the Cannolis were in financial straits.

In early March 2001 Luisa decided to visit her oldest daughter Rosanna in Boston for her twentieth birthday. She had been contacted by Freedom Insurance and asked to schedule an appointment with a psychiatrist, Anil Chabad, who worked for the company, but she decided to put off the session until after she had returned from Boston.

Luisa had a wonderful time with Rosanna. They took a sightseeing boat tour on the Charles River and spent many happy hours sightseeing and having lunch together. Rosanna had decided to move out of the Boston University dormitory where she was living and rent an apartment with several of her friends. She showed her mother the apartment, and Luisa approved of Rosanna's selection.

The move would mean that Rosanna would have to learn money management and assume grownup responsibilities. Luisa was confident that her eldest had matured quite a bit since going off to college and that she would be able to handle her new independence. Rosanna and her friends all had part time jobs, so Luisa was not concerned about the girls ability to pay the rent. When Rosanna asked her mother if she would sign the lease for the apartment, Luisa happily agreed.

As Luisa's three-day visit came to an end, she knew that she and Rosanna had truly bonded. The realization brought tears to Luisa's eyes, and she stored the magic memories of her time with Rosanna away in her heart.

When Luisa returned home, she faced both her meeting with Dr. Chabad and more jaw surgery. Before surgery she would have to undergo 25 hours a week of various treatments that included injections, ultrasounds, and exercises.

Her doctor explained to her due to health care insurance policies, conservative treatment was mandatory before surgery. Surgery can be risky and death can occur.

"But if my MRI showed damage and displacement to my jaw, why do I have to go through all this expensive pre-surgery treatment?" Luisa asked.

Her doctor explained that her body and brain had gone through so many traumas that they had to prepare her mentally and physically for the surgery. From the onset of the horrific accident, the doctor told her this would take time. She had no idea that it would take five plus years for all the necessary medical treatments to take place.

Despite her misgivings about all the pre-surgery treatments she would have to endure, Luisa remained confident that her excellent doctors had carefully structured a recovery plan that would help her return to normal health.

Dr. Williams – a jaw specialist and Mr. Rogers look-a-like, was to perform her jaw surgery. To prepare Luisa for the operation, he sent her to see Dr. Peter Bronz, a pain psychologist. When Luisa met with Dr. Bronz she told him another pain psychologist, Dr. Chris Stuart, had previously treated her.

Bronz spoke highly of Dr. Stuart's Pain Care Management Recovery Program. He went on to tell Luisa that he agreed with Dr. Williams that her head and neck pain was chronic and permanent due to the horrific accident on July 22, 1997.

When Dr. Bronz had finished examining Luisa, she brought up the subject of her coming psychiatric examination by Dr. Anil Chabad, who worked for the insurance company defense team.

Dr. Bronz looked thoughtful for a moment, and then said, "I know Anil, but I wasn't aware that he did defense work for insurance companies."

Luisa said, "Is there any advice you can give me about how I should handle my interview with Dr. Chabad?"

"I can tell you this," Bronz said, a sober look on his face. "Whatever he puts you through, be sure to tell him at the end of your session that your injuries are due to the accident of record and that I will testify to that fact."

Bronz smiled mischievously. "Oh, and tell him I said hello."

"Thank you, Dr. Bronz," Luisa said. "You have no idea how

helpful you've been to me."

Luisa's appointment with Dr. Chabad fell on a sunny Wednesday afternoon. She called Tom to let him know she was at the doctor's office. He gave her reassuring words to build up her confidence. Luisa's stomach was churning as she waited for the stressful encounter to take place.

She had a sudden urge to go to the bathroom. Her entire insides felt like they were exploding. Fear of the unexpected reached its peak. She had cried in the car driving to his office. All the flashbacks of what she had been through just overwhelmed her. She prayed to the Lord, for strength.

She even called on St. Jude, patron Saint of Lost Causes and situations of despair, to help her through this ordeal. Then she prayed to St. Michael the Archangel to protect her from the enemy. She has faith and desperately needed the immediate heavenly help. Finally she got her emotions in check and readied herself for the meeting with Dr. Anil Chabad.

As Luisa walked into the psychologist's small inner office she was surprised to discover that he was Indian. As if the session wouldn't be stressful enough, she found his heavily accented English to be extremely hard to understand.

Before sitting down Luisa's eyes swept his office, nervously checking out every detail. There was a small oak desk, file cabinets, three occasional chairs that looked comfortable, and a small table with a lamp on it.

Dr. Chabad motioned Luisa to an armless chair and sat down facing her. On the floor beside his chair were boxes piled high with papers. On his lap was a legal pad covered with notes.

He began with the accident description. "I see by my notes that only one tractor trailer hit your car. Not the two that you have contended."

Luisa took immediate offense. "Where did you get that little gem of misinformation?" she asked.

"From the defense lawyer for Freedom Insurance, Lee Sleazer, who in turn was given the information by the driver for Oceanic Transportation."

"Despite what Mr. Sleazer may have told you, there were two tractor-trailers involved. One hit the driver's side of my car, the other the passenger side. I believe the police report will verify that."

Chabad continued asking her questions. He had some correct information about her education and doctors and Luisa didn't object. However, he then went on to state that she was involved in business fraud and that was why she had losses on her tax return.

Luisa looked Chabad directly in the eye and said, "I have no idea what you are talking about. I have never been involved with fraud. I defy you to show me a single document that even suggests I did anything wrong."

Chabad sidestepped the challenge and instead asked her about the post-traumatic stress she claimed to have suffered.

Luisa said, "For one thing, I've had repeated flashbacks of the accident. I was also afraid to drive for a long time, and even now I'm extremely nervous behind the wheel. There are other examples, if you'd like me to go through the entire litany."

Chabad shook his head no. "Tell me about your marital relations with your husband. I understand that you and he had problems with intimacy prior to the accident."

"That's simply untrue," Luisa flared. "We never had any problems before the accident. Look, I'm willing to sign a release giving you the right to obtain any information you want about my relationship with my husband."

"That won't be necessary," Chabad said.

The psychologist next told Luisa that the defense would be calling her mother to the stand to testify about her daughter's emotional and physical state prior to the accident, and her past history of law suits.

"My mother's eighty years old," Luisa objected.

"She's not too old to be called to the stand," Chabad said coldly.

Luisa was infuriated but – knowing that Chabad was baiting her and trying to get her upset – she wisely kept her temper under check. Besides, the psychologist had inadvertently given Luisa some valuable information.

Obviously, Chabad would not have threatened to call Luisa's mother to testify unless he was privy to private conversations between the two women during which they'd discussed Luisa's emotional and physical problems. And the only way he could have learned of these conversations was if Freedom Insurance snakes had tapped Luisa's phone.

"Your defense team will be wasting its time if you try to call my mother to the stand," Luisa said. "She's already told me that she'll testify on my behalf, but she'll take the Fifth Amendment before she testify for Freedom Insurance."

The muscles around Chabad's mouth twitched in annoyance, but he dropped the subject and moved on. "How do you feel about coming to see me?" he asked.

Suspecting that there might be a listening device in the room, Luisa chose her words carefully. "I do what I have to do, Dr. Chabad," she said.

"Does that include doctor shopping?" he asked, throwing her a curve ball.

"I don't 'doctor shop,'" Luisa said, keeping her voice calm despite her growing anger. "May I remind you that I am being treated by physicians who belong to the Maxfield Group – perhaps the most prestigious group of doctors in Cincinnati."

Chabad studied his notes for a moment, then said, "I'd like to talk about the actions of the truck driver, Frank T. Walker, immediately after the accident."

Luisa's face screwed up in disgust. "That bastard! He got out of his truck after the accident and I thought he was going to help me. I was trapped in my car. But he stopped fifty feet away and just stared at me. I pleaded with him to get me out, but he refused. I'll never forget the cold look on his face. He didn't care what he'd done. He didn't give a damn about the excruciating pain I was in."

Luisa's heated words seem to give Chabad pause. He was obviously uncomfortable with the subject. For the next ten minutes he questioned her about her family, their careers and where they lived. Then he delved into her medical records.

"You've been diagnosed as being bi-polar. Is that true?"

"Yes, I was diagnosed with bi-polar disorder in January 2000."

"Were you ever treated for a bi-polar condition prior to July 22, 1997?"

"No."

Chabad noted her answer on his pad and went on. "What do you intend to do with your life after the trial and assumed settlement?"

"I don't know for sure," Luisa answered truthfully. "I'm taking life one day at a time and reevaluating my goals."

"Give me an example of your goals," Chabad said.

"I hope to do volunteer work with children. There's a program called Rotating Olympics for All Ages that I'm interested in."

"That's all I have for today," Dr. Chabad said, rising from his chair to signify that their meeting was over.

Luisa gathered up her files and stood. "Oh, by the way," she said as casually as she could. "I had a conversation about you with Dr. Peter Bronz. He said to say hello."

A look of shock came over Chabad's face and he dropped the files he was holding. His formerly confident demeanor suddenly took on a nervous air.

"It's time for you to go," he stammered.

"Thank you for your time," Luisa said, delighted that she had rattled the flinty psychologist.

As she drove home she realized how exhausted she was after being grilled by Chabad for two hours. Yet she also felt a sense of gratification. She had kept her composure during the trying session, despite the psychologist's numerous attempts to unnerve her. Undoubtedly, Chabad would report back to Lee Sleazer that Luisa was not a woman they could easily bully.

That night was a living nightmare for Luisa. She tossed and turned all night. About 3: a.m. she found herself at the footboard of her queen bed hitting the foot poster with her head. She had rotated in the bed like a hand on the clock. Hitting the post at seven o'clock. She was ringing wet from the nightmare of Chabad's mind-boggling examination. The psychological harassment was so damaging to her. She fought in the nightmare with Chabad hanging upside down on a cross bar with snakes crawling up his legs and coming out of his ears and mouths. Papers were burning at his feet. The cross bar would spin like a clock hand which was being pushed by other snakes of the ones following Luisa thus far. They, too, had snakes coming from their ears and mouths. It reminded Luisa of **Raiders of the Lost Ark** with Harrison Ford.

As Luisa straightened herself back into the rumbled up bedcovers, she prayed to St. Michael the Archangel to protect so much as she fell back to sleep.

That next morning, Luisa was thoroughly drained from hardly any sound sleep. Sofia called her to see how everything the day before with Chabad. Luisa told her everything down to the very last detail.

Sofia told Luisa to stay home that day and to just rest and to read her books to settle her mind down. Luisa took her sound advice and thanked her for calling. Luisa took her morning Jacuzzi bubble bath with candles around the tub burning a fresh lavender scent to calm her.

She put on the casual gray jump suit that she bought at Target. She nestled in her cozy bed and read her two books. One of which was **The Notebook** by Nicholas Sparks. This book captured Luisa's heart as it too revealed triumph over tragedy, as Luisa so much wanted in her life. Her other book was *Illuminata* by Marianne Williamson.

She kept reading the verse on Forgiveness. She was having so much trouble forgiving Frank Walker for causing this horrific accident, his refusal to help her as she screamed for help, and his walking away from her calls just haunted her daily. The mental and physical pain that she was in kept those flashbacks fresh in her mind. Oh, how she reread that verse to hope that someday she could forgive that man.

Freedom Insurance may not be so eager to go to trial now, Luisa thought, smiling to herself. ***Perhaps today was a victory for the good guys.***

Luisa's Vision of the insurance lawyers - nothing but snakes.

Chapter 18

More Strange Events

Two weeks passed and there was no report from Dr. Chabad. Luisa wondered whether he was delaying releasing his report because he was bothered that a prominent colleague, Dr. Bronz, now knew that he supplemented his income by working for an insurance company defense team.

Unable to do anything to speed up Chabad's report, Luisa put her energies into other urgent matters. One of the first things she did was to call Car Owners Insurance to file a homeowner's claim for the items that had been stolen from her home.

An insurance company representative told her that forms would be sent to her home for her to list the stolen possessions by the first week of June 2001. Before filling out the forms, she decided to do an inventory of her house. After taking stock, she was able to put together a comprehensive list of the things that were missing.

To her horror, Luisa discovered that her home security box that had held legal documents and school records was now empty. Her valued Treasure Box that contained irreplaceable mementoes of her youth was also missing.

Moments later she found that the Venetian white Lace Christening gowns that she had bought in Venice in June 1999 for her future grandchildren were also gone. In addition, two

$250 dollar U.S. Saving bonds issued to Rosanna and Carmella had apparently been stolen, as well two Disney stock certificates.

The list kept getting longer as Luisa went through her home: CDs, family photos, keepsakes, all were gone. The thefts angered Luisa so much that she just knew she had to take a proactive stance and report her family's losses to law enforcement authorities.

She called the Clarksville FBI office and a woman answered. When Luisa asked her for her name, the woman told Luisa that she was not allowed to give her name out. Luisa accepted the woman's explanation for withholding her name and explained why she was calling. The female FBI worker told Luisa to give all evidence of the thefts to her attorney. Luisa thanked her and hung up the telephone. She thought that justice would prevail from her telephone call to FBI.

She then made arrangements for a claim adjuster and an investigator to come to her home. Patricia Reading was the claim adjuster and Frederick Knox was the investigator. As soon as she met the pair, Luisa sized them up as inept. The 20-year-old Reading tried to come across as older and more experienced, but her act didn't quite come off. She was plainly a babe in the woods.

The tall heavyset Knox was cocky and rough around the edges, and seemed to spend half his time trying to get his tape recorder to work. Luisa answered his general questions but gave him limited information, as she just did not trust him.

After thirty minutes, the two insurance company hacks left. The next day, Knox called to schedule an interview with Anton. Luisa briefed Anton on the investigator's tactics. His appointment was for the next night after work.

The following night Knox appeared on time for Anton's interview. Luisa decided to be present when Knox questioned Anton. Her husband's responses to Knox's questions were general and vague. Luisa couldn't understand why he was giving Knox such non-specific answers. One of his replies especially irked her.

"How long have you and your wife been married?" Knox asked.

"I don't know for sure, about twenty years," Anton answered.

Luisa bristled. They would mark their 25th anniversary on August 7. They had plans to celebrate the occasion with a vacation in Hawaii. How on earth could Anton forget such an important milestone in their marriage?

Luisa was totally perplexed by Anton's vague responses. He had always drilled Luisa and the girls in the importance of providing exact information – who, what, where, when and why. And now here he was dancing all around the facts.

Luisa knew that Anton played things close to the chest – rarely revealing his inner thoughts. She wondered whether he would repeat the evasive performance he had given tonight at her personal injury trial, scheduled for July 1, 2001.

Knox finished his questions and told the Cannolis that he would continue processing their theft claim.

The next morning, Marshall Kent called Luisa to tell her that Knox had contacted him and inquired about Luisa's medical history.

"What did you tell him?" Luisa asked.

"That his inquiry was totally inappropriate and that it was illegal for me, your doctor or anyone else to release information about your medical history without your written consent," Kent said. "He should have known that. The kid's still wet behind the ears."

Luisa smiled at Kent's colorful words. "Thanks for keeping me advised, Marshall," Luisa said. "I'll talk to you soon."

Luisa hung up and made a note of what Kent had told her in her records.

That evening, Tom called the Cannolis to tell them that Lee Sleazer wanted them to submit to another deposition before the July 2001 trial. The deposition was scheduled for May 28, 2001 at 9:00 AM at Tom's office. Tom advised her that it would be an all day deposition for the two of them, and that night Luisa told Anton that he would need to take that day off from work.

Luisa knew Tom Freeby had told Lee Sleazer about the illegal computer chip and the prior robberies in May 2001. She was now facing that dreaded deposition with Lee Sleazer that next week.

On May 28, 2001, Anton and Luisa arrived at Tom's office at 8:30 AM to prepare for the deposition with Tom and Rocko. Luisa's stomach was upset and her body pain was a level seven that morning. Tom told Luisa to relax and all would be fine.

Lee Sleazer arrived about 8:50 A.M. Anton, Luisa, Tom, Rocko and the court reporter, Alice Hinkle, were ready for the deposition by the time Sleazer arrived.

The deposition started with Sleazer inquiring about Luisa's two business lawsuits. Sleazer asked her to explain the cases. She simply said they were for invoice resolutions. The individuals she had sued resolved the situations most amicably.

Then Sleazer brought up business fraud deals that she was allegedly involved with. Luisa asked him to explain what he was talking about, as she had no knowledge of any fraud suits against her.

Sleazer was apparently caught off guard by her response and replied, "Well, I don't know where my office got that information. Let's move on."

Sleazer then delved into Luisa's relationships with Anton and her girls. He was most blunt in his questions about marital sex.

"Does your husband sleep in the same bedroom with you?" he asked Luisa. "I understand that there has been a lack of marital relations between you two for some time."

Luisa responded that due to her many surgeries Anton did sleep in the other bedroom to get his rest as Luisa recuperated. Her response put an end to Sleazer's suggestive and misleading questions.

As to her daughters, she explained that due to the extensive rehabilitation program that her doctors prescribed, she was not able to attend all the activities of the girls for the past four years.

Sleazer then turned his attention to Luisa's interior design business. He questioned her about the losses on her tax returns. She explained that since the accident she had had to hire others to do much of the work she normally did.

Sleazer then asked her how much she expected to lose in wages. Tom interrupted Sleazer and told him that at trial he would prove losses somewhere around $167,000, all backed up by documents from Luisa's accountant.

Sleazer continued with his questioning of Luisa. "Who is Marshall Kent and what does he do for you?"

"Marshall Kent is a private detective I hired to help me investigate the thefts at our home," Luisa said.

"What was stolen from your home?" Sleazer asked.

"Many things," Luisa said. "If you wish, I can give you a complete list."

"I'd appreciate that," Sleazer said, then moved on to question Luisa about her current medical condition.

Luisa told the insurance company lawyer about her physical therapy and her medically prescribed aquatic exercise at Tri- Health Pavilion.

Sleazer then asked about her schedule of therapy and medical appointments. Luisa thought his questions were just like Chahad's a few weeks ago. She told Sleazer her schedule, including her various medical appointments.

This question concluded Luisa's deposition and Sleazer turned his attention to Anton. He told Anton that he only had a few questions for him.

The first question to Anton was to explain the frequency of their marital relationship, as spousal consortium was one of their claims. Anton told him that they had had relations a few weeks ago. This was so embarrassing to Luisa that she wrote a short note for Tom to stop Sleazer from his slimy questions. What would be next in this line of inquiry?

Tom told Sleazer that Anton had answered his question and to move on to another topic. In response, Sleazer began questioning Anton about their daughters, asking him to explain how Luisa's accident had affected them.

"A hell of a lot," Anton answered emphatically, ending his part of the deposition.

As Sleazer rose to leave, he extended his hand to shake to Luisa. She ignored the gesture and walked downstairs to the bathroom. Her stomach was churning again.

Upon her return to Tom's office, Tom and Rocko told Luisa and Anton that they did quite well in handling Sleazer's line of questioning. They then escorted the Cannolis to the front door, telling them that they would get back to them to schedule more trial preparations. Before Luisa and Anton left, Tom asked Luisa to update their witness list sometime in the next ten days as he would need it.

As the Cannolis walked to their car, Anton told Luisa that he had asked Tom when she was in the bathroom about their dating relationship many years ago. This was a surprise, as Anton had never expressed curiosity about Luisa's relationship with Tom before.

"What did he say?" Luisa asked.

"Nothing, really, except that he had enjoyed dating you."

Luisa was touched that Anton was interested but shocked that he had actually asked such a question of Tom.

"He also told me that that he was working really hard on getting the full settlement amount of $775,000," Anton said.

It was dinnertime when they arrived home. Anton put steaks on the grill while Luisa and Carmella prepared vegetables and set the table.

After dinner, Luisa went to bed to read her book Simple Abundance, as Anton cut the grass and Carmella hit tennis balls against the house.

Tom called Luisa that evening and explained that Lee Sleazer wanted to go to mediation on Friday, July 13th at 10:OO A.M. He told Luisa that Judge Perrino had reprimanded Sleazer for requesting another delay in their jury trial.

Tom added that Sleazer had told the Judge in a conference call that he needed more time to get ready for trial. Judge Perrino had told Sleazer in return that he had had four years to get ready for trial and to stop trying to delay the proceedings. The judge then extended the trial date until August 13, 2001 if the matter could not be settled in mediation.

Before Tom hung up, he assured Luisa that he had worked very long hours preparing her case and he was ready to go to war with Sleazer and fight for the fair settlement of $775,000.

Luisa thanked him and said goodbye.

During this troubling time, Anton did his best to help Luisa by researching the interaction of drugs on the Internet. The information he gleaned stressed how Yoga and natural healing could effectively substitute for drugs in the relief of chronic pain.

Concerned for his wife's addiction to prescribed drugs, he replaced the narcotics in her prescription bottles with vitamins. When Luisa discovered that the drugs she was taking were actually vitamins, she insisted vehemently to Anton that she needed her narcotics to relieve her severe pain.

The strong disagreements between the two over Luisa's addiction to strong narcotics were heated at times. Good and patient man that Anton was, he understood that Luisa was so crazed with drugs that she was not thinking clearly.

Luisa's addiction and aberrant behavior reached the point that her family and friends insisted that something had to be done before Luisa destroyed herself.

During the first week of June 2001, Luisa found herself becoming more involved in the planning of the Children's Dream World Organization Rainbow Rotating Olympics

Function.

A month earlier, she had become a volunteer for the organization. Their office was in the same building where Luisa was receiving her medical rehabilitation treatments three times a week. As she had been advised to do, she had deep massages and underwent physical therapy under the care of experienced therapists.

Luisa met with the organization's director, Edward Brownfield, who had placed flyers in the medical office, hoping to find volunteers to help the ill children with their needs. The flyer explained that there was a need for people to visit the sick children and to share their creative and caring talents with them.

Luisa noted that a meeting was scheduled for the following evening and decided to attend. At the meeting, the director showed a video of the children. Hearing the tearful stories of their illnesses and the limited chances of survival, which many of them faced, touched Luisa deeply. She volunteered that evening and received the name of a five-year-old to visit. The child's name was Coletta Bird.

The next morning, Luisa contacted the Bird family. Since she had no medical appointments that day and the family lived near the Cannoli home, Luisa made plans to visit that very afternoon.

The director had suggested that the volunteers might wish to bring a small gift on their first visit. On the way to the Bird home, Luisa stopped and purchased a stuffed teddy bear for Colletta.

Luisa arrived at the Bird's home. It was a small cottage with a few small two-wheeler bicycles in the yard. She rang the doorbell and silently whispered a prayer for this family, thinking about the enormous medical bills she had been told they were facing since Colletta's terminal bone cancer had been discovered two years before.

The young Dad answered the door. As he opened it, Luisa saw Mrs. Bird cuddling her young daughter. Colletta had blurred watery eyes and very pale skin, and the child had lost all of her hair. Luisa kept her concern for the family to herself as she introduced herself.

Colletta smiled as Luisa handed her the small teddy bear. Luisa returned the little girl's smile and asked if she'd like to give the teddy bear a name.

In her soft, young voice, Colletta whispered, "Lucky."

This brought tears to Luisa eyes, as she thought of her own girls and remembered when Rosanna and Carmella had been that young. She thought of their childhood illnesses and how she and Anton had been so afraid for their lives when they had been in isolation at Children's Heart and Body Hospital, and her heart ached for this family.

Colletta and her parents walked Luisa to the bedroom Colletta shared with her seven-year-old sister, Lucy. There, they showed Luisa the many colorful paintings that Colletta had created.

The visit was short and sweet. Before departing, Luisa invited Colletta to go with her and Carmella to a young children's beauty and self-esteem class at the medical rehabilitation center where Luisa was having treatments.

Her parents approved of the outing, and they arranged it for the following week.

Luisa had been thinking for many years to return to teaching. Now as she was nearing her fiftieth birthday and her daughters were getting older, her thoughts prompted her to plan the Rainbow Rotating Olympics Outing. She chose the date of July 22, 2001 for the function, wanting to plan something good for every future July 22 of her life, hoping it might help her put the horrific past behind her.

The planning associated with the project was becoming overwhelming to her. Luisa intended to invite 50 family members and friends to her home for a fun day of outside activities. She designed the invitations and t-shirts, and planned the refreshments for the 50 families expected to attend the function at her home. She also placed orders for needed supplies and contacted a music company to play the CDs for the event. It was especially difficult for her to coordinate and find all the volunteers she had enlisted, most of whom she did not know well.

The Children's Dream World Organization listened to Luisa's ideas for the function. They approved of the plan to play games such as wiffle ball, badminton and some table board games like Clue, Sorry, Risk, chess and checkers.

Among the 50 families, there would be eight teams, each of which would have six players who would participate in the games by rotating to each game site. Points would be tallied for each team and the highest scoring team would receive an Olympic-type medal.

To add color and atmosphere to the outing, Luisa decided to select character costumes for the volunteers to wear as they assisted the families from game to game. She chose five costumes – Beauty and the Beast, Mr. Blue, Elmo and Dorothy. Although Luisa did not know the five volunteers personally, they helped at the Children's Dream World Organization once a month.

Planning the outing was a way for Luisa to try to focus on something else, rather than the daily horror in her life.

Unfortunately, the horror did continue. The clicking sounds returned to her telephone lines, there were additional thefts from her car, and the garage door opener was missing for a week. The security system for her 1993 Nissan Quest still was not working, nor could it be fixed due to the high cost. In addition, charge card bills and other mail disappeared from her desks after she had placed them there, just as they had during the period of January – May 2000.

The many drugs she was taking affected Luisa's mind. Her doctors, as well as her family, insisted she was paranoid, and their disbelief caused her tremendous stress. Luisa wanted so much to prove to them that they were wrong.

The items were just gone! As if that was not enough,

additional acknowledgments came from her design venders, but merchandise ordered was coming to her home rather than the designated warehouse.

Who was doing this to her again? Were the snakes from Freedom Insurance trying to really drive her crazy and have the doctors overmedicate her to kill her? Her mind desperately tried to filter through all the strange violations occurring once again in her life.

During one afternoon in early June, Luisa went to Tri-Health Pavilion for her normal treatment session. She changed into a swim suit, put pink hand paddles on her hands and blue flippers on her feet – her injuries had left her unable to swim without the aids – and entered the aquatic therapy pool.

Careful to stay in her own lane, Luisa began her exercise routine. After covering about two-thirds the length of the pool, she noticed a dark-haired lady in her fifties hop into the lane ahead of her. There was no one else in the pool, and Luisa thought it was rude of the woman to enter her lane when there was so much room in the pool.

The woman made no effort to get out of Luisa's way as she paddled near. Luisa noticed that the woman was wearing a yellow Sony headset on her head and was using hand-paddles, although they were not the pink color that the Pavilion normally issued.

Although Luisa tried to avoid the woman by switching lanes, the stranger swam up to her and began a conversation.

"I just bought these paddles at the store here and I don't know how to use them yet," she said.

"They take some getting used to," Luisa said, attempting to move away.

"Why are you here?" the woman asked.

The personal question – coming out of the blue from a stranger – made Luisa instantly suspicious. Could this woman be yet another insurance company snake? She had told Dr. Chabad her treatment schedule, including her times for going to Tri-Health.

Perhaps Chabad had tipped off Freedom Insurance.

Luisa kept her answer vague. "I'm here under doctors' orders to do aquatic therapy. Why are you here?"

The woman ignored Luisa's question and hurriedly changed the subject. "How do you use these paddles? I can't figure them out."

"I was taught how to use them by an instructor," Luisa said. "It might do you some good if you had a professional teach you as well."

"So what sort of injuries are you recovering from," the woman asked.

Why is she asking me about injuries? Luisa thought. I never told her that I'd been injured.

Tired of playing games with the woman, Luisa decided to tell the woman about her car accident in July 1997 and her lawsuit against Freedom Insurance. If the woman were a snake for the insurance company, she already knew all the details. If she was simply being curious, Luisa had nothing to lose.

"I was badly injured in a car accident in the summer of 1997," Luisa said. "A truck smashed into me. The driver was drunk. I've been receiving medical treatment ever since."

"Did you sue the trucking company?" the woman asked.

"Yes. My suit is rescheduled for trial in August."

"Are your injuries permanent?"

Luisa nodded. "My doctors tell me that I'll have to endure physical pain as a result of my injuries for the rest of my life."

Luisa then turned the conversation to the defendants in the case. She told the woman that she did not think the defendants had a case; that all they did was lie and keep changing the trial date. Luisa added that she had had to go through two hours of harassment at the hands of the insurance company's psychiatrist.

As Luisa talked, a trapped look came over the woman's face. Suddenly she started to back away from Luisa.

"Where are you going?" Luisa asked.

The woman muttered something unintelligible and frantically

tried to get out of the pool by climbing backwards up the ladder as fast as she could. When she reached the concrete fringe around the pool, the woman snatched off her swim fins and hurriedly disappeared toward the women's dressing room.

Watching her go, Luisa thought, she must be a snake. Why else would she want to get away from me in such a hurry? What lengths would Sleazer go to in this Conspiracy that keeps getting worse and erupting every time a trial was scheduled? Luisa recalled the last Judge at her first Mediation in November 1999 who told her that the high profile trials often get cancelled so many times!!!

Even though Luisa's relaxation in the pool had been ruined, she decided to finish her routine, get an orange juice to drink and a yogurt to eat and go home. It was 10:00 p.m. when she left the Tri-Health.

Luisa arrived home mentally exhausted. Once again Freedom Insurance had violated her personal life. She went to bed only to find that her sleep pattern was completely out of kilter. She had numerous flashbacks of all the violations she had sustained. Through the sleepless night she prayed to the Lord to free her of these nightmares and pain. It was getting to be too much for her.

The next day Luisa had Carmella drive her around as she visited the companies involved with the Children's Dream World Fund fundraiser. That afternoon, she received a phone call from Linda Harrison, a prior customer from 13 years ago.

Linda was buying a 1960's home that needed a 20th century update; carpet, interior lights, a sunroom, new furniture, sound system, new paint, new window treatments, new bath fixtures, tile and cabinets - this would be a major job. Luisa explained that she just had jaw surgery, and could not drive around to gather product samples for Linda to chooe from, as she normally would. Linda sais she understood, and the next morning, her huband, Gus and Linda picked Luisa up to pick up the samples together. The Harrisions would be moving in four weeks and wanted the redecorating to be finished in time for the move. Luisa also wanted to have job completed before her trial date.

The Harrisons also needed to arrange the financing for the job. The project cost would be approximately $65,000, so a deposit of $15,000 was needed to begin work. In order to raise the funds, the Harrisons decided to a bridge loan from the bank. At this point, Luisa suspected that they may be overspending, and this was not a good sign. But she went to meet them at the bank the next day to pick up the deposit, and found they had only raised a total of $10,000. Luisa reluctantly agreed to begin work, while they would raise the additional funds later in the week.

As the week progressed, Luisa found herself snowed under with work for the Children's Dream World Fund. She was also inundated with calls from Linda Harrison asking where her carpet was.

She made the decision to pull her workers from the Harrison job after that Saturday. She simply could not continue the project until she'd been at least received the full deposit of $15,000.

Luisa called the Harrisons and told them that she was at the Embassy Suites, and that she would talk to them after mediation.

Three days later, Luisa received a call from Tom's law partner informing her that Tom had had a minor heart attack and was in St. Margaret's Cardiac Unit. Luisa was shocked.

"He was working all hours – often to 3:00 AM – on your case," Tom's partner told her. "I guess the exhaustion finally caught up with him."

"How long will he be in the hospital?" Luisa asked.

"Three to five days. Why don't you give him a call. I'm sure he'd like to hear from you."

Luisa said goodbye and promptly called the hospital. Tom's nurse came on the line and she identified herself as a friend of Tom's.

"How is he?" she asked.

"His vital signs are stabilizing and his prognosis is good," the nurse said.

"Please tell him that Luisa Cannoli called to wish him well," Luisa said.

The nurse promised that she would pass on the message and Luisa hung up, and then called the florist and ordered flowers for Tom.

About four days later, Luisa received a call from Tom. He was back at his office and feeling well rested. He thanked Luisa for the flowers she had sent and told her that the bouquet had cheered him up during his hospital stay. Luisa was glad to hear he was well enough to continue her case. Before she hung up she told Tom that she was getting ready for jaw surgery the following morning.

A Maxilfacial surgeon, Dr. Alexander Winston, was chosen to perform her second jaw surgery by her TMJ specialist doctor who had been treating her since March 2000. She had had prior jaw surgery in mid December 2000 on her right jaw and in the beginning of January 2001 she had the left jaw operated on to remove built up scar tissue.

This time surgery was scheduled on both jaws. Her permanent jaw injuries were due to her accident on July 22, 1997. During the surgery, Luisa experienced so much pain that she was put on Percocet.

Months before Dr. Ba had prescribed Lipitor, Relafen, Neurontin, Dulcolax, Lotres, Ativan, Hydrocholorothiazide, Restoril, Zyprexa, Prevacid, Hydrocodone, and Rhinocert. Now – on top of all her other prescriptions – Luisa was also taking Percocet, a powerful drug by itself.

Leery of taking so many potent medications together, Luisa had asked Dr. Ba what the side effects of the drugs would be. The physician skirted the question and simply told Luisa to comply with her recommendations.

The cocktail of strong drugs that Luisa was taking upset her family, friends and lawyers. They all insisted that Luisa was once again being over-medicated. Luisa's stress level rose as she found herself in constant arguments with both her family and her legal team.

Yet she was at a loss as to what to do. Since her January 2000 hospital stay she had been off most of the medicines. Now her internist, jaw surgeon and psychiatrist were ordering her to take 19 different medicines (Darvon, Methocarbamol, Relafen, Tylenol #4, Zantax, Oxycondin, Sulfameth, Buspar, Ranitidine, Trazodone, Promethazine, Roxicet, Hydrocodone, Cipro, Guaifenesen, Paxil, Prevacid, Lorazepam, Lipitor). Who was she to listen to - her physicians or her family?

The next afternoon, Tom called Luisa and asked for her witness list. She told him that she had most of the names but needed to track down Renee Jones and Lori Chantell, the two main witnesses at her July 1997 accident. Tom told her that he would like her to fax to him the names of the witnesses that she had and Luisa did so as soon as she hung up.

Then she contacted Marshall Kent to help her locate the two main witnesses. Within hours, he called back and told Luisa that they had moved and both now had unlisted telephone numbers. Nevertheless, he had obtained their numbers and had spoken to both of them.

He told Luisa that Lee Sleazer had contacted them months ago. They both told Marshall that the attorney had spoken to them in a harassing and insulting way, adding that Sleazer had inferred that Luisa was crazy.

"Because of the way Sleazer acted on the phone, both the witnesses are now worried that he will go after them if they testify at your trial," Marshall said. "I suggest that you contact them in person and tell them how much you need their testimony."

Luisa agreed and called Lori Chantell first. Lori didn't answer the phone and there was no answering machine. Renee Jones answered on the second ring. She repeated what Sleazer had told her and recommended that Luisa do an interview on 20-20, 60

Minutes or Dateline to get her story out to the public. Luisa thanked Renee for her recommendation and promised that she would consider the idea.

Luisa then told Renee of the thefts at her home, the illegal telephone tap and her harassment by Sleazer's snakes. Upon hearing of all that additional horrific violations of Luisa's life, Renee told Luisa that she should contact the FBI.

Luisa then told Renee that Tom Freeby was now her attorney and that he would be contacting her in a month or so to testify at her trial. Renee asked for Tom's telephone number to contact him. Luisa gave it to her and they closed their conversation on a friendly note.

Within 10 minutes, Tom called Luisa. "What in the hell are you doing talking to the witnesses?" he said in a loud agitated voice. "Renee Jones called a few minutes ago and told me that she'd just spoken to you. She said that she thinks you're crazy after hearing what Lee Sleazer had to say about you. Now she will not even testify. And what is this about the FBI? Did you contact them? If you did, I am withdrawing from your case immediately!"

Luisa was shocked that Tom would speak to her in such a demeaning manner. She gained her composure as best as she could.

"I called Renee because you asked me to locate her," Luisa said. "Marshall Kent got me her number and I simply followed your instructions. As to the FBI, Renee suggested that I contact them, but I haven't done so yet."

Tom settled down and calmly said, "Alright Luisa, I believe you. I have a lot of work to do. You get a goodnight's rest. I'll call you as I need to for the rest of trial preparations. I am sorry if my words just now were harsh. Goodbye."

"I'll talk to you soon," Luisa said. "Goodbye, Tom."

After Luisa hung up she poured herself a glass of Merlot and went to bed. She did not tell Anton about her conversations with

Marshall, Renee, and Tom.

The next morning Luisa called Cathy at the Mid West Telephone security office to report a return of the clicking sounds on her telephone. Cathy told Luisa that a security technician would be at her home by mid-morning.

Within one hour, the technician arrived. He told Luisa that he suspected the felons were monitoring her calls to the   telephone company and moving their tapping equipment before the security team could get there.

Luisa told him of the additional robberies at her home and the technician recommended that she contact her garage door company again and change the codes to her garage door keypad. He also told her that if she heard clicking noises on her phone again she should call the company from a pay phone.

When Luisa used the phone later that day she noticed that the clicking sounds had stopped.

The next day Tom Freeby called to tell Luisa that Dr. Winston had given him written verification of Luisa's medical claims and was ready to testify at the July 2001 jury trial that was coming up.

Tom went on to say that the trial was expected to last four weeks and would include all necessary testimony from doctors, therapists, family, friends and the two main witnesses to the accident.

Tom assured Luisa that he was thoroughly prepared for the trial and would do his best to win her a fair settlement. Luisa knew in her mind and heart that Tom was indeed doing his utmost to see that she was rightly compensated for her suffering as a result of the accident.

Listening to Tom, she thought of her grandmother's words of Italian wisdom: ***L'unico merito d'un e il buon senso, ma il maggior valore di donna 3 nella sua bellezza*** – The only merit of a man is his good sense, but the greatest merit of a woman is her beauty.

After hanging up with Tom, Luisa decided to put $50.00 in

pennies in a wishing well in their backyard for the children to collect during the upcoming Rainbow Olympics event at her home. She went down to the local Lock Bank to get the pennies. Since she was under doctor's orders not to lift anything heavy, she asked the manager to help carry the pennies out to her car. To Luisa's shock, the woman refused.

When Luisa told the manager that she wished to speak to the bank vice president she reported to, the manager reluctantly put the call through. The vice president told Luisa that Sue, as a bank manager, did not have to help load pennies. Luisa told the vice president to keep the pennies and stormed out of the bank. The manager followed and locked the door behind her. Luisa drove home resolved never to use Lock Bank again.

Later that day Luisa had some medical appointments scheduled. It was also the day that Carmella and Colletta were to go to a beauty and self esteem class with her. Fortunately, the two-day class fell on the same days as Luisa's treatments at the medical rehabilitation center. Colletta had had chemo treatment the day before but was feeling well enough to go. Luisa and the girls had a pleasant outing together.

The next day Luisa began experiencing severe pain from her jaw surgery and called Dr. Winston to ask for a strong narcotic to give her some relief, as she wanted to be able to take Carmella and Colletta back to the beauty class that was scheduled the following day.

Dr. Winston prescribed Percocet and warned Luisa that she should not drive while taking such a strong narcotic. Since Luisa needed a way to get around to her various medical treatments and other commitments, she called her friend Adrian at United Cab and gave Adrian the dates and times of her medical appointments. Adrian scheduled cabs for Luisa for the next ten days.

To add to Luisa's stress at this time, the Harrison project was nearly finished when she learned that the couple had overextended themselves. Their home had not sold as they planned and they could not pay her as promised. Luisa used her limited funds to cover the Harrisons' shortfall.

Several days later Anton emailed Rocko to get his opinion on whether they should attempt another mediation session. Rocko responded with an email to Anton:

A trial is best described as a judicial examination of the issues of fact of law disputed by parties for determining the rights of the parties. It is a costly and expensive way to settle an argument. Mediation can be described as an attempt to bring about a peaceful settlement or compromise between disputants through the objective intervention of a neutral party.

While in law school, I was an undercover agent for an insurance company and later a claims adjuster. Since admission to the practice of law I have tried and settled cases on behalf of insurance companies, individuals and other entities. Only after many, many trials did I come to understand the saying 'nobody wins at trial.'

Experience, a good teacher, repeatedly has demonstrated to me that litigants who can effect settlement without the rigors of trial are best served because they do not carry the frequently bad memories of trial. Many of my trial lawyer friends have expressed the belief that when both sides feel they gave away too much in exchange for too little, they have achieved a fair and adequate settlement.

Finally, in answer to your question, I believe intelligent people who enter mediation in good faith have a better chance to settle and walk away in good spirits and without the trauma of trial. In all the cases I have tried, I have not found the experience of trial to be a catharsis even when my client hits a home run.

Rocko

After reading Rocko's email, Anton and Luisa agreed to try mediation once more, and the mediation meeting was scheduled for Friday, July 13th at 10:00 AM.

Chapter 19

The Steps to Settlement

Shortly before dinner, Tom called and told Luisa and Anton that Freedom Insurance was going to offer $300,000 at mediation to settle the four year old case. He told them they would stay at $775,000 firm, as that is what the case was worth per his team of advisors from the University. They set the mediation day for Friday, July 13th, 2001. Luisa thought the attorneys heard her tell her friends that she read her horoscope at the end of the day, as she tries not to project her day from reading the paper in the morning.

On Thursday, July 12th, Luisa called Dr. Ba office to set an appointment for that Saturday.

Luisa had to prepare for the mediation during the week before the July 13th date. She decided to check into the Embassy Suites for Wednesday and Thursday to mentally prepare in solitude for the coming mediation.

Luisa checked into the hotel and began preparing for mediation. Part of her preparation was to call friends she knew in the legal field to seek their advice and the settlement terms she should agree to. Everyone she called told her to stick with her demand for $775,000, insisting that the serious injuries she had suffered in the car accident warranted that amount.

After regaining her emotional strength and focus in the

peaceful atmosphere of the Embassy Suites, Luisa returned home and got ready to go to mediation on Friday, July 13th. Shortly before dinner that Thursday night, Tom called and again told Luisa and Anton that Freedom Insurance was going to offer $300,000 at mediation to settle the four-year-old case. He said that he would continue to insist on the $775,000 figure.

Anton, on the morning of July 13th, was out of sorts. Luisa chose not to speak to him that morning. There was no radio or conversation for the 50-minute ride to Tom Freeby's office. They arrived at 8:45 am for the 9:00 am meeting. To their dismay, Tom was not there. His secretary, Janet, told the Cannoli's that Tom was at the Mediator Sonny Benson's office already. The look of total shock and upset ran across Anton's face. Luisa stood there silent as Anton quipped, "Some boyfriend you had - he could not even call to tell us where to meet him."

Janet eased this situation and wrote down the directions for the Cannolis' and called Tom to advice him of their comments, and that they were on their way.

On top of that, Anton fumbled in his pocket, and could not locate his car keys. He found them lying on the concrete by his driver's door.

Anton said, "Luisa, just get into the car and say nothing to me nor turn on the radio as you usually do.

Let's find this place and get this over with."

Shortly after driving a few blocks, they found Benson's office. As they entered the old historic late 1800's building, the secretary in the mediation room greeted them.

Freedom Insurance had sent from their distant office from out of North County two young and cocky rookies. They handed their business cards to the Cannolis. Their names were Timothy Bremmer and Dan Field. Immediately, they stated in unison that the offer was $75,000 not $300,000 as Tom had told her. Luisa's thoughts were intense; her hatred of these snaky liars was growing by the minute.

During the hearing, the mediator was shown photos of the accident scene. After viewing the photos, he told Luisa that Freedom Insurance had insisted that there was only one truck involved. Luisa could not believe what she was hearing. She drew snakes in her notebook. Her mind was spinning with all the horrific flashbacks.

Tom pulled from his folder the actual photo of the totaled car, which showed extensive damage to the entire front of the car and the two sides.

Adamantly and speaking loudly, Tom said, "Sonny, here are the photos and clearly you can see that both sides are damaged. Luisa screamed for her life as her car was smashed by the second tractor trailer as the car went under it."

Sonny took the photos and just shook his head in disbelief as he now heard the truth of what occurred on 7-22-97.

Luisa knew this was another of the mental games Freedom enjoyed playing. She lost interest in the mediation, which she now considered useless.

She sat there with a sudden state of anxiety rising within her. Tom noticed a change in Luisa as well as her husband, Rocko and Sonny.

Sonny left the room. Rocko Marciene expressed his strategy to raise the demand higher than the $775,000. As an experienced plaintiff and defense trial lawyer, Luisa listened to him as she believed he was on the right track.

Rocko, a Larry King type of a guy, spoke quite harsh and direct of adding Anton's workplace, parental consortium along with spousal consortium. In addition to these, the Cannolis' personal health insurance, home and auto would be added to the defense. He further recommended adding Rosanna and Carmella to the case.

Hitting a home run, the Cannolis' could see his legal strategy to making this a higher profile case than it already was. They asked Rocko about the duration of a legal case by adding all these entities to it.

Simply but bluntly put, Rocko said "Years!! But these huge insurance companies and lawyers eventually settle cases like these."

Anton told Tom that Luisa had spoken to other friends of hers who were in the legal field. Tom told him that he felt "bruised" that the Cannolis had consulted other attorneys. Luisa placed her left hand on his right arm and told him that he would get over that bruising some day. Tom told her thanks for the vote of confidence.

Luisa was badly stung by the fruitless negotiations. What was she to do now? Yet – mentally – she was getting stronger as she steeled herself to go to a jury trial on March 13, 2002. During the waiting period, Lee Sleazer – obviously nervous about a jury verdict that might award Luisa an astronomical amount – offered a $100,000 settlement. When the Cannolis rejected the offer, Sleazer upped the ante to $150,000. Again, Luisa and Anton refused to settle.

In response, Tom pulled out an amended complaint that he was prepared to file in the court. The complaint detailed Luisa's medical expenses as a result of the accident, a list of permanent injuries, her lost wages, and their desired compensation for lost spousal and parental consortium.

The money damages totaled $91,000 reducing it from the established $350,000 bills that included all prescribed medical treatments and medicines along with professional drivers as the prescribed drugs prevented Luisa from driving, specialists for home care nursing and medical treatments not covered by the Cannoli's personal insurance carrier. Her own doctors referred her to these specialists with her type of injuries. The documented lost wages and paid out salaries to Anne, Suzanne and William of $167,000 was set aside for the trial but had been calculated into the total along with the onset of this major motor vehicle accident the high cost of gasoline and car maintenance with so many medical visits prescribed.

Luisa had professional letters from the Toyota Used Car Manager who knew her particular 1989 Toyota Cressida and the Dealership Service Manager. Both letters stated that the value of the car to be $9200 and it was in excellent condition. Tom told that he would address the car property damage at trial. In addition to those letters, Anton had provided to Tom the reports from the Kelly Blue Book and the Nada book plus newspaper car ads. All of which verified the value between $8900- 10,000.

Luisa was distraught that the total amount of compensation that Tom asked for was a mere $91,000. When she leaned over to Tom and whispered to Tom that she was most unhappy with the amount he was willing to settle for, he reluctantly showed her Lee Sleazer's medical summary of her injuries.

The report stated that her displaced ovary was due to her C-sections in 1981 and 1986. It went on to say that her chest, neck, jaw, head and back injuries were not caused by this accident. The Doctors of Maynard Ernonet and Martin Jung would testify to that statement.

Luisa shot at Tom, "These money hungry doctors did not even see me on the day of the accident nor treat me at all." Tom responded, " They do this for money, Luisa."

In addition, Dr. Chabad had testified in the report that Luisa was not suffering from Post Traumatic Stress Disorder.

Tom showed Luisa the damaging report from Dr.Ba that Luisa did not suffer from Post Traumatic Stress Disorder and that she could not see any correlation with what occurred on 7-22-97. Luisa sharply told him that Dr. Ba had told her while at her office that she despises lawyers and all the twisting of the truth. Luisa went on to tell him that Dr.Ba did not want to participate in this personal injury case.

In addition to that blow, her displaced right ovary treatments and surgery from the seatbelt syndrome was also thrown out, as the surgeon now would not testify.

The growing conflict between good and bad doctors has been going on for years. The legal system has lost its importance in getting justice served, Luisa told Tom and Rocko. They agreed that the system has decayed so much so that they face that in cases like this. Money dictates the process. Good doctors do not want to get involved and the money hungry ones lie for the defense, Rocko explained to the Cannolis.

Luisa read the legal paper that Sleazer wrote for the Judge Perrino, which stated that Luisa caused the accident on 7-22-97. But the Judge gave to Luisa the liability judgment in May 2000.

Her thoughts were probably, Sleazer and his team of investigators along with the police, namely Detective Crosswell, that Luisa contacted were probably getting paid money from the million dollar policy that Oceanic Land Transportation had with Freedom Insurance.

Over the past years, many of Luisa's friends voiced these same opinions and referred it to the Mafia way of thinking of protecting your own before others are paid and what goes on to make money does not go into the home.

Just like the movie, Return to Perdition, with Tom Hanks. This compelling story really crossed Luisa's mind many a time with all she and her family have been though. This day was another day; it came forward in her innocent and somewhat still naïve mind.

This infuriated Luisa so much that she decided to speak her Italian mind to these men with the stories told to her by her new friends who heard her horrific story and her massive injuries.

Luisa said, "Tom, who do you think you are?? You are taking the side of the defense!!!! We hired you to represent our damaged family!!! How dare you become a Pontius Pilate in this case!!!"

As to Rocko, Luisa said, " Rocko, you are trying to line your pocket with more money and delay the resolution of this trial for many years to come!!!"

To both of them she expressed, vehemently, "you are traitors like John Wilkes Booth who killed Abe Lincoln and Judas who betrayed the Lord. In today's world, you are like Robert Hasson's lining your pockets at our expense and adding severe insult to injury. You deleted the most related injuries in the case. It took the doctors 11 months of extensive treatments before finding and confirming the cause of anemia and the severity of pain in my right groin area since the accident."

She went on to tell all the men in that room the stories to get her point across and let them feel the pain she was and had been in.

Shooting cannons at these greedy and selfless men, Luisa told them that "Men can talk about and fondle women's breasts all they want, but now let me tell you about your precious testicles to knock you in your place.

Luisa began, " Edna May Sue from the hills of West Virginia, my true friend of many years at the Ketch the Chicken Shop in Leland Community Center, told me about her precious 16 year old niece, Annalisa Beth. In her thick West Virginia twang, poor little Annalisa Beth who was born with mental deficiencies, was raped by a drunken S.O.B. in the hills of our homeland and left crying frantically for hours before her cries were heard by her kinfolk. For weeks, Annalisa Beth wondered endlessly, thoughtless and holding her tattered teddy bear as she had the mentally of an eight year old.

Suddenly, a fast moving weaving red battered pickup truck struck her and killed her instantly with her teddy bear flying into the air only to land beside her broken body on the gravel road as the driver continued on in his haste to escape. Her death struck the entire caring community hard to find that driver. As it turned out that S.O.B drunk that had raped her was the same man who killed her mercifully and most brutally.

The community of hardworking miners found that bastard in the hills stone drunk. They dragged him into an abandoned cottage in the thicket of trees in an isolated area and tied his hands and legs to the old wooden chair. Taking his pants off the old drunkard and his penis falling on the floor, they nailed that floppy penis to the floor. Filling up ice cold buckets of water, they poured those buckets on his nefarious looking face as they knew of the mental anguish this bastard put Annalisa Beth through and now her brutally battered beautiful body was destroyed and her Spirit was in the Heavens of God.

The drunk woke up and yelled so loud through those late evening howling dogs, "Come help me." Those men for yelled back to him, "Justice is now served on you in the name of Annalisa Beth."

Luisa summed up that story all those in the Ketch in the Chicken Shop told Luisa that Sleazer should be nailed to the floor in the same fashion for the living hell that he has put her precious daughters through plus the harm to her and her loving husband.If that story was not enough, Luisa told them about Ted.

Luisa said," Let me tell you about my friend, Ted. The story was that Ted and his friend, Willard were chasing pigs in the grassy green farmland in Central Kentucky a few years ago. Willard's pig went through a hole in the barbed wired fence and split rail. Without thinking, Willard tried hopping over the 3' foot fence but his jeans and short legs could not make it. He got caught in the barbed wired fence, which cut right through his blue jeans and into his right testicle tearing it right off as Willard flipped over the fence screaming his head off throughout the hill of Kentucky and echoing into the mountains of Tennessee. "Where in the living hell is my testicle and Oh, Teddy; I am in such howling pain. Oh, shit, IT HURTS!!!!! Ted, help me quickly!!!!"

Blood was shooting everywhere on Willard and into the summer air as he lied on his back moaning and screaming, Ted tore off his undershirt off his back and tied a tourniquet to stop the bleeding.

Ted was an Eagle Scout and knew his first aid and knots. He wrapped his best friend's right bleeding testicle most carefully in his shirt.

Assisting Willard to his care, he drove to the nearest hospital, which was 20 minutes away. To help ease Willard's screams, he started singing '99 Bottles of Beer on the Wall' as Willard joined into singing with Ted.

Once there, the admitting nurse told them that in that small medical facility that the staff was not adequate for this type of surgery. She introduced the two of them shaking with fear and still the mumbling Willard in severe pain and crying his heart out to the beautiful young 30ish doctor, Doctor Angela Felds. She had flowing long blond hair just like a model from Glamour.

Ted and Willard, seeing her, now blushed like a tomato as the thought of her assisting sew the right torn testicle on.

Dr. Felds led them to the scrub room and they readied themselves for the procedure. Willard was put on the operating table and the bright lights glared onto him lying there with his private parts exposed. She applied the numbing needle as Willard continued to scream, 'Oh, Shit!" over and over again. The sweat from his forehead was dripping onto the floor.

Ted was speechless through his surgical mask as Dr. Felds asked him to hand to her the surgical knives and needles and thread along with scissors. Music played in the freezing cold room, the sounds of Dolly Parton.

After the hour-long surgery was over, Willard was able to hobble to Ted's car. He was given a shot of morphine to ease his pain as he just mumbled to Ted, " I hope it still works." Ted soothed his ego and macho concerns with his response " Willard, only time will tell- just calm down now, Good Buddy! The Lord would know your needs!!!"

Finishing the story, Luisa spoke to the men in the room that Sleazer should hop a fence without jumping so he can personally relate to her severe pain for the 11 solid months." The looks on those men faces will never leave Luisa's mind.

Luisa saved her story for last as another shooting of the loaded cannon at these lawyer men. She told them firmly and solidly to adamantly tell Sleazer and all his ruthless investigators from Freedom Insurance as she looked Benson square into his face that they should all pull their testicles for eleven months at 4 inches to know the severe pain that she was in and still in from that most severe injury due to the lap seat belt.

The men started moving in their seat and clearing their voices when Luisa finished with her descriptive and most unexpected stories to get her point across after reading those lies by Sleazer.

Tom regained his composure and reconfirmed all her injuries with his legal description. The meeting soon dissolved into a swirl of mutual accusations between Luisa, Tom Freeby and the Freedom Insurance Company representatives. Mediator Sonny Benson finally threw up his hands and declared that he saw no hope to settle the matter except through a jury trial. He declared the meeting over.

Sonny Benson chose not to even challenge Luisa anymore. He told her that Sleazer thought that Anton should become Luisa's guardian immediately.

Benson, being macho and an egotist, told Luisa that in all his years of being a mediator that he never failed in arriving to achieve an amicable settlement. Luisa advised him to stick to the truth as perhaps this could have been worked out with Sleazer. Furthermore, Luisa expressed that when you spoke to Sleazer you obviously did not challenge him like you did to me.

Sonny announced that the two-hour mediation session was over and requested his fee of $225 to Tom. Tom quickly, told Benson that he would mail the check. Luisa, just as quickly, told them both that the payment would be in a bucket of pennies swirling and buried in sauerkraut so he could smell the stench in the air created that day by lawyers and his lack to resolve.

The tension mounted in that room with those forceful words from Luisa, as she continued that the topping for the sauerkraut would be sauerkraut dressing. As he picked each penny from the bucket, he would have delight in counting all 22,500 pennies reeking in the stench he created for those two hours.

The litigants all filed unhappily from the room.

On that evening of July 13th, 2001, Luisa felt the effects of a huge Black Cloud hanging over her. Anton was still out of sorts and Carmella stayed over a friend's house that weekend to leave her parents alone.

Anton absorbed himself in yard work and Luisa read her books and prayed to the Lord, St. Jude and St. Michael the Archangel.

On that Sunday, her sisters had decided to have a family gathering to ease the Cannolis' into a happy atmosphere. So they grilled out and played wiffle ball for hours into the summer night.

Upon returning home at 11 PM, Luisa readied herself for bed with the planning of a Jacuzzi hot bubbly bath. The front door rang with Carmella answering it. To their surprise and total dismay, it was the Harrisons.

"The Harrisons are downstairs, Mom," Carmella said.

"What!" Luisa exclaimed, flabbergasted that a client would arrive so late on a Sunday evening. "Go back down and tell them that I'm in the Jacuzzi and I'll call them tomorrow morning."

"That won't work, Mom," Carmella shook her head. " They said they're not leaving until they see you."

"Oh, for heavens sake! All right, Carmella, tell them I'll be right down in a few minutes."

As Carmella trudged back down the stairs, Luisa got out of the Jacuzzi, hurriedly dried herself and dressed, and went downstairs.

"We want our carpet samples board back," Mrs. Harrison said as Luisa approached them in the front hall.

Luisa suspected that the Harrisons did not have the money to pay their bill and wanted to buy the carpet somewhere else.

"First of all, I don't appreciate you showing up at my front door at eleven o'clock on a Sunday night," Luisa said. "Secondly, I can't get you the carpet samples until the distributor opens tomorrow morning. Thirdly, you have not paid your bill yet."

"We'll pay you tomorrow," Wally Harrison said firmly.

"I'd appreciate that, Luisa said, doubtful that the Harrisons would fulfill that promise.

The couple turned on their heels and left, leaving Luisa to shake her head to herself at the strange visit. It was yet another bizarre incident in her life – a life that had been plagued with weird events ever since her car had been crushed on the freeway on the fateful day in July 1997.

That Monday, she arranged for her friends at Mike's Fast Delivery Service to pick up her carpet sample and deliver to the Harrisons. She received on Monday on her telephone answering machine, seven messages from the Harrisons asking for her carpet. "Where's my carpet?" sounded like to Luisa "Where's the beef?" Just like the Wendy's Commercial.

Luisa knew that stress could wear down your body and mind and lead to heart disease, cancer, extreme weight shifts and other physical maladies. Stress can also cause psychological   damage. She was faced with yet another medical issue.

That Saturday, Luisa and Anton went to the Print Shop to pick up a Print Shop's clerk had overcharged Luisa. She showed him the quote she had been given when she brought the order in, but he kept telling her she was wrong.

As Luisa tried to reason with the stubborn clerk, her breathing became increasingly labored. She finally reached the point where she knew she was in trouble and called 911 for help. Within minutes the life squad came. The paramedics took Luisa's pulse rate. It was high. She was having a severe anxiety attack.

The paramedics took her to Spirit of Body Healing Hospital. The ER doctor kept Luisa for observation until 11:00 that evening. He gave her Ativan to calm her down and also gave her some extra Ativan to take home. He told her to follow up with her doctors. Anton took Luisa home to rest.

Luisa was both emotionally drained and over-medicated. The Rainbow Rotating Olympics for the Children Dream World fundraiser was scheduled for July 22, 2001. All the arrangements were made and the responses were favorable from the 50 families invited. Luisa was torn between her commitment to this cause and the realization that her world was crashing in on her. The prescribed drugs were damaging her personality, her business and now her reputation to those who did not know what she was going thru.

Anton continued to vehemently insist that the physicians were overmedicating his wife. Luisa's psychiatrists were only interested in Freudian analysis. They refused to listen to Rosanna's concerns, even though she was a dean's scholar college grad who had studied medicine. Dr. Ba further insulted the family by telling them that Rosanna was only a 21-year-old without a medical degree.

Luisa and Rosanna met with Dr. Ba, and Rosanna asked if the psychiatrist had read the Mayo Clinic's report about chemical interaction. Dr. Ba replied that she had not seen the report.

With that, Rosanna told the psychiatrist, "You are not treating my mother anymore." Rosanna and Luisa then left Dr. Ba's office for good.

When they got home, Luisa reluctantly agreed with her family that she needed medical help to get her off the powerful drugs that she was taking. Subsequently, urgent visits were scheduled for the week of July 16th, 2001.

Dr. Stuart met with Luisa and Rosanna on Monday morning. He discussed quite openly with them that he believed that Luisa should go into detoxification as she had done in January 2000. On Friday, July 21st, Rosanna, Anton and Luisa went to see Dr. Ted Grizzly.

Despite her urgent medical problems, Luisa was so concerned about her obligations for the coming fundraiser that as they sat in Dr. Grizzly's waiting room she worried constantly about arrangements for the event.

Rosanna had her cell phone with her and Luisa asked to use it to check on the fundraiser. Rosanna told her Mom to settle down and not to think of the fundraiser but her health.

But Luisa's mind was focused on the fundraiser and the people coming to her home at 3:00 P.M. to set up chairs and tables. To make matters worse, rain was in the weather forecast. "But it's already two o'clock!" Luisa nearly shouted.

When Rosanna refused to relent and Anton would not tell her to let Luisa use her phone, Luisa left the room to use the office telephone.

Luisa reached the company that was providing the tables and chairs, and a representative agreed to delay arrival at her home until 5:O0 P.M. Luisa returned to the examination room somewhat relieved.

Dr. Grizzly finally came in to the examination room and saw the tension between the Cannolis. He told Luisa that he had never, in the three years he'd been treating her, seen her in her present state of mind.

Then he threw Luisa a curveball. Standing six feet tall, his 350 pound frame hovering above her, he bluntly told her, "You are way over medicated, and you are being admitted to the hospital today."

Dr.Grizzly's startling pronouncement, made Luisa wonder if this medical doctor, to whom she had entrusted her medical care, had overdosed her with drugs along with Dr.Ba. Were they both on the defense team? Was it a conspiracy to kill her?

With those thoughts in her mind, Luisa jumped off the examination table and stood right in front of the huge Goliath. She pounded his chest with her finger, telling him that she would go on Tuesday, after the social function. "I am not going today!" she said, punctuating each word with a jab at his chest.

With that, Dr. Grizzly told Luisa loudly and firmly, "You are going today." In a stern voice, he added, "This is a public place, and I am calling the Sheriff of Harrisburg to take you to Harrisburg Hospital now!"

Luisa was shell shocked into reality. The fundraiser! Despite all the preparations for the function scheduled the next day, Luisa had little choice as the Sheriff came to escort her to Harrisburg Hospital. She was completely humiliated.

Rosanna and Luisa rode together, as Anton followed them to the hospital in their Lexus. During the twenty-minute car ride, Luisa gave Rosanna the fundraiser folder and asked her to contact the volunteers to cancel the event unless the volunteers were   willing to take over.

While they were in the hospital waiting room, Luisa decided to call the people herself to let them know what was happening. She asked the desk clerk for permission to use her phone.

"You may make one call," the clerk told her, "but no more than one."

Luisa looked around, but there was no pay phone in sight. Luisa asked Rosanna to use her cell phone, but Rosanna refused.

Luisa became frustrated and agitated. The two of them, Anton and Rosanna, arranged for this whole medicine/doctor evaluation, Luisa thought, wondering what was going to happen.

Finally, they were called in to talk to the social worker. One by one, he spoke to each of them. He decided that Luisa could go home, but insisted she go to a hospital of her choice the following week.

Anton, Rosanna and Luisa left the facility to go home. Again, Luisa asked Rosanna to use her cell phone. With Rosanna sitting in the front seat of the car and Luisa in the rear, Luisa kept asking Rosanna if she could use her cell phone.

For some reason, Rosanna kept saying NO! Finally, Anton told Rosanna to give her mother the cell phone.

Luisa tried to call one of the companies bringing amusement items for the fundraiser. The cell phone would not work. Luisa had had enough. Pushing the button to open the window, Luisa said, "The hell with this phone," and she threw the cell phone out the open window.

All hell broke loose in the car. Anton screamed, "We're taking you to the hospital right now!"

Rosanna screamed, "Why did you throw my cell phone out the window?"

Luisa's mind was racing with all kinds of thoughts. Dr. Ted Grizzly, Rosanna and Anton were smothering her. Luisa wanted to escape from them. As Anton pulled off the exit to take Luisa to the hospital, Luisa told him, "To hell with you. I am not going to the damn hospital."

Feeling that she was being forced into a situation that was out of control, Luisa opened the car door.

To her surprise, two police cars pulled up. The officers got out of their cars to talk to Luisa, and then Rosanna and Anton got out of the car.

Luisa told the officers what happened. She told them about the fundraiser.

One of the officers said, "Your focus should be on your health, not on a fundraiser. Listen to your husband and go home amicably."

Reluctantly, Luisa did so.

When they arrived home, Luisa learned that the fundraiser was already in the hands of others. It had been canceled.

Luisa was extremely stressed. She was on overload. She finally admitted to herself that she had to get medical help.

Luisa had read "***Battlefield of the Mind***" by Joyce Meyer. During mental overload, the power of prayer is necessary to uplift you through difficult times and periods of depression. Meyer's book and ministries have helped thousands of people through crisis of life.

This book helped Luisa reach the point of realizing the need to do something about her health before it was too late. The simple references to the Bible and the crisis of life are written together in the book. The understanding of the message was clear as Luisa reread the book.

Emotionally drained and over-medicated, on Wednesday, July 25th Luisa checked into Spirit of Healing Body Hospital for treatment.

Chapter 20

Life in the Cuckoo's Nest

Although Luisa believed that she was being admitted to Spirit of Healing Body Hospital to undergo detoxification, she found herself being unceremoniously ushered into the psychiatric ward.

Luisa's younger sisters, Sophia and Anna, accompanied her. They too believed that Luisa was being admitted to detoxification to be weaned off the numerous potent drugs she had been taking.

Dr. Gunson, who admitted Luisa, had an odd look about him. He perpetually cocked his head upward – as if he wanted to be taller – and wore eyeglasses that had huge frames that were much too large for his thin face.

As the doctor examined Luisa, he ignored the concerned questions of her sisters. They had brought with them a bag full of the prescription drugs Luisa had been taking. Despite their determined attempts to show him the bag of prescription drugs, he continued to ignore them.

Casually pushing the bag aside, the physician began asking Luisa questions about her early sexual encounters. Luisa could not believe that her early sex life could have any relevance to her present condition and refused to answer the doctor's questions.

She felt like screaming, "I'm over–medicated, you idiot! Can't you see that!"

Her family and friends – even her attorney Tom – knew that she was over–medicated. This doctor was on the wrong track. To compound his folly, the physician diagnosed her as bipolar, a diagnosis that Luisa, her husband and her family all strongly disagreed with.

After her examination, Luisa was admitted to a semi-private room in the psychiatric wing. She soon learned that the other patient in the room was a heavily drugged woman named Rachel.

Rachel was beautiful with flowing long blond hair. She wore Ralph Lauren stylish washed-out blue jeans and a freshly pressed long-sleeved white cotton blouse. The blouse was unbuttoned at her neck and the gold chains she wore flowed over her ample bosom as she lay on her side facing Luisa. Her eyes were glassy and very green.

As she lay on the bed, a cotton sheet at her feet, she mumbled words to her husband who stood over her on the right side of the bed. She asked him to tell their children where she was.

The striking man who resembled Paul Newman assured her that he would. His baby blue eyes sparkled as he spoke to his wife, expressing his love and concern for her. He leaned down and gently pulled her hair away from her cheek as he kissed her goodbye and goodnight.

She mumbled, "I love you and I'll be fine," before she closed her eyes and fell asleep.

Luisa saw the horror of prescribed drug overdose right before her eyes. She too just wanted to sleep and escape this nightmare of her thoughts.

Luisa learned that Rachel was under the care of Dr. Ba and thought; I guess I'm not the only one that Dr. Ba has overmedicated. That woman has no business practicing medicine!

Luisa continued to contemplate filing malpractice suits against Dr. Grizzly, Dr. Ba and Dr. Gunson, and she decided she would speak to Tom Freeby about it.

An hour later Dr. Ba came in and began talking to her groggy, glassy-eyed patient. Rachel did not acknowledge Dr. Ba at all.

"I am ordering more medication for you," Dr. Ba said, seemingly oblivious to the woman's near comatose state.

As the physician left the room, she glanced at Luisa but said nothing.

Luisa shook her head. Obviously, Dr. Ba believed that her prescription pad was a magic wand that could solve any medical problem.

I wonder how big a kickback she gets from the pharmaceutical companies for writing so many unnecessary and ultimately harmful prescriptions, Luisa thought. She's making big bucks while her patients sink into the hell of drug dependency.

Luisa had no doubts about Dr. Ba's unethical methods because her family had researched the physician's medical record. Suits had been filed against her. Although the information did not surprise anyone, it also did nothing to help Luisa. The damage had been done. Luisa was addicted to a host of powerful drugs. And now it was Luisa and her family, not Dr. Ba, who were left to clean up the mess.

Luisa knew that her road to recovery would not be easy. She could not speak coherently, and she had zero interest in anything around her. The doctors adjusted her medications in an attempt to stabilize the chemical imbalance she was suffering, and numerous blood tests were taken.

Dr. Glen Lockwood came to see Luisa. He was compassionate and understanding. Luisa told the internist the horrific story of what had happened to her. He listened and suggested that it might be of benefit to her if she wrote down her inner thoughts and feelings during this hospitalization.

Luisa recalled that Dr. Stuart had advised her to do the same thing. During the months of the strangest events in her life, she had taken Dr. Stuart's advice and made many visits to Sorrento's Inn to write her story. She wrote on their placemats while she drank glasses of merlot and amaretto, trying to escape the weird events and forget about the thefts at her home, if only for a while.

Dr. Lockwood listened to her difficult breathing and ordered x-rays of her lungs. Test results proved the collapse of her right lung in the lower area, and the drugs she was taking were determined to be the definitive underlying cause.

The caring Dr. Lockwood disagreed with doctors prescribing harmful drugs to people, and he advised Luisa to change doctors. He encouraged her to relax and suggested that she have her family bring her things she might enjoy doing during her hospitalization since she was accustomed to keeping herself busy.

Luisa only saw him three times during her stay. He knew some of her Italian relatives and offered his prayers for her recovery. Dr. Lockwood was so different than Dr. Gunson.

Luisa was tempted to complain about Dr. Gunson, but decided to hold off, believing it might be best to take up the matter later with the medical insurance company who recommended him to admit her to the hospital.

Rosanna brought her books, watercolor drawing pads and paints. Her cousin, Angela, brought her Backgammon Gameboy to ease the boredom. Behind the scenes, her other cousins were helping with Carmella. She was on the high school tennis team and needed transportation. Rosanna pitched in to help as well.

Luisa had a hospital room with a view. The huge glass picture window showed the bright summer sky and the trees in full bloom. As she lay there on August 7th she was overwhelmed with sadness as she thought about the plans she and Anton had made to vacation in Hawaii in celebration of their 25th wedding anniversary.

As her heart ached, the nurse, Megan, walked into her room with a large colorful bouquet of flowers from her most loving family. The card read, "Mom, we love you dearly and you will be home soon! Forever love, Anton, Rosanna, Carmella, Princess and Fish."

Luisa thought of the Italian verse she had learned from her

mother – La beautitudine de essere amato raddolciisce qualunque dolore. Foscolo - The happiness of being in love sweetens whatever pain exists.

The surprise bouquet brought a smile to Luisa's face and lifted her heart. She remembered the lovely times over the years at Hilton Head with family and friends. The recollection prompted her to do a watercolor of her fondest memory of Hilton Head with the boats and tall trees and sounds of the rolling ocean waves. The watercolor was so meaningful to her that she decided she would make copies of it to share with the many people who meant the most to her.

Dr. Stuart came to visit Luisa that afternoon as she was finishing the watercolor. He expressed admiration for her talent and told her that he had not been aware of her broad creative abilities. He expressed further admiration of the slide she had of her top award-winning statue of the Virgin Mary at the Guggenheim Museum in New York City from many years ago. Luisa painted a similar watercolor for him to have, and the watercolor now hangs in his home.

That evening, Dr Gunson made his rounds at the hospital. When he came into Luisa's room and saw all the items Rosanna brought, he cocked his head in that most peculiar position. He then straightened his oversized eyeglasses and spoke to Luisa.

His words a reprimand, he told Luisa that he wanted her to have nothing to do in order to slow down her mind with the drugs he was prescribing her. He stood there and waved his arm like a drill sergeant. With his finger stabbing the air, he told Luisa to call her family and have the items removed.

Luisa's disgust with him gave her the courage to tell him that no drugs were going to slow her down. She told him that her family cared very much about her.

"They are dysfunctional!" the doctor said.

The doctor's audacity to call her family dysfunctional infuriated Luisa even more so. Although the surroundings of this hospital were better than they had been at Good Spirit Hospital during her stay in January 2000, this doctor's egotistical and arrogant personality were too much for Luisa to bear.

Luisa told him to leave her alone. She went on to tell him that the drugs he prescribed were making her worse emotionally, and she needed an outlet to express her true inner anger over this whole horrific episode caused by doctors.

With those words spoken firmly to him, he turned his body sharply, cocked his overly proud head, and left her room.

Luisa sat down, feeling finally relieved.

Her roommate, Rachel, witnessed the encounter. She told Luisa that she was right to speak up. She explained that Dr. Ba had diagnosed her as bipolar and she had been hospitalized repeatedly because of the drugs Dr. Ba prescribed for her.

Rachel complimented Luisa on having the courage to use her creative talent. She told her that the watercolor was beautiful and it brightened up the room.

Rachel looked around the room and said, "This place is so dusty." She got up from the bed, picked up a towel and began dusting the room. "Maybe I can help brighten up this room too," she said to Luisa with a smile.

As Luisa began to detoxify and regain her senses, she became aware of a disheartening number of heavily medicated and non-coherent patients in the psychiatric wing. There was one unfortunate man named Rodney, who had many of his teeth missing and could not conduct a conversation. He wore the same cloth pajamas every day and kept asking the nurses and his fellow patients for money for cigarettes. His condition saddened Luisa and made her feel like she had somehow become trapped in the movie "One Flew Over the Cuckoo's Nest."

Luisa knew she could not check out of the hospital. She didn't know how long she would be there. Her doctor told her it might take two to four weeks to get her chemical imbalance under control and restore her mental health. Sometimes it could last months according to some of the trusted pharmacists she had spoken to.

She felt like she was in prison. The psychiatric ward had locked doors, and no one except authorized personnel could enter or leave. Her freedom had been taken away from her and, once again, she had to adjust to an extremely difficult situation.

Her stress level had reached an all time high. Her doctors wanted her to mingle with the other patients and she attempted to do so. She started going to the gym and joining in table conversation at meal times.

Luisa had a headset so that she could listen to music as she walked around the ward. She had several favorite songs, among them Andrea Bocelli's Mistero Dell'Amore – The Mystery of Love CD that touched her heart with her love for Anton. Another was Puff Johnson's Over and Over Again as Luisa waged her internal battle with those lawyers and doctors who challenged her so much.

She also enjoyed Bette Midler, Diane Keaton, and Goldie Hawn's You Don't Own Me. Other favorites included Frank Sinatra's Fly me To The Moon and New York, New York. Sometimes she noticed other patients following her through the corridors.

When she listened to Judy Garland's Somewhere Over the Rainbow, it reminded Luisa that the Rainbow Rotating Olympics for families had to be put on hold.

She listened to Ray Charles's America and Louis Armstrong's Between The Devil And The Deep Blue Sea and prayed for release from the devils from Lee Sleazer's investigative team. And she longed with a passionate desire to go to Hawaii some time and see God's beautiful Deep Blue Hawaiian Seas, and recalled movies like South Pacific which she loved watching as a child with her father, mother and sisters.

Listening to her music as she walked through the ward brought peace to Luisa's mind, and she could see smiles on the some of the faces of the poor drug addicted victims she passed on her walks through the corridors.

One day on a whim she turned the volume up and took off the earphones so that the patients around her could hear the music. The music put smiles on everyone's faces. The back ward had senior drug addicts there. The walls in that ward were soft pink, rather than the ocean blue walls of the ward Luisa was in.

One day an elderly lady called for Luisa to come to that side of the ward. Luisa saw her pleading look as she called out, "Luisa, I want to join you!"

Luisa welcomed the opportunity to help this kind and lonely soul join her. Her group of followers had grown to eight. They danced in the hallway, moving their arms as if they were flying. The purpose was to exercise all muscle groups.

Luisa pushed the elderly lady, Gloria, in her wheelchair around the u-shaped corridor. They hadn't gotten very far when Nurse Gertrude called Gloria and told her to go back to her side of the ward.

Nurse Gertrude was a large stocky lady with a thick German accent. Since Nurse Gertrude was in charge, Luisa quickly complied with her request. As Luisa wheeled Gloria back to her ward, Luisa thought, A sergeant in this hellhole of a prison. How long has Gloria been locked up in the pink ward with Nurse Gertrude? Luisa wondered.

The rest of the group applauded and thanked Luisa for helping Gloria have a moment of happiness, cheer and music. The group continued walking the corridors, listening to music and doing their dance for eight days straight. The nurses in the ocean blue ward supported Luisa in her efforts to entertain the group.

Luisa also established a routine, which she felt would help prepare her to go home. While the other patients wore their pajamas both day and night, Luisa chose to wear her normal clothing during the day and her pajamas only at night. She also continued to pray to the Lord for Him to help her get through this ordeal.

In an effort to interact with her fellow patients, on the eleventh day of her hospital stay Luisa approached a lonely looking young man in the cafeteria and asked him if he'd like to listen to music.

"Yes," he replied, "I'd like that very much."

As she reached up to take off her headset, the young man suddenly grabbed her around the waist and pulled her against him.

"Stop!" Louisa yelled, struggling to pull away. "What are you doing? Let go of me!"

Fortunately, a male nurse heard her shouts and came rushing over. "That's enough, Steven," the nurse said, pulling the young man off Luisa. "What's the matter with you? Go to your room immediately."

The nurse turned to Luisa. "Are you all right?"

Luisa took a deep breath. "Yes, I think so. He really threw a scare into me though. Thank God you were nearby."

"Steven's never pulled this sort of stunt before. Then again, nothing the patients in this ward do surprise me."

"Nor me," Luisa said, a rueful smile creasing her lips. "I guess I'd better be more careful about who I try to make friends with."

The nurse nodded. "That might be a good idea."

After the incident, Luisa made up her mind that the psychiatric ward was no place for her to be. Determined to go home, she went to the front nurses' station and asked to be checked out.

The head nurse refused. "You have to be discharged by your doctor and signed out by your husband," The nurse said adamantly.

Luisa stubbornly stood her ground and said, "May I please use your telephone?"

The nurse eyed Luisa suspiciously as she handed her the phone. Luisa called information and got the number for United Cab. She told the dispatcher that she knew Adrian and then asked the dispatcher to send a cab to Spirit of the Healing Body Hospital.

"I just told you that you can't leave," the nurse said angrily as Luisa hung up.

"Who said I was leaving?" Luisa answered calmly. "I ordered the cab to come pick up some of my things and bring them to my home. Now, please call my husband and tell him that I will be ready to leave tomorrow."

Sensing that Luisa was not about to change her mind, the nurse called Anton and handed the phone to Luisa.

"You've got to get me out of here, Anton," she pleaded. "I'll recover much faster in the security of my own home than I will in this hellish place."

"All right," Anton said. "I'll call your doctor and arrange for you to be released tomorrow. I'll pick you up."

Luisa breathed a sigh of relief. "Thank you, Anton. You have no idea how much better I feel."

During her 28-day stay in the psychiatric ward, Luisa had come to understand that prescribed drugs were as dangerous as illegal drugs. Addiction to either could cost an individual dearly. Even though she had been the innocent victim of doctors all too ready to prescribe powerful drugs, it was she who had lost her freedom and not her unethical physicians.

Luisa's stay at Spirit of the Healing Body Hospital had helped her get her detoxification off to a good start. However, it took another two months for the chemical imbalance in her body to subside. During this time, her willpower and determination to be drug free - as well as the love and support of her family and friends - gave her the strength she needed to gradually stop taking the prescribed medications.

Chapter 21

The Beginning of the End

Although Luisa found great gratification in her recovery from addiction, her victory over drugs was tinged with sadness that her hospitalization had forced her and Anton to cancel their 25th wedding anniversary celebration.

Luisa resolved to reschedule their vacation as soon as she could. Although Luisa and Anton had talked about going to Hawaii with their timeshares for this anniversary, with the upcoming trial they decided against it. Instead of Hawaii, they decided they would go to Hilton Head Island. Nonetheless, Anton advised Luisa to wait for the trial to be over before making any reservations. Luisa agreed, since they both knew reservations for a get-away trip through Interval International could be made on as short as 24 hours notice. The airlines and Interval International would issue their reservations.

Louisa made telephone calls to the airlines and Interval International. The airline representative she spoke to was Gloria, and Interval International's representative was Bernardo.

Luisa told both Gloria and Bernardo about the July 22 automobile accident and explained the tremendous stress she had been under due to insurance company tactics. Neither Gloria nor Bernardo could believe the atrocities Luisa had sustained and both company representatives said they would be happy to accommodate her in securing airline and hotel reservations for Luisa and Anton.

Next, Luisa made medical appointments with OBGYN and her internist for thorough examinations. Both doctors told her that she could go to Hilton Head with Anton after the trial. Aware that Luisa and Anton's marriage had certainly been tested through the ordeal that had begun on July 22, 1997, both doctors believed that the trip would be a good opportunity for the couple to restart their marriage and renew their commitments to one another.

Luisa was elated that her doctors encouraged the rekindling of their romantic relationship as they told her that many of their patients needed this type of distraction to rebalance their marriages. Dr. Joseph, her OBGYN, told her that such a trip could save a marriage. Husbands and wives needed time together from the normal headaches of life. Those who could get away for a week or weekend could do wonders, he told Luisa.

Louisa's doctors both wrote letters to assure Anton they believed the trip would benefit her:

To Luisa Cannoli

Regarding Anton's concern for your health and trip to Hilton Head. I see no problems and hopefully this could even be helpful.

Sincerely,
Ted Grizzly, M.D.

Dear Anton,

Luisa is in fine health today except for the chronic pain. Enjoy your 25th Silver Wedding Anniversary in Hilton Head. Treat her like a bride. Carry her over the threshold and she will have wine, cheese and chocolate covered cherries waiting for you. Have fun and stay young and healthy!!

Most sincerely
Dr. Joseph
OBGYN

In Luisa's collection of favorite Italian love quotations, she found a particularly appropriate one from *Aore la spinge e tira, (Treasury of Italian Love).*

Non per elezion ma per destino. Petrarrca – Love drives on not by choice but by fate.

Eagerly, Luisa and Anton packed their bags and made arrangements for Rosanna to stay with Carmella, since Rosanna didn't start school until after Carmella.

The girls were looking forward to their time alone. Anton reminded the girls that there would be no partying or drinking in their home while they were gone. He gave them a list of responsibilities, such as taking care of Fish and Princess, along with keeping the home secure and well lit. He gave them grocery money, and Luisa gave the girls the telephone numbers of her nearby cousins in case they were needed. She also reminded the girls to stay in touch with their grandmother. Laundry could wait until they were home.

Luisa was still experiencing withdrawal systems from the 24 drugs she was taking. Having lived through the eye-opening drama and horror at Spirit of the Healing Body's Hospital and having to face reality was not easy for her. In addition, her weight had reached 267 pounds, and Luisa's self-esteem was destroyed.

She was scheduled to attend a six-week outpatient program under Dr. Gunson at his hospital, St. Jude Rehabilitation Center in mid- September and the month of October.

The shakes and sweats of withdrawal kept Luisa up at night

but she was determined to lose the weight and become her old self again. Knowing this would take time, and the first step was to flush the 24 vials of prescription drugs down the toilet in her bathroom. It took seven flushes – and a chemical explosion before her eyes! - as she watched the drugs to go down the toilet drain.

No wonder she was taking prevacid for her stomach acid build-up. The damage to her internal system would be permanent. When she spoke to her plumber about the bubbling chemical explosion that took place in the commode, he told her it probably took the enamel off the inside. Now she knew why she needed that prevacid everyday.

After the incident, Luisa wondered why the pharmaceutical companies did not warn consumers of the hazards of chemical interaction when their drugs are mixed. Did they even warn the doctors when they provided their drugs to the doctors? Or was it the doctors who did not pass on the warning? Didn't the doctors take chemistry in school?

Enough wondering and worrying, she told herself. Now she was ready for the honeymoon vacation with Anton. They decided to put the stress of the trial - now delayed until March 2002 - on the back burner. They would also deal with the Car Owners Insurance claim when they got back. Tom was notified of their much-needed vacation, and then they were off.

Once in Hilton Head, Luisa had a complimentary facial at the beauty shop and had her hairstyle changed. Although she needed new clothes, she decided not to shop for clothes until she managed to lose some weight.

Anton planned their simple outings. He chose to walk the beach and ride bicycles and to have picnic lunches all week. He treated Luisa to a bottle of wine and dinners out on the waterfront. Luisa remembered that her best friend, Diana, had reminded them to try Raspberry Gelato at Rita's and to eat at Spargetti's Inn off the waterfront.

Luisa recalled the Italian proverbs - *Chi amo assai, soltante parlo poco. Castiglione - One who loves much often talks little.* Luisa remembered what her late father thought of Anton – still water runs deep.

As Anton sat on the beach and read his book on real estate and the Search for Excellence, Luisa knew she had married Mr. Right. Tom Freeby would remain in a warm place in her heart, but he would only be there as a friend.

Anton and Luisa were on the road to romantic recovery.

The week ended with fond, warm and private moments for the Cannolis. As Carmella wrote in her school paper, their family had become closer since July 22, 1997.

Luisa knew that the Lord kept her alive for a deeper purpose in her life. Perhaps her journal notes would fulfill that unknown purpose as P.H. Atwater had in the *Beyond the Light* book and video.

Upon their return home, they were delighted to discover that their girls had managed to keep the home front just as they had expected they would. Luisa's cousins, Angela and Jill, along with her sisters Sofia and Anna, had helped the girls with getting Carmella to tennis and waking them up in the morning so Carmella would not be late for class.

Luisa readied herself for the outpatient program for the prescribed drug program. The program would last all day long for six weeks. Realizing to her utter disappointment that her design world and business were gone, Luisa resigned herself, with the support of Anton, her family and closest friends, hoping that participation in this program would benefit her.

She cheered herself with the realization that she could still meet Suzanne, Caroline and Anne for breakfast to plan the family gatherings with the kids. During one morning breakfast at the Country Breakfast and Lunch Inn, Luisa's mind was foggy as she tried to stay focused on the conversations, but the withdrawal systems continued as they had in Hilton Head. From her experience during the January 2000 episode, Luisa knew that this could last up to five months.

At the rehabilitation sessions, Luisa met and saw victims from suicide and car accidents. The devastating stories of these innocent victims deepened Luisa's understanding of the difficulty that men sometimes have expressing their inner feelings and reminded her of the way Anton kept so many of those thoughts to himself. Two of the women spoke of voices telling them to commit suicide.

Luisa knew that when it was her turn to speak that it was important to tell the truth of her inner thoughts. She had firsthand knowledge of the damage of low self-esteem that she wanted to share with these men and women. She decided to bring in some of the books she had read that helped pull her through her horrific trauma. The books she brought were *Simple Abundance, Illuminatta* and *Teatime with God.* The group leader, Sarah, mentioned to Luisa that she should teach the class and help others because she was an example of strength to this group. The six weeks went fast and Luisa valued her time there.

Carmella made the tennis team at her school. Luisa was able to attend but had some embarrassing moments with pain and severe spasms. She knew she had to overcome the embarrassment of being stared at by a public who did not realize all she had been through. It was tough for her. She remembered Erin Brocovich's father's word: Tough. That word sometimes describes life as it is. But the TOUGH keep on moving.

It was time for Anton and Luisa to meet with Tom regarding their theft claims. Car Owners Insurance sent them a certified letter about having a legal examination with their lawyer, H.S. Witt. Mr. Witt would question Luisa and Anton about the thefts, and the examination would take place under oath. Now they needed a lawyer to represent them.

They had no idea of what they would be facing. Tom Freeby prepared Luisa. She had photos and receipts verifying her claim.

After being questioned earlier that summer by their investigator, Luisa was not looking forward to the examination. She already knew the lack of professionalism and lack of integrity by the representatives who had come to her home.

Anton listened as Luisa spoke to Tom about the missing items and their value, which totaled thousands of dollars for the valued goods. Next, Tom prepared Anton. The examination was scheduled for Friday, December 17, 2001.

Luisa arrived first at Witt's office. She eased into a navy wingback chair with her folder of detailed records that listed the items stolen from their home, as well as photographs of the missing things. It was her understanding that she would go under oath first with her evidence.

Anton and Tom Freeby arrived almost at the same time that wintry Friday afternoon. H.S. Witt came in shortly afterwards. Luisa noted that he was slightly under six feet tall and of medium build, and had dark brown hair.

As soon as he entered the room, he handed his secretary his laptop and barked, "This damn thing won't work. Fix it!"

As the secretary fiddled with Witt's computer, Tom said, "We want Mrs. Cannoli to go first. She knows more about the missing items than her husband."

Witt shook his head no. "Forget it, counselor. I want to interview Mr. Cannoli first. Or do you intend to tell me how to conduct my examination?"

"The ball's in your court," Tom replied. "Interview the Cannolis in whatever order you wish. I was just trying to make things easier on us all."

"Sure you were," Witt said in a nasty tone, then whipped around and confronted his secretary. "Have you fixed that stupid computer yet?"

"Yes," the secretary said, a look of disgust on her face as she handed the laptop to Witt. "You put a floppy in the A-drive backwards."

Without a word of thanks, Witt snatched the laptop from his secretary's hand and disappeared into the examination room. "Send Anton Cannoli in," he shouted from within.

Luisa shuddered knowing that this Goliath S.O.B would slaughter the mild mannered Anton. The interview started and through the glass doors Luisa could see H.S. Witt's growling face as he threw rapid-fire questions at Anton.

Four long hours into Anton's interview, Luisa could see that her husband was both mentally exhausted and distraught. True to her premonition, the hard-edged Witt had beaten Anton into the ground.

Luisa saw the drained look on Anton's face. She decided to level with Tom as he stood across the table in the outer conference room.

She turned to Freeby and asked, "Tom, what the hell's going on? Witt's treating Anton like a criminal."

Her former passionate lover threw his long arms upward, and told Luisa in a very smooth sounding voice, "I do not want you to think anything less of me."

Luisa did not know what to think except that she had told him in May 2001 that she still loved him and he knew that. Luisa thoughts went to a Frank Sinatra song - I got you under my skin – and then back to their most loving and very warm relationship.

But then her thoughts flew back to Anton. I chose Anton as my husband because of the freedom he provided to me. I just could not be controlled. Anton gave me more choices in life.

Brought out of her reverie, Luisa sat down when she heard Tom suggest that she sit down and review some papers that needed more explanation. Then Tom went on about the approach taken by the Car Owners Insurance lawyer.

"I had a phone conversation with Witt earlier today," Tom said. "I hadn't wanted to bring this up until I was sure he wasn't bluffing, but Witt told me that he was prepared to charge Anton with insurance fraud. You and Anton made a claim for a $15,000 to $20,000 loss, and Witt insists that entire claim is bogus. I'm afraid that Anton could face felony charges. So could you. Naturally, I'll fight the action."

Luisa sat back in her chair ashen-faced."

"How could this be happening?" she asked in a suddenly hoarse voice.

"For one thing, during the break in the interview a couple of hours ago Witt told me that Anton was being purposely vague about the value of the stolen items. That sort of vagueness arouses suspicion in an investigator."

Luisa thought a moment then – convinced that she could not win against unethical lawyers and nefarious insurance company tactics – she sighed deeply and told Tom to drop their claim against Car Owners Insurance.

"We've had Car Owners for six years and never once before filed a claim," she said. "And the first time we do, they threaten us with fraud charges. The little guy just can't win, huh Tom?"

Tom looked away for a moment, then went to the examination room door and knocked. He held a brief whispered conversation with Witt, and then Anton emerged from the room looking green in the gills.

"Before we leave I want to tell Mr. Witt something in Italian," Luisa said, seething inside.

A worried look came over Tom's face. I don't think that's a good idea, Luisa."

Witt added, "I have no interest in hearing anything you might say, Mrs. Cannoli."

Luisa charged on. "You're going to hear it anyway. Fasha la gul, Witt (your face is like your Glutaeus Maximus)."

The court reporter took it all in. Witt glared at Luisa for a long moment, then handed Tom a release statement for the Cannolis to sign.

Without another word being exchanged, the parties rose to leave Witt's office. Tom walked with Anton and Luisa to the elevator.

"I'm still negotiating with Freedom Insurance," Tom said. "Their offer is up to $550,000, plus $9,200 for your totaled '89 Cressida. I want you both to sign this memo paper for this new demand offer. Give it some thought."

Luisa told him to get the case settled. Rosanna was ready to have Sleazer take her deposition. Her maturity at 21 years enabled her to see right through the unethical tactics by the S.O.B. investigators and their defense lawyers. Carmella, on the other hand, was so sensitive to the messy situation.

Luisa reminded Tom that it was Carmella who discovered the red flashing light on the garage door analog keypad. The code had been "1225" for years, symbolizing the date of Christmas. Carmella had chosen that code, and it had been she who had discovered the missing treasured Christmas ornaments.

With the emotional concern of a mother aware of the deep emotional toll taken on her family, along with her concern for the friends who would be called as witnesses for the March 13, 2002 trial, Luisa pleaded with Tom to ask if Judge Perrino would meet with them and Sleazer to help settle the case without a jury.

Tom told Luisa that the case had been filed with a jury demand, so a motion would have to be entered for a bench trial.

Tom advised her that he would take her concerns into consideration. He told her that if anything developed between then and Christmas, he would call them.

Tom wished the Cannolis a Happy Christmas holiday as they shook hands and parted ways, opening up their umbrellas to the pouring rain. With temperatures dropping, the rain would likely change to snow by Christmas.

A few days later the Cannolis received a structured settlement letter offering $300,000 – there was now no mention of $550,000 – that would be paid once Luisa reached 65 years of age.

At 65 a small portion monthly amount would be paid. This letter added more insult to injury. It was rejected. The Cannolis focused on their Christmas holidays. Anton made bows and bought new ornaments to replace the old ornaments that had been stolen.

Tom called after the holidays and told Luisa that he was working very hard on her case. He told her that Freedom was one of the worst insurance companies that he had ever come up against. Sleazer would not bend.

Luisa was sick of it all. They had a family wedding in April to start thinking about. Rosanna had plans to go to the California coast for spring break. This never-ending situation was hindering the Cannoli family from moving on. Luisa told Tom to do his best.

Tom said he would keep on negotiating with Sleazer.

It was cold and snowing outside as Luisa resorted to read her *Something More - Excavating Your Authentic Self* book written by Sarah Ban Breathnah. The book had been a Christmas gift from Mary Ellen, her best soul mate for many years.

As the book starts:

"What we'll be searching for are the moments that have made a difference in the trajectory of your life. To do that we'll need to dig deep: through the successes and failures that have defined you; through the loves and hates, gains and losses, promises and pain that have bound you; though the risks and ruins, tumults and triumphs that set you free. We'll exhume all the perfectly reasonable choices that derailed your dreams and brush off the clinging soil hiding the half-truths that have haunted you all these years.

Pay dirt."

Luisa was ready for this excavation to start. She spent the next weeks reading this most interesting book and writing notes in her journal.

In mid-January 2002, Luisa visited her mother, who lived over 50 miles from her home. Her mother had invited her daughters - Luisa, Anna and Sophia - and their families over for the day and to stay for dinner. Since Carmella had homework to do, Anton stayed home to help her with it so Luisa drove to her mother's home alone on that Sunday afternoon.

The gathering was relaxing. They sat in the family room and watched the Super Bowl game. Teresa was in the kitchen fixing the pot roast. Sophia was baking her delicious homemade apple pie with a touch of carmel, for which she had won a blue ribbon baking award. Their Aunt Gwinnete showed her the trade secret to the crust and Sophia had taken it from there to improvise her own apple pie ingredients. Anna and Luisa set the dining and kitchen table for dinner.

All said prayers of thanksgiving and the eating and family chatter began. Topics included sports, school and the upcoming wedding of Laurie and Stu in April. The nieces were all in the wedding party and chatted about their dresses and hairstyles.

After the game and the delicious meal, it was time to go home. Luisa was the first to leave. Less than two miles from her mom's home, she heard a loud popping sound as she drove along the interstate. It was her right front tire, and it went flat instantly.

Luisa tried to stay calm, but the flashbacks of her demolished Toyota came to mind and she had an immediate anxiety attack. She had activated her car cell phone for 911 calls only, and she dialed 911 for someone to come and change her tire.

The 911 operator realized that Luisa was shaken up from the sound of her voice. In the next moment, Anna appeared at Luisa's car window. She told Luisa to settle down. Anna's husband, Jack, would change the tire.

Just then an ambulance pulled up behind Luisa's car followed by a police car. Anna told Luisa that she was having a severe anxiety attack. The EMS attendant opened Luisa's driver's door to check her blood pressure. It was elevated to 250/140. The

EMS attendant told Luisa and Anna that they were taking Luisa to the local hospital, St. Margaret, to be checked.

As the ambulance drove off, Jack told the policeman that he would change the tire and drive the car to his nearby home. Anna called Anton and told him to meet them at the hospital.

The EMS arrived at the hospital, and Luisa was admitted into emergency. The attending physician, Dr. Peters, recognized Luisa's anxiety attack. He hooked her up to an IV with a strong sedative. For two hours, Luisa remained there.

Anton arrived and was aware of the severe anxiety Luisa was suffering. He told Luisa that perhaps she was pushing herself too hard and needed to better pace herself since being off the medications.

Dr. Peters gave Luisa Ativan and discharged her after advising her to tell her doctors what happened. Anton and Luisa left the hospital around midnight. Luisa asked Anton if she should call Tom Freeby. He suggested she wait until they got home.

Once home, Luisa made the call to Tom Freeby. At that hour she expected to get his answering machine and was surprised when Tom answered. Luisa told him what had happened on the expressway.

He told that he appreciated the call and that he was preparing her case for the March 13th trial. He ended the conversation by reminding her of the importance of relaxing and encouraged her not to give up on driving. Then they hung the phone. The ativan helped Luisa relax and she got a good night's sleep.

Driving was still difficult for Luisa, but she had had to let William go and she had no funds for United Cab to drive her to her medical treatments. What was she going to do? She had tried six sessions of hypnosis, which was paid out of pocket. Unfortunately, it did not work for Luisa.

On February 14th, Tom Freeby called, with devastating news. Tom had received a very strange message on his computer screen. He explained to Luisa that it said, "Tom Freeby, you are full of shit!"

He went on to say that when he hit the delete button a pornographic scene appeared. He inadvertently pushed delete again and to his dismay all his data files were destroyed. Tom's voice was quivering as he told Luisa this bombshell that he was faced with.

Freedom Insurance had refused to negotiate beyond a final offer of $287,500. In an upset voice Tom explained that he had tried for weeks to get them to $550,000 and when that failed had sought $300,000. Her lost wages, all medically prescribed out of pocket expenses along with the total car expenses was not included in that amount. Luisa told him that by shaving her extensive and legitimate medical bills that Freedom Insurance just multiplied his low partial figure of $91,000 by three.

She reminded him adamantly of his damn cheapness when they dated seriously many years ago. Now the truth comes out between the two of them.

Anton allowed Luisa to express her talents and treated her to plays and music concerts. They dined out by themselves. She told Tom that she understood his law school bills but his control and most frugal ways really bothered her. How controlling would he have been in a marriage? Luisa told him that at that time of her life she planned ahead. She cherished his compassionate ways and verbal conversations, his ideals in thinking of where he would be in five years.

Anton was so reserved that he would not even discuss his future goals at that time of his life. As a lawyer, Tom knew the potential for his future.

The tormenting decision that Luisa faced 27 seven years ago drew her to marry Anton, but often during her married life she thought of Tom.

Her medical misdiagnosis of being bipolar, paranoid and delusional brought her to Tom to take on her personal injury case because he was so compassionate. Their passionate love relationship never left Luisa's mind and heart. Their relationship followed that old Italian proverb spoken to Luisa from her Grandmother, Nonni, who married her Vincent when she was only eighteen years old.

L'amore cert l'amore, fuoco e fiamme per un anno, cenere per trenta. Lampeedusa - Love, certainly lover, fire and flames for a year, then ashes for thirty years.

The openness of this conversation with Tom gave Luisa pause to consider another compelling decision of her life, just as she had done twenty-seven years ago.

The importance of dining together as Anton did often with Luisa read just like the phrase in the Treasure of Italian poems, Quotations and Proverbs book Senza Bacco a Cerere, Venere trema pel freddo – Without wine and food, Love grows pale.

This is why in their dating relationship many years ago Luisa was torn apart between Anton and Tom. Those chats over candlelight showed Anton as a true Italian romantic in his quiet loving ways.

With his thoughtful B.C. cartoons on the library table in college and the Cracker Jack box and its hidden treasures, Anton romanced Luisa for seven years before marriage. The little gestures went a long way. He might not have spoken with the compassionate words that Tom did, but his outward simple generous surprises kept Luisa at bay.

To this day in time, Luisa still has those treasures. She thanks the Lord that the snakes of Lee Sleazer that robbed her home only took the vinyl Treasures box of her youth, but Anton's gifts of silent love remain with Luisa, safely locked away.

When Tom told Luisa her months prior to this February 14th – "I do not want you to think less of me," – she didn't know what he meant, and she still doesn't know.

The destruction of his legal files had to have been done by Lee Sleazer's ruthless investigators. They would have known from their eavesdropping that a previous relationship had existed between Tom Freeby and Luisa.

Luisa was very upset. How in the 21st Century could a lawyer not have a backup system? Even Luisa's four-year-old niece knew it was necessary to back-up computer files.

Tom's self-pitying announcement that it was now going to cost him $500.00 to buy a back–up system did not move Luisa. Five hundred dollars was pennies compared to the Cannoli debt of over $250,000. And with college tuition and current and future medical bills that needed to be paid, a low settlement of $200,000 would leave the Cannoli's with only $120,000.

In the Treasury of Italian Love, Luisa remembers the one her grandmother and mother repeated to her over and over again many years ago - Amor non viva quando muor la speranza love no longer live is dead.

Luisa's inner feelings for Tom melted away as he spoke to her. How could he not have a back-up system for his files? This affected not only Luisa but would have certainly affected his other clients as well. Tom had gone to law school and ranked high in his class. He kept the scales of justice on his desk, but his frugal ways conflicted with the interests of his clients. Did he not realize that not having a back-up system for his legal files could open him up to malpractice? Should Luisa file a claim with the North County Legal Bar Association for this breech of legal services by Thomas Freeby?

Luisa now had to decide whether to accept the offer of $287,000. In reality, she would only receive $200,000, with Tom getting the balance of $87,500 as his attorney's fee. Her debt load as a result of the accident had now reached more than $250,000, which meant she would be losing $50,000 if she took the offer.

Part of her wanted to fight on until she was justly compensated for all her physical injuries and emotional pain. Yet she was both mentally and physically drained after her five-year battle with the unscrupulous people at Freedom Insurance.

Reluctant to endure any more torture, Luisa said, "I just can't keep living with this thing, Tom. I'm worn out. Tell the bastards that I accept their offer."

"Are you sure you want to do this?" Tom said, disbelief in his voice.

"What choice do I have, Tom? My family and I have to get on with our lives. The insurance company has the resources to keep us mired in litigation for the next ten years. I need to put this whole thing behind me."

"I think you've made the only decision you could, Luisa," Tom said. "As wrong as this outcome is, Freedom Insurance is a powerful financial giant that's almost impossible to fight. Maybe someday Congress will enact laws to give the average Joe an even playing field with the insurance behemoths."

"I doubt it, Tom," Luisa said dejectedly. "Not as long as there's a well-funded insurance lobby in Washington."

"I'm afraid you're right," Tom said. "I'll arrange for the settlement check to be processed. It should only take a couple of weeks."

As Luisa hung up, her shoulders sagged and she felt as if an icy hand had gripped her heart. She had suffered so much and fought so hard only to end up with an insurance settlement that wouldn't even pay all her medical bills and business losses. Wearily she sank down on the living room couch and began to weep bitterly.

Luisa made plans to drive to her niece's shower in Macon, Georgia. The road map was marked for construction zones. She decided to leave on Friday before the shower. She planned to visit and stay with Diana, her very best friend.

The following week, around 7:OO p.m., Luisa was lying in bed in her master bedroom reading Beyond the Light book by P.H.Y. Atwater, who nearly died three times in 1977 resulting from miscarriage complications.

In her most enlightening book on after death experiences, she wrote about the victims of trauma and their path to recovery over seven years.

It had been five years for Luisa, so she was hopeful that in two more years, perhaps her life would be somewhat back to normal. Her perceptions of viewing life, however, would be damaged as a result of the trauma to her brain and the PSTD, which causes permanent damage.

There are many different opinions on this subject worldwide. With the tragedy of September 11, 2001 in New York City and the loss of so many lives and damage to so many families, Luisa heard more and more about the real systems and treatments for PSTD. If nothing else, more people than ever before are now aware of its existence.

As she nestled comfortably in her bed covers, the telephone rang in her office downstairs. She decided to let the recorder pick up the call. It was Tom Freeby, but Luisa had no desire to talk with him.

He left a message – "Luisa, this is Tom. I'm at home and I'm listening to the local radio station 55. There is a product that I thought could help you with your pain. It is called Therma Care from Proctor and Gamble. It will be cheaper than your costly body massages. Take care and tell Anton hello. I'll see you soon. Goodbye."

Hearing Tom's message, Luisa thought that he was feeling guilty over getting such a low settlement. He deserves to feel guilty, Luisa thought.

Her lawyer friends had encouraged her to report Tom to the local bar association with a malpractice grievance. She was still sorting in her mind what to do. In any event, she chose not to call him back.

Instead, Luisa called her mom to tell her about Tom's message. Teresa told Luisa that Tom tried his best to recover all her financial losses. Her mom reminded Luisa that life has many ups and downs and in her 80 plus years she had experienced many of them. Dealings with insurance companies and the defense lawyers that help them keep their insurance money rather than paying their claims were more of the same.

Luisa reminded her mom that she would be heading to Macon, Georgia in the morning. It was 9:00 P.M. and time for an evening bath. She told her mom that she would talk to her later. They said, "Goodnight" to each other and hung up.

As Luisa drew her hot water for her hour of relaxation, she reflected on the past two years and getting to know Tom again. Aware of his four-day cardiac care hospitalization for his heart irregularity, she knew that he was also under stress with health worries. It was something he would have to sort out.

Tonight's telephone call showed Luisa that he cared about her, but his frugal ways had driven them apart again. Now his law license could be in jeopardy as a result of the choices he had made in life.

She retired to sleep thanking the Lord for still being alive. The Lord will guide me in the future was her last thought as she dozed off.

Luisa was ready to leave for Macon, Georgia. Anton expressed concern for her driving due to her difficulties with PSTD.

Luisa tried to reassure him that she had to conquer the problem, and reminded Anton that she had driven to Atlanta many times before her terrible accident.

What Luisa did not anticipate was that just south of Big Bone, Kentucky, the feelings of anxiety started to hit her. Her heart raced and her hands were clammy, and her anxious feelings would not go away.

The speeding cars and tractor-trailers flying past her with their turn signals on unsettled Luisa. With no cell phone, she regained her composure and dried the tears that rolled down her face. Will I ever have my life back? She screamed aloud in the car.

She took the next exit to call Anton and let him know where she was, but chose not to worry him, so she said nothing to him about her feelings of anxiety.

She got on the interstate again, but got only as far as Lexington, where she decided to stay that night. She called her family, and they reassured her that she had made the right decision by choosing to stay overnight.

Very early the next morning, Luisa rose to venture out on the interstate again. Determined to get to Macon, she prayed to St. Jude to help her overcome the black cloud that unexpectedly hovered over her.

Approaching Knoxville, Luisa decided that she would stay at the Clubhouse Inn and leave early again the next morning. She called Diana who truly understood Luisa because of their many, many years of friendship.

The Clubhouse Inn in Knoxville had a hot breakfast to start the next day. Luisa called Anton to reassure him that she was doing fine, but admitted she had been anxious. Anton told Luisa to call him immediately if she experienced any more anxiety attacks. She told him that she would.

Finally, 48 hours later, Luisa arrived at Diana's to get ready for the bridal shower. Manicures and pedicures for $15 for Diana and Luisa fit into their beauty budget.

So many friends were there to have a fun bridal shower. The luncheon was a sit-down affair, with lit candles adorning the Southern Living table. They enjoyed filet mignon, asparagus and Waldorf salad, and the meal was completed with chocolate mousse cake topped with ice cream and cherries.

Reminiscing with her niece, Laurie, they shared stories of when she was a young girl and the stories delighted all at the table and the room was filled with laughter.

They all had stories to share. From her white parakeet going everywhere with her to the making of homemade pizza with the family in the Cannoli kitchen as they watched the way Momma Mia Pizzaria made it. Except they left flour dough everywhere on the first floor of the Cannoli home, so much so that it took weeks to find it all. Only the two of them knew the whole story!

For dinner, Diana and her daughter, Lynda, took Luisa to the English Pub. They talked about their trip to London in 1999. The English Pub was very much like Cheshire's where Charles Dickens and Sam Johnson had dined. They discussed their vacation trip to Ponde Verdre that would be coming up over the Fourth of July holiday in a few months.

The next morning, Luisa awakened to the aroma of a blueberry pancakes, hot Peppermint tea and homemade cinnamon rolls. It was a real Southern breakfast prepared by Diana, a genuine Southern beauty and very talented hostess and cook. Luisa loved receiving her recipes.

The journey home began after the delicious breakfast. Luisa was determined to make it home in one day. She took numerous 20-minute breaks to help her regain her confidence, and after each break, she continued north. She vowed she would not give up. Come hell or high water, she would succeed. Luisa made the journey home in ten hours.

On March 15th, Luisa and Carmella arrived at Tom's law firm. When they walked into his office he looked tired. He rose and shook their hands, then indicated two chairs before his large cherry-wood desk.

Reaching into his desk drawer, Tom handed Luisa a Freedom Insurance Company check for $200,000 and apologized again for the low amount. Luisa told him that they would invest it conservatively and wisely. After a 40-minute meeting, Luisa and Carmella rose and shook hands goodbye with Tom. Luisa had mixed emotions as they left his office.

As they drove home Luisa spoke to Carmella about the true value of $200,000 in today's money. She spoke of home and car costs, as well as the cost of college educations for both Carmella and Rosanna. It was a brief lesson in economics for the teenage Carmella.

They arrived home and together prepared a spaghetti dinner for Anton. It was a quiet evening for the Cannolis and Luisa went to bed at 9:00 PM. Before tucking herself in, Luisa got down on her knees and thanked the Lord for the insurance settlement that would finally end her five-year long hellish ordeal.

The next day Luisa woke up feeling better than she had in a long time. It was time to rebuild her life and the lives of her family members. She called her best friend Diana in Georgia and they arranged for the two families to vacation together in July in Florida. When Anton came home Luisa told him about her plans and he agreed that the vacation would be a great idea. Carmella and Rosanne were also enthusiastic about the trip.

At long last it looked like the Cannoli family would once again begin enjoying life.

Chapter 22

The Rocky Road Back

Following the settlement with Freedom Insurance, the Cannolis prepared for their niece's coming wedding in Atlanta. Although Luisa was looking forward to the happy family event, she was also readying herself to take on her next daunting task – writing a book documenting the violation of her life over the past five years by Freedom Insurance.

Turning her painful experiences into a book would not be easy, for she would have to take mounds of notes, records, receipts and legal documents and weave them into a coherent story of her battle against the insurance company's injustice and deceit.

Time flew, and in April the Cannolis boarded a Great Wings airliner for the flight to Atlanta. The wedding was a joyous event – the niece who was getting married was a special favorite of Luisa and Anton – and all too soon the weekend was over and the Cannolis were back home in East Hills Valley.

They would soon find themselves on a plane again, however, thy soon would take their long-awaited Florida vacation with their very best friends, Arnold, Seth, Laura and Diana. The three couples had started vacationing together in the early 1990s. This year they planned to get together over the fourth of July holiday at Ponte Vedre Resort in Jacksonville Beach, a quiet and pristine beach resort with a beautiful golf course.

Luisa had been experiencing numbness in her arms while doing weight exercises and she now began the Post Analysis of Systems Therapy (P.A.S.T.). This was a four-week process to help patients learn how to ease pain. The support group included physical therapists - Dan and Ben - Dr. Stuart and many nurses were there to help.

At the same time that Luisa was beginning her P.A.S.T. rehabilitation, Carmella tried out for high school tennis and once again made the team. This made Luisa's all-day participation in the P.A.S.T. program most difficult. Faced with a major decision, Luisa chose to spend her time supporting Carmella's quest to excel at tennis.

Luisa's muscle spasms continued – sometimes so severely that she was embarrassed to go out in public – but she was determined not to take any medication to ease her discomfort. She had made up her mind never to take mind-altering drugs again, no matter how bad her physical pain became. Instead, she sought relief through thrice-weekly body massages.

One day that spring of 2002 Luisa received an unexpected letter of apology from Ocean Land Transportation, Inc., the company that owned the truck that had smashed into her car five years before.

Although Luisa appreciated the apology – however late – she still sometimes wished that she had had a jury trial, if only to have the chance to ask the members of the jury if they were aware of the severe injury she had sustained.

Luisa's latest task was to straighten out their credit rating, which had been ravaged by huge medical expenses and her loss of business income over the past five years. It took three months of constant communication to get the lateness status removed from twelve of their credit reports.

Luisa and Anton found not only lateness notices but also incorrect information, which in turn lowered their credit score. Somehow they managed to get all their credit information corrected and forwarded to their mortgage company and to credit bureaus.

As Luisa continued her physical and mental recovery through the spring of 2002, she decided one day that it was time to make a hair appointment at Mitchell's, her favorite spa and salon. Her friends at the salon had supported her through the past five years of living hell and had encouraged her plans to write a book about her painful experience.

Luisa was greeted warmly when she arrived at the salon. Hairdresser Annie Faye spotted several new gray strands in Luisa's hair and made them go away.

Another ten years off my age, Luisa thought.

Sara Marie, the salon's manicurist and pedicurist, helped minimize Luisa's arm, hand and foot pain with a nice long steam water treatment.

Adam, the masseuse, treated Luisa for one and a half hours with steam and a very deep tissue massage to help release pain. When Luisa's friends at Mitchell's had finished with her she felt like a new woman. Waving goodbye to everyone, she fairly skipped out the door ready to take on the world.

During the weeks before the Cannolis were to leave for Florida, Luisa was contacted by many of her friends and vendors who had heard of the closure and of the low settlement she had received in her personal injury case. Almost all insisted that legal/criminal action should be taken against both those perpetrators who had violated her life and the defense team that had schemed to deprive her of a just settlement.

Several of her friends volunteered to organize a bike marathon fundraiser – together with a collection and a raffle – to raise money to help the Cannolis pay Luisa's continuing medical expenses. Everyone knew that Luisa's design business had been destroyed by her ordeal, and that the family was hard-pressed financially.

Because the Cannolis were planning to leave at the end of June

2002 for a five-day holiday, Luisa would do this fundraiser in four weeks. It had to be organized. The vendors donated their wares. Luisa called some former students of hers from years past to ask them for suggestions. They had been special students to her 22 years earlier; special because that was the year Luisa was pregnant with Rosanna. At Christmas, the students had given Luisa special Baby Christmas ornaments – Hallmark, Lenox, handmade ornaments, Baby's 1st ornaments. Luisa and her family cherished those ornaments for many years of fond memories. Those ornaments were the ones stolen by defense attorney Sleazer and his team of snake investigators.

How violated their lives have been. It was so painful for Luisa to think about the audacity of illegal eavesdropping at Thanksgiving time, to realize that strangers had been listening to the Cannolis sing their Christmas carols in their great room and heard them playing their player piano.

They joyfully decorated their home traditionally at Thanksgiving school break to bring holiday cheer during all the weeks before Christmas. Nineteen Ninety-Nine was the very last year for those precious ornaments to be hung by Luisa's beautiful daughters on their trees.

Over the years, they would go and find real trees to set the holiday spirit and the fresh evergreen scents filled their home. The girls loved the weeks-long holiday spirit in their home with decorations throughout – Santas, candles, Christmas decorated picture frames, ferns, poinsettias, stockings and garnishments on the stone fireplace.

As Luisa spoke to her past students, they told her of their young families. They were now the same age that Luisa was when she taught them twenty-two years ago. Tracy and Jackie expressed a willingness to help, despite the fact that they had busy lives of their own.

Tracy suggested that she contact businesses for varied donations – car washes, massages, dinners, hotel get-aways. She was knowledgeable about marketing and promoting for good and worthwhile causes.

Within two weeks, donations were coming in. A beautiful sage green over white wool yarns Oriental rug was received from KAS in New York, and they received a contemporary brown-toned rug from Aria's Rugs in Cincinnati, Ohio.

Luisa gave her organizers - Betty, Nicole and Patti Jean - her Rolodex with all her friends, relatives and business vendors' names and addresses in it. They compiled a list and wrote letters for Luisa explaining the atrocities she had suffered since her major motor vehicle accident on July 22, 1997. The letter was simple and to the point, and Luisa signed it.

The organizers took charge of the mailer. The Raffle drawing date would be July 22, 2002. Luisa chose that date to give new meaning to the date. She hoped that by telling 450 of her friends what had happened to her that they would be more knowledgeable of insurance company tactics and lawyer games.

Luisa readied herself for the Ponte Verde trip. She felt some embarrassment for this fundraiser raffle as she had always been self-sufficient with her successful interior design business for twenty some years. But the support of so many people convinced her that their need to help and serve others was genuine.

One evening in June 2002 as the Cannoli family was planning their Florida vacation there was a sudden hard knock on their front door. Luisa answered the door and found a good-looking, well-groomed man dressed in a shirt and tie standing there.

"Yes?" Luisa said.

"Good evening. Are you Luisa Cannoli?"

Luisa nodded. "Yes, how can I help you?"

"I'm Detective Quaker from the East Chester Police Department. May I come in?"

"Of course," Luisa said, leading the policeman into the living room and indicating a chair. "May I ask what this is all about?"

"I'm here about the fundraiser being organized for you,"

Quaker said as he eased himself into the chair. "We're concerned that the fundraiser may not be entirely legal."

"What's the problem?" Luisa asked.

Quaker rubbed his palms together thoughtfully. "We know that the fundraiser itself is entirely legitimate. However, the raffle is another matter. It's a form of gambling. We're in the process of contacting the State Attorney's office to get the specific rules."

"This is so embarrassing," Luisa said, turning red. "I'm sure my friends who suggested the raffle had no idea there would be any problem. They're simply trying to help me pay off some medical bills I incurred after a terrible automobile accident five years ago."

Quaker nodded. "Don't worry, Mrs. Cannoli, we know you and your friends did not intentionally break any laws. However, we have received an inquiry about the raffle from the manager of one of the hotel chains that tickets were mailed to. He wanted to know whether this was a legitimate raffle, and – naturally – we had to look into it."

"This is so upsetting," Luisa said. "What would you advise me to do?"

"Like I said, we're waiting for a ruling on this from the State Attorney. In the meanwhile, I suggest that you stop your mailing and try to recover the raffle tickets that have already gone out."

"We're planning on going to Florida on vacation in early July," Luisa said. "Does this mean we have to stay home and await word from the State Attorney?"

"No, not at all," the detective said, rising from his chair. "Go on your vacation. I'm sure this matter will be straightened out soon. Good night."

Luisa let Detective Quaker out and sank wearily into the couch. She had thought that after the settlement had finally been won – even if the dollar amount was far below what it should have been – things would start going right for her and her family. Now she wondered if the difficult times were really over.

Luisa contacted an attorney and her accountant to be certain of the law and IRS requirements for such a fundraiser. She was advised to keep clear records and receipts and to treat the fundraiser like a business. Luisa was accustomed to this type of recordkeeping.

It took two weeks for the organizers to organize names, confirm donations, prepare the mailer and do the actual mailing. The mailings were in the hands of the US Postal Service one day before Luisa was leaving for Ponte Verde.

On Wednesday, July 1st, Luisa flew down to Florida. Rosanna was scheduled to arrive that night. Anton and Carmella had decided to drive down together and wouldn't get there for another day or two.

A rental car was ready for her at Dollar Car Rental at the Jacksonville Beach Airport. She checked into the Best Rest Hotel as their suite at the Ponte Vedra Resort wouldn't be available for a couple of days. Luisa was aware that since her accident she had quite frequently talked to total strangers about what was going on in her life. She had never been this outgoing before and she wondered whether her frank revelations about herself were another result of surviving her near death experience on the freeway that day in the summer of 1997.

In her extensive reading since the accident she had come across numerous accounts of other survivors of trauma going through mental, emotional and physical changes in their lives.

After checking in, Luisa decided to take a drive along the Atlantic Ocean. Not far from the hotel she noticed a roadside sign reading, Miss Loretta – Psychic. Although she had never consulted a psychic before, Luisa's curiosity got the better of her and she pulled into the parking lot before the red brick building where Miss Loretta's had her office.

She slowly got out of her rented car and tentatively walked up the four concrete steps to ring Miss Loretta's doorbell. A young woman about 20-years-old with long blond hair opened the door and asked Luisa how she could help her.

Luisa asked to have her Tarot cards read to her. Miss Loretta told Luisa that there would be a small $30 charge. Although Luisa was on a strict budget, she agreed to the psychic's fee. Miss Loretta led Luisa to a table and chairs in the middle of the room and began turning the cards over one at a time. To Luisa's surprise, Ms. Loretta told her that there were stressors in her life.

"I sense that you were in the hospital last year," the psychic said.

Luisa nodded but said nothing.

"I see that you and your family have been through much suffering over the past several years," Miss Loretta continued. "The cards tell me that you have either two or three children – girls. Am I correct?"

"Two," Luisa said. "And, yes, they're girls."

Miss Loretta went on to reveal several other things about Luisa that were uncannily true. Finally, at the end of the session, the young psychic gave Luisa a clear crystal quartz pendant to wear close to her heart to relieve her of her stresses.

As Luisa was leaving, Miss Loretta handed her a business card in case she needed her psychic help in the future. They parted most amicably and Luisa drove back to the Best Rest to prepare to meet Rosanna at the airport later that night.

Rosanna's plane was on time and they found a small diner for a late dinner. Luisa was thrilled to have her oldest daughter with her. As they ate they chatted excitedly about all the fun they were going to have on the beach, although they did worry a bit about the forecast for rain over the next several days.

They decided to wait for Anton and Carmella to arrive before they made any final sightseeing arrangements. After dinner they went to the beach fronting the Best Rest and took a long walk on the sand as the stars and moon shone high above the ghost white surf.

The next morning Rosanna rose early to walk the beach while Luisa relaxed around the pool. The rest of the day passed lazily as mother and daughter caught up on each other's lives and basked in the warm Florida sun.

Despite the stress-free day, Luisa had another restless night. When would this stop? When would she finally be able to let go of the memory of the torturous years she had lived through? It didn't help, of course, that her physical pain was a constant reminder of the accident and the terrible times that had followed.

As Luisa lay tossing and turning, she thought of the family's precarious financial situation. Rosanna's final year of college would cost up to $21,000 for tuition and board, and Carmella would be entering college in only two more years. Where would she and Anton get the money?

Luisa hoped to return her design business to the successful level it had once enjoyed, but the business would take time to rebuild. Then there was the problem of the fluctuating stock market where they had much of their savings.

Lying there in the dark Luisa wondered how she could relax on the beach for five days with all those worries weighing her down. Desperately seeking relief from her stress, she concentrated on remembering all the happy times she had had with her family and friends over the years.

She then thought of the solace she had found in prayer. She had prayed to the Lord, St. Jude, and St. Michael the Archangel and she felt that her prayers had done much to get her through the roughest times.

The steps to recovery are like the layers of an onion, she thought, remembering Erika Coleman's award-winning poem the *Onion Told.*

> *I was once told of a onion stink*
> *and the juice that makes you cry,*
> *was the replacement of a bitter heart*
> *with in no one shall pry.*

Unforgiveness is the force that bring
the onion to the door.
The ones that try to get inside makes
the onion grow some more.
Even though you seem to do all you can
to get the onion away.
The toughness of each and every layer
gets stronger every day.
A needed help came along with a voice
real soft and warm.
Take your time in forgiving the ones
you think did you some harm.
As you peel and cry layer by layer
until you get to the core,
rip it out and tear it up and
bitterness no more.
-- Erika Coleman

The next day Luisa and Rosanna checked into the Ponte Vedra Resort to await Anton, Carmella and their friends. Everyone soon arrived and the fun began. The children played on the beach and swam in the ocean and pool.

Arnold and Seth played golf every day while Anton relaxed beside the pool with a book. Luisa, Laura and Debra sprawled out in beach chaises sipping cool Mimosas. The three women also went to the resort Spa on July 4th for a total therapeutic massage and Spa treatment. The treatment greatly lowered Luisa's pain level and she was finally able to relax.

That evening they all went down to the beach to enjoy a wonderful fireworks display that was a fitting tribute to America's Independence Day.

Unfortunately, the next day the quartz necklace the psychic had given Luisa fell from her neck and simply vanished. Luisa heard it hit the hardwood floor but she could not find it anywhere. For some reason, the loss of the pendant upset Luisa more than she could have imagined.

On July 6 everyone packed to head home, taking with them fond memories of the fun and sun they had enjoyed together in Florida.

A month after the Cannolis returned from Florida, Rosanna returned to college in Boston while Carmella prepared to go enter her junior year in high school and resume her tennis play.

With her family all occupied with their own pursuits, Luisa did not know what to do with herself. Her sister, Anna, tried to convince her to restart her design company. Luisa agreed that it was a good idea, but decided to start out slowly by helping Anna choose a color scheme for the remodel and redecoration her family was doing on their suburban home.

At the same time, one of Luisa's designer friends, Dolores Parker, needed an expert designer for her business in hopes that sales would increase. She called Luisa to ask if she would join her company. Luisa told her that she could not join her at that time as she was still undergoing some medical treatments. Possibly in the fall, she told her friend.

Shortly afterward, Luisa spotted an ad in Home Bargains magazine about a design show scheduled for early fall. The cost to participate was low. All one had to do was set up a booth with a display. She contacted Dolores and suggested that she participate in the show. Dolores declined. Luisa could not figure that one out. Her friend wanted business but would not advertise.

Luisa still saw possibilities in the show and called one of her business vendors, Kate, owner of Kate's Light Shop. She suggested to Kate that they share the cost of the booth. Luisa would highlight her design work, and Kate could advertise her lighting talents.

Kate thought it was a great idea and the two women agreed to share costs. Financially, they were both on tight budgets, but they soon got some unexpected and deeply heartfelt help from a lot of very wonderful people.

When Luisa's former vendors found out that she was trying to rebuild her design business and would be hosting a booth at the show, offers of assistance started pouring in. Wallpaper, paint, wood and trim, carpet, fabrics, furniture, and labor were all donated to help restart her in the design world.

As Luisa's rehabilitation continued to progress and she began to slowly ease her way back into design work, her mind turned more and more to her coming book *Violation*.

Luisa Cannoli had no way of knowing whether her book would truly help others. Yet she felt deeply that if making her story public brought solace to even a single other human being, then all her years of suffering would not have been in vain.

As bad as her pain sometimes got, Luisa continued to do all she could to get her life back on track. She, Suzanne, Anne and Caroline devoted much of their time to the monthly dinners they hosted at Ronald McDonald House. The four women would meet for breakfast at Marx Bagels, Pannera Bread or First Watch to plan their meals before beginning their busy days.

Although Luisa's schedule was now becoming increasingly busy, she applied for teaching jobs at four local schools. She got several calls concerning her applications, but no job offers. Although she had been a teacher for eight years, she had not set foot in a classroom for the past 20 years, and apparently her long absence dissuaded prospective employers from hiring her.

Anton tried to help by giving Luisa numerous books on resumes and how to begin a new career at age 50. All the books helped but Luisa knew that the real difficulty lay in the tough competition she was getting from newly graduated teachers who were willing to work for a lower salary.

Luisa next tried advertising her design abilities. She prepared a flyer highlighting her talents and considerable experience but – much to her dismay and discouragement – no calls came in.

Determined to find a job, Luisa gave her resume to Betty Bloom – the mother of one of the other players on Carmella's tennis team – after Betty expressed an interest in having her basement remodeled and her living room painted.

One day in September 2002, Luisa happened to browse through a local publication called Reach Magazine, which featured ads for area vendors, and saw an ad for Home Builders Association Housetrends for October 2002. Fall was approaching and – Luisa knew from past years – fall was a great time for home updates for the holidays. Luisa called Housetrends and spoke to Michael Keley about the show and learned that participating would be reasonable.

Knowing her friend Kate at the Light and Interiors Showroom needed to advertise, Luisa called her to partner and she agreed. Dolores was also called to participate, but she declined.

Plans went forward, and all her business friends who participated in the fundraiser were at Luisa's show. Once again, Paxton Woods donated the display boards and crown mouldings, Ante Carpet donated the golden carpet, and the paint store helped out with wallpaper and paints. Light and Interiors Store, Designs for your Entire Home Studio and Dolores came through with some accessories. Boone Fabrics discounted fabrics, Franks discounted potpourri for the guests, and Hancock's discounted the netting for the sachet for the handouts along with ribbon.

The booth was fragrant with the smells of fall floral lavender and there was mint in the air. It was colorful too, the maroon back wall contrasted with soft golden shades of sage green with deep blue touches in the fabric of the window treatments designed by Luisa and sewn by Suzanne. And there were colorful window swags, triangles and country swags.

As it turned out, their design/lighting booth was the only one of its kind at the show and was a big hit. Luisa also met some wonderful people who – when they heard about her plans to write a book about her ordeal – encouraged her literary effort and promised to buy copies of her book.

Luisa's plans to write her book were gathering more steam with each passing day. She had kept a daily journal for the past years, recording much of the raw material that would go into telling her tragic story.

She wisely decided to seek the help of those in the literary field, and visited Little Reader's Book Store in an East Hill Valley shopping center. She told the owner about her goal to publish a book and he advised her to research the talented editors and ghostwriters listed in Writer's Digest. That was a huge stepping-stone.

She spoke to many other people in various vocations about the possibility of publishing her book. She needed to get a feel for marketability of such a book. At every turn she was encouraged to go forward. The professionals she spoke to even gave her their business cards, and told her that they wanted to buy a copy of her book once it was published. Some even volunteered to put her in touch with people they knew in the media. She was also advised to put the book online and to get a publicist.

Wanting to do all she could to realize her dream of being published, Luisa and Anton went to one of Peter Lowe's Success seminars, events highlighted by high profile speakers. At the seminar she and Anton attended, George and Barbara Bush gave the keynote speech.

It was a small crowd and everything was very personable. Peter Lowe showed a movie on how he became successful. He revealed how he had started out by asking people on the street what their meaning of success was. He found that their answers comprised a very valuable tool.

By August 2002 many people had responded to the mailing about the Cannoli fundraiser. It brought tears to Luisa's eyes as she read the many prayer groups notes and beautiful cards. Her feelings of embarrassment left her as she recognized the uncritical selflessness of those who help others in need.

On her road to recovery this was another baby step, as Jim Borgman's 9/11 editorial cartoon so aptly portrays.

By permission of John L. Hart FLP, and Creative Syndicate, Inc.

By August 2002 Luisa had lost more than 100 pounds and now the Liz Claiborne clothes she'd bought in 2000 were too big. She knew she couldn't afford a new wardrobe so she took her old sweaters, slacks, jackets and skirts to Robby at Quality Alterations to be altered. Robby promised to have her winter clothes ready for her by October.

From Robby's Luisa went to Specialized Undergarment Design Studio, as she had a gift certificate from her sister Alexia. Like her clothes, her underwear was way too big and at times embarrassing to wear. Luisa had fun choosing new underwear and pajamas.

Her huge weight loss had made her feel youthful again and she had regained her long-absent sense of self-esteem and self-worth.

Luisa had taken the first steps on her still rocky road back to the life she had known five long years before.

Chapter 23

Moving On

In October of 2002, Luisa started calling mortgage companies to see if she could refinance their high interest mortgage. She found that the mortgage officers at World Mortgage Company were exceptionally helpful and decided to refinance through them.

The Cannolis began getting their financial records in order in preparation for submitting their paperwork to World Mortgage Company. They applied for an interest-only loan at a rate of 3% for ten years, but the closing costs were $6,000, which was included in the first mortgage loan at a cost of $6,500.

It was explained to the Cannolis that the reduced interest rate would result in an $800 savings per month that would lower their payment significantly by paying only the interest on the loan. The other option would be to invest the difference for ten years in a safe investment. The decision would be Anton's, as ongoing medical and tuition costs were his responsibility and the priority was to keep from borrowing any further.

Luisa got back into her charity work and just before Thanksgiving she made a huge pot of succotash to take to the Drop Inn Center for the homeless to enjoy with their turkey dinner. Helping the needy was a Cannoli family tradition, and for many years they had been providing food gifts to the Drop

Inn Center.

As Luisa drove downtown with the hot succotash she prayed endlessly that the coming holidays would bring joy to both her family and the unfortunates at the Center. She also prayed over whether she should contact the FBI again about the items stolen from her home. She wanted so much to go to the FBI, but she was still angry and disappointed with the Bureau for not returning her call when she had contacted their office in June 2001.

As she pulled up to the Center, her friend Donald Mellow – who worked at the facility – was standing outside on the sidewalk. He greeted her warmly and took the heavy pot of succotash from her.

Needing badly to talk to someone about her dilemma, Luisa told Donald of her indecision over whether to once again report the burglaries of her home to the FBI.

"Perhaps it would be best if you left your decision up to the Lord," Donald said. "In time, He will provide an answer."

"You're absolutely right, Donald," Luisa said, giving her friend a hug. "As a matter of fact, I have been praying over this."

"Have faith, Luisa. The Lord will answer your prayers."

"I know," Luisa smiled. "I guess I'm just impatient to know what to do."

"I'll pray for you as well," Donald said. "And thank you for the succotash. I'm sure everyone at the Center will enjoy it at Thanksgiving."

As Luisa drove home she was warmed by Donald's comforting words. He was truly a man of God in his selfless work and in his giving heart. That night, Luisa slept well for the first time in weeks.

After a wonderful family Thanksgiving, the Cannolis began planning for Christmas. Anton bought new Christmas ornaments to decorate the tree and before long Rosanna arrived home from college.

Much to the Cannoli's shock, when the day arived to close the
new loan for refinancing their home, the underwriter cancelled
the closing at the last minute. Luisa and Anton called to find out
what happened, and were shocked to hear that the underwriter
found twelve late payments on Luisa's credit report, and had
decided to back out as a result.

Luisa was extremely upset to say the least. She knew that she
had reported a case of identity theft in January of 2000, but had
not realized that it would still be coming back to haunt her again
now, when she and Anton were trying to rebuild their life. She
resolved herself to the news, and began the process of contact
the three credit bureaus, and disputing the late payments. To
her surprise, when the bureaus re-examined her credit report,
they found that she had never been late at all! The credit report
was updated, and the closing on the house was rescheduled for
two months later by the underwriter. Another delay, but at least
the problem was resolved. The bureaus suggested that Luisa
contacted the Federal Trade Commission to report any further
instances of identiy theft, or unusual activity on her credit report.
Luisa agreed, and tried to focus on the upcoming Christmas
celebration.

To everyone's surprise and dismay, Rosanna found two
crumpled computer paper boxes in the attic containing several
of their missing Christmas ornaments. When Luisa saw them,
she knew for certain that they were part of the original boxful of
ornaments stolen by Freedom Insurance Company snakes - the
expensive Waterford, Lenox and Christopher Radko, along with
the handmade petit point needlework ones given to her by Mary
Ellen many years ago. Only one remained in the crumpled box,
and only one Lenox one for the dog, Princess. This devastated
Luisa, but it verified to her doubtful family this strange and
ruthless theft.

The only explanation that Luisa could think of for the
reappearance of some of the stolen ornaments was that Lee Sleazer

had had his operatives return a few of the bulbs to further torture her.

This blatant cruelty so appalled Luisa that she suddenly started crying. Rosanna and Carmella tried to console her by reminding their mother that they'd all embarked on a new beginning. Although Luisa greatly appreciated her daughters' caring words, the sight of the few old ornaments that had been returned made her remember all the other family treasures that the snakes had stolen.

During the weeks before Christmas, Luisa worked hard on picking up her holiday spirit. By Christmas Day, she had recovered her composure and was brimming with the spirit of the season. Her gift to her loving family that year was a long-postponed two-week Hawaiian Holiday. The Cannolis would spend 14 glorious days in June 2003 enjoying the wonders of Maui, Kona, Kauai and Oahu.

Anton, Rosanna and Carmella were all surprised and delighted with Luisa's Christmas gift, and they embraced her with big hugs and happy kisses.

"This is wonderful, Luisa," Anton said. "Lord knows we could all use two weeks in paradise. But what about the expense? We're on a pretty tight budget."

Luisa smiled. "Don't worry, Anton, our Hawaiian vacation is going to cost very little. Our airfare and accommodations are mostly paid for already through credits we had with the airlines and our travel club. And Charlotte Booby from World-Wide Travel has arranged for an inexpensive car rental and found us budget tours of the islands."

"Fantastic!" Anton said. "Tell you what, I'll bring the camcorder and take videos of our vacation. We can show them to the family when we get home."

"Can I bring my friend Ashley along?" Carmella asked excitedly.

"I think that would be fine as long as her parents pay for her airfare and extra activities like snorkeling and surfing," Luisa said.

The Christmas of 2002 turned out to be one of the most joyous holidays the Cannolis had ever known. The player piano and Sony recorder were going all day, filling their home with traditional Christmas songs and carols. Luisa felt so blessed as she laughed and sang together with her beautiful daughters and her wonderful husband.

With the holidays past, Luisa spent the three months from January to March 2003 doing design consultations and small projects for new clients she had met through her display at the Housetrends Kitchen and Bath Show.

She also continued to work on her book, and shared her progress with her family, clients and friends. Everyone encouraged her, and it seemed like almost every day more people told her that they would buy her book when it was finished early in 2004.

Luisa also resumed her rehabilitation at Tri-Health Pavilion Spa to deal with her chronic pain syndrome. Her masseuse Kevin used LaStone Massage, an increasingly popular form of thermotherapy.

Most of the medical world had come to view thermotherapy – the alternating application of heat and cold to the body to alter physiological responses – as the most effective massage technique yet discovered. The purpose of the therapy was to intentionally disturb the body's balance, or homeostasis, by alternating hot and cold treatments.

The alternating of hot and cold increases – or decreases – blood flow to specific areas more effectively than either one separately. The healing that results from more efficient blood flow in turn enhances the immune system.

Luisa's schedule through the early winter months of 2003 was flexible and she had time to do research on the next step along her road to the publication of her book: finding a good ghostwriter and editor. Working with Writers Digest, she was put in touch with Richard Moran, a best selling author who also ghostwrote and edited books.

Luisa called Richard at his home in Carson City, Nevada and the two hit it off immediately. After giving Richard a detailed synopsis of her story, they agreed to meet to discuss the project.

She took a hot bath, applied Tresor Lancôme Lotion from head to toe, put on her make-up and dressed in a sage Capri skirt and matching sweater from Liz Claiborne. She was now ready for her first exciting first day exploring the world of literature and book promotion.

When she walked outside she found Anton washing both his own car and Carmella's. A typical male, washing and waxing cars was a Saturday ritual for Anton, and she knew it would take him a good part of the day.

As Luisa neared, Anton straightened and looked at her strangely. "Do you have a bra on?" he asked.

Men! Luisa thought. The first thing they notice about a woman is her breast.

"I'm wearing my thin black bra today because I'm going to negotiate business with men! Put it down to a woman's wiles."

Anton didn't find Luisa's little joke amusing. "I think you should change bras!"

"Naturally, you're my husband. Bye."

Flashing her wickedest smile, Luisa leaned forward and gave Anton a loving kiss, then started her car and drove away. In her rearview mirror she could see Anton standing in the drive with a dripping sponge in his hand staring after her.

Beside her on the seat Luisa had a stack of information packets on her coming book which she intended to hand out that day. Her first stop was at the Little Readers Book Store.

She went into the store to see Paul, the owner, but he was not there today. Instead, a friend of Paul's – a Chinese man from Taiwan named Litsu was busy dusting book spines on the shelves. He introduced himself and the two exchanged pleasantries.

"I was hoping that Paul would be here today because I'm writing a book and wanted to talk to him about it."

"Really, you are writing a book?" Litsu said, a look of interest in his eyes. "What's it about?"

Luisa told Litsu her story. When she finished she added, "The primary reason I'm writing a book about my ordeal is to help others who have been cruelly treated by insurance companies."

"That is a worthy objective," Litsu said. "Perhaps I can help you. I am a journalist. I write a daily column on events in America for a Taiwanese newspaper. I believe my publisher would be interested in your story. If your book is translated into Chinese, you might make many sales in Taiwan."

Luisa was thrilled. "I can't tell you how much I'd appreciate your help," she said. "If you'll give me your card, I'll call you when my book is done."

"Of course, Litsu said, handing Luisa his business card.

Luisa looked down at the card. "It says here that you're also an author."

"Yes, I am presently finishing a book on the old Taiwanese language. My goal is to keep it flourishing in Taiwan."

Luisa and Litsu talked for another half hour, then Luisa thanked him again and the two said a warm goodbye. What a fortuitous meeting, Luisa thought as she drove away. Or maybe it was fate.

Luisa's next stop was at the Book Store to meet Steve Kissing, author of *Running from the Devil.* He was there to sign his book and meet potential readers. Luisa had heard of him through one of her HBA House Trends clients she had met last fall at the show.

After waiting in line, she met Steve Kissing and he signed his book for her. She then told the author about her book project.

"Please email me some information on your book and I'll do what I can to help you," Kissing said. "I'd also appreciate an email telling me if you enjoyed my book."

Luisa promised to email the author, and then went to have

lunch at The Pub. While ordering, she started a conversation with her waiter Jason and ended up sharing her story with him. Like most people, Jason was shocked at what he heard.

After lunch, she met with her copyright attorney Alfred Scott to go over her book project and Richard's credentials and contract. Luisa was excited by Scott's overall support and enthusiastic endorsement of Richard.

"I'm in your corner, Luisa," Scott said. "I can't tell you how appalled I am at how ruthlessly and shamelessly Freedom Insurance has treated you. I wish you every success in your publishing endeavor."

Luisa next contacted her travel agent Charlotte Booby and arranged for an economical roundtrip airfare to Nevada and back. She then gathered up her stacks of legal files, records and manuscript pages and in late February 2003 boarded a plane for Reno, the nearest city with a commercial airport to Richard's home.

For two days Luisa and Richard met at his home overlooking the western slopes of the majestic snow-capped Sierra Nevada. During their intensive discussions of Luisa's story and how best to present it to the reading public, they poured over legal documents, medical files and Luisa's handwritten records.

Richard's wife Annie, a novelist and editor in her own right often joined them. Annie added many valuable insights to their literary talks, and by the end of Luisa's visit the three writers were in complete accord about the direction of the book.

"This is not going to be an easy book to put together," Richard cautioned. "But if we persevere I believe we'll be able to create a work that we will all be proud of."

Luisa flew back to East Hills Valley feeling that the writing of her book was in good hands, and that she had made two wonderful new friends as well.

Following her return from Nevada, Luisa called her typist and asked her to help prepare a letter about her book to the members of her Elite 450 Club. She wanted all her friends and colleagues in the design industry to have a chance to buy her book, and indeed – even before the book had been written – she had already sold several copies.

A month later – in April 2003 – Luisa sent her attorney Tom Freeby the following letter:

Dear Tom:

I am back from my trip out west.

This letter is a formal request for written clarification of what you told me that February 2002 afternoon regarding what happened to your database – which caused you to say to me that you had to withdraw from my personal injury case because all of the data was lost.

I need this written confirmation immediately.

Thank you very much.

Most sincerely,
Luisa Cannoli

Two days after sending Tom Freeby the letter, Luisa received a letter back from him. Her heart thudded in her chest and her hands got sweaty as she opened it up.

Dear Luisa:

I am in receipt of your April 9, 2003 letter addressed to me. I do not know what you are talking about. I did not have any of your data on my database. I did not lose any of your information. I have given you your entire file. I did not tell you that I had to withdraw from representing you in your personal injury case because all your data was lost.

Your case is over. You received more in settlement than I believe a North County jury would have given you. You have got to close this episode in your life. My representation of you is over. I am not going to respond to any more letters I receive from you concerning your personal injury case.

I wish the best to you, Anton and your daughters.

Very truly yours,
Thomas Freeby

Luisa could not believe Tom's reply. How could he deny that he had lost her data files when he had specifically told her and Anton that this had indeed happened?

Luisa had taken notes during the conversation with Tom in February 2002. Those notes read, "Tom says that all of the data in his computer was lost including e-mails, except one received from Anton about settlement amount possibilities."

As Luisa reread his response letter, her thoughts flashed back to a movie that she had rented from Blockbuster when dealing with Michael Wright in April 2000. It was *Liar, Liar* with Jim Carey. This movie depicts the dual role of living as both an honest and dishonest lawyer.

By permission of John L. Hart FLP, and Creative Syndicate, Inc.

Good ole Mr. Thomas Freeby fits that mold, Luisa thought bitterly. She knew from working with Tom on her case that his memory was still good at age 54. So how could he not know what she meant? And how could he add insult to injury by writing, "You received more in settlement than I believe an North County jury would have given you."

If he'd had so little confidence in winning a large settlement, why did he have Anton and Luisa sign demand letters for $775,000 and $550,000? Luisa was both baffled and hurt by Tom's letter, and she crumpled it up and tossed it aside.

Reflecting on the fact that she had once almost married Tom but had instead chosen Anton, she realized once again that she had made the right decision. Anton's support, understanding and endless patience through the past five terrible years had been the rock she'd anchored her shipwreck of a life to.

Although they had at times had disagreements and heated quarrels, their shared ordeal had also drawn them closer together. They had walked through the gates of hell and somehow emerged from the flames singed but whole.

They were talking to each other frequently again and – perhaps more important – understanding and empathizing with what the other was saying. Their romantic life had also been rekindled. Two weeks ago they had even gone out on a "date," enjoying a night together at the symphony.

Unfortunately, during the performance Luisa's neck injury began causing her excruciating pain and they were forced to leave early and return home. Through the entire episode Anton was nurturing and supportive, and even though she was in considerable pain Luisa felt a surge of love for her kind and considerate husband.

The next morning was a Saturday and Luisa awoke feeling much better. She had several appointments that day to promote her upcoming book.

On the way home, she decided to visit her old friend Geraldine who now worked at USA Quik Stop where she sometimes bought gasoline for her car. Their friendship went back many years, as she had once dated Anton's brother, Joseph. They used to play ping-pong in Anton's back yard when they were both dating the Cannoli young men.

Geraldine had already told others about Luisa's motor vehicle accident and subsequent battle with Freedom Insurance. She gave Luisa the names of several people who wanted an information packet on Luisa's coming book. Luisa was surprised and delighted, and gave Geraldine a big hug. As Luisa drove home, she thought about all the support she was getting from good friends like Geraldine.

Another friend, Tony Spacetti, had translated her book promo letter into Italian for her relatives in Sicily and for his friends throughout Italy.

She had also received letters from friends who encouraged her to write her book.

Luisa received the following letter from a friend who lived in Spain and South America:

April 23, 2003

My Luisa,

Autoaotinfacaïin noso tros noticia por merecedor tgriunfo, pora. Usted ofectuoso felicitacin.

We heard news of your worthy triumph, with affectionate congratulations.

Joy
Adielo

One of Rosanna's close friends, Jessica, wrote to the Cannolis following her graduation party.

Dear Mr. and Mrs. Cannoli,

I am so glad you were able to celebrate with us on Sunday! It was really nice to see you both. We will have to find another reason to celebrate soon! Have a great summer and good luck with the book! Thanks again.

Love,
Jessica

They were deeply touched by the Jessica's support and her letter prompted Luisa to continue Sarah Ban Breathnach's Something More Excavation of Herself, a journey begun at the beginning of the 2001 year and which take a long time to complete.

Luisa called Jessica and thanked her for the nice card. She shared with Jessica a goal that she had set for herself four years ago during the worst time of her life, a time filled with violations and financial decisions to face.

She had told herself then that if she set her priorities right and was selfless in reaching her goal, she would set up the Cannoli Foundation to help those with financial needs because they had been robbed of their savings, or to help defray the costs of medical specialists and co-pays not reimbursed by the insurance companies.

It would take substantial funding, but with God's guidance to help her find the right people to be in charge, this goal could be attained. The sales of millions of books could pave that path, and to do so was Luisa's dream.

The next day the Cannolis went to Palm Sunday Mass to Praise the Lord. It was a beautiful service that renewed them all. As they left the church, Luisa felt more strongly than ever that both her recovery and her book project would be successful.

The Lord was with her, and she had complete faith that He would guide her down the path to her journey's end.

Chapter 24

True Friends

In early 2003 Luisa started receiving telephone calls from people wanting Swanstone products, which she used in her bathroom and kitchen design work. Swanstone is a synthetic material for shower walls, tub surrounds, basins, sinks, vanity tops and kitchen counters. The product comes in a variety of colors: solids and granite type.

That February one of the calls materialized into an appointment with a client. Conveniently, the client lived in Luisa's neighborhood. He wanted a bathroom design and Luisa agreed to meet him at his home the following week.

In preparing for the call Luisa organized her resume and decided to include her book packet in the hope that the client might be interested in her story. She arrived on time and Mr. And Mrs. Patrick Cruise greeted her at the door.

She gave Mr. Cruise her resume and book packet. He glanced briefly at the packet, and then said, "Why don't we go take a look at the bathroom and you can fill us in on your design ideas and prices."

Luisa thought at first that she should not have brought her book packet to their first meeting. However, when they returned to the kitchen to discuss the project Mr. Cruise picked up the packet again and began reading. Soon he was shaking her head in wonderment. Although Luisa was dying to ask him what he thought about her proposed book, she decided that for now it was best to concentrate on her redesign of the Cruise bathroom.

She and the couple discussed the project for several minutes more, and then arranged a second meeting for the following week.

"I can come over on either Tuesday or Thursday," Luisa said. "Which day is best for you two?"

Mrs. Cruise looked at her husband and said, "Honey, what night next week are you volunteering at the firehouse?"

"Thursday," Mr. Cruise answered.

"Do you by any chance work at the East Hill Valley Firehouse," Luisa asked sheepishly, wondering if Mr. Cruise had been one of the volunteers who had come to her home during her medical crisis in January 2000.

"Yes," Mr. Cruise said. "I was one of the fireman who helped load you into the ambulance when you had that medical emergency a couple of years ago."

Luisa's face turned beet red. "Were you in my bedroom?"

"No, I was out in your driveway the entire time. I must say; you look a lot better now than you did that night."

"I'm so embarrassed," Luisa said.

"Don't be," Mr. Cruise said. "These things happen to all of us."

Luisa and the Cruises shook hands goodbye and Luisa headed home, heartened by the fact that Mr. Cruise had seen her at her absolute worse yet was still willing to entrust her with a design project in his home.

Plans finally materialized for Luisa, Suzanne, Anne, and Caroline to volunteer once a month at the Ronald McDonald House for families with children needing extensive medical treatments at Children's Hospital.

The close friends met for early morning breakfast at Perkins Pancake House to discuss the dinner meals for that month. They planned to rotate a main dish, salad, dessert, and breads each month. Suzanne organized the schedule.

Luisa looked forward to this volunteer project. She knew that the worthwhile work would fulfill her inner desire to help children and at the same time provide support to their families in their time of need.

Luisa decided to serve meatloaf as her main dish for the first meal they would prepare. The others brought green beans, mashed potatoes and cherry cake. The families really enjoyed that meal. They thanked the friends for taking the time to help.

While helping out at the Ronald MacDonald House, Luisa saw the pain in the parents' eyes as they spoke about their children stricken with terminal cancer, liver disease, lung problems, and heart and circulatory failure.

She prayed for the recovery of the children, yet many remained at the House for long periods of time. One night, a young blond three-year-old hugged Suzanne and called her his friend. All of Luisa's stresses were put on a back burner.

As the friends cleaned up after the evening meal they always knew that they did their job with unselfish love in their hearts for the children and their families. They scheduled their next planning session at Marx Bagels for the next week.

Luisa looked forward to this gathering with Anne, Suzanne, and Caroline. They laughed. They joked. They spoke of their own kids and life in general. For those two hours bi-weekly, Luisa's mind was distracted from the violations of her life by Freedom Insurance. Caroline said that their luncheons were cheaper therapy for Luisa than seeing a psychiatrist.

Luisa treasured the love and support of her true friends. They had stuck it out for Luisa, and she knew that she would not have had the strength to expose the violations of her life without their diligent help.

By helping out at the Ronald McDonald House monthly, Luisa found herself better able to adjust to the priorities in her life. A smile on an ill child's face melted Luisa's heart as she served the child a dessert and a surprise toy from the basket Suzanne brought.

She realized that the struggles in life can be overwhelming but in serving others unselfishly you can get much more in return. Luisa's life was getting to be more balanced, even though she still had to struggle to focus on the task at hand.

In April 2003 Luisa attended a seminar to learn how to set up a website to promote her upcoming book. While there she met a private investigator that became interested in her story.

The PI advised her to contact cowboy attorney Hoss Cartman and ask him if he would represent her in a criminal and civil action against Lee Sleazer and his investigators. The next day Luisa sat down and wrote a letter to Cartman.

She followed this up with a fax to Greg Madison on March 25, 2003 inquiring about the statute of limitations on pursuing legal action against those who had robbed her home and tapped her phone.

A week later Luisa received a faxed reply from Madison saying that he would require a $1,000 retainer before he could advise her about the statute of limitations for criminal and civil action. After reading Madison's fax, Luisa weighed her options. With her debt load, low insurance settlement and, hardly any secondary supplemental income, it would not be easy to pay the attorney's requested retainer. Besides, Madison's legal fees would only continue to grow.

She contemplated writing a detailed letter to the ACLU to ask if one of their attorneys could handle her case but decided to wait until she had exhausted all possibilities to hire her own attorney on a contingency basis.

In early April 2003, Luisa wrote back to Greg Madison giving him additional information in the hope that he would take her case on contingency. Unfortunately, the attorney wrote back declining to participate in her case without being paid a fee upfront.

A week later Luisa went in for her annual breast examination. As she waited for her mammogram test results, she noticed that the elderly lady sitting next to her was reading a paperback and smiling.

Wanting to be friendly, Luisa turned to the woman and said, "It looks like you enjoy reading."

"Oh heavens yes," the woman replied.

Her response opened a conversation between the two of them and before they left the doctor's office they exchanged names and telephone numbers. The woman's name was Rebba Marie and she was a retired art teacher. Within a couple days, Rebba Marie called Luisa and they arranged to meet for dinner. It was the beginning of a new friendship for Luisa.

Over dinner, Luisa explained her art school concept to Rebba Marie. An exchange of creative ideas followed and over time Rebba Marie became a valued advisor to Luisa as she made plans to establish her art school.

Soon after her dinner with Rebba Marie, Luisa decided to send her new book packet to Oprah Winfrey along with a complimentary box of Italian dessert cannolis. She had some cannolis specially baked at the Wyoming Pastry in Wyoming, Ohio and arranged to have them packed in dry ice for shipment.

That spring Luisa received two requests for design work: her sister Anna asked her to help pick out new furniture, rugs, and accessories for her home, and Dolores Parker called to request her assistance on a project. Luisa appreciated both opportunities

Luisa also felt that it was time for her to switch doctors and medical treatments. Kate, her friend from the Light and Interiors Store, recommended Dr. Theodore Cole, an internist specializing in innovative therapies for both the body and mind.

Dr. Cole was head of the Cole Center for Healing and had impressive medical credentials. He had doctorates in both Naturopathic and Osteopathic medicine and a degree in psychology. The American Association of Integrative Medicine had also named him a Fellow.

As a result of her horrific car accident, Luisa had twelve damaged discs in her cervical and thoracic areas, which were touching her spinal cord, along with severely torn and heavily scarred muscles.

To bring relief, Dr. Cole applied oil treatments and massage to Luisa's back and spinal cord. The oils penetrated deep into her nerves and her pain dissipated as the treatment soothed damaged nerves.

Anton had done extensive research on rehabilitation over the past year and urged Luisa to try Yoga and Tai for exercise and relaxation. Rosanna encouraged her mom to try these methods as well. Luisa, however, decided that – for now at least – she would stick with aquatic therapy, thermotherapy and massage.

She found oil massages and deep tissue massages the most beneficial. Due to her tight budget, she had to shop around and find the best prices for her treatments. Hearing that the School for Massage had reasonable rates, she made an appointment and met with massage teacher Mark Michelson.

Luisa was gratified to hear that Mark felt that deep tissue massage was especially beneficial to those he treated. Equally heartening, the cost of the school's massage service fit into her budget. Luisa scheduled an appointment with Mark and soon found that his strong hands did wonders to relieve the pain she was experiencing in her trapezoid muscles.

If Luisa could not get an appointment with Dr. Cole, she scheduled an appointment with the School for Massage.

As Luisa's rehabilitation continued to progress and she began to slowly ease her way back into design work, her mind turned more and more to her coming book Violation. Richard Moran was scheduled to finish the editing of her manuscript in March 2004 and she gave increasing thought to her purpose in writing the book.

She didn't want the book to simply tell the story of her tragic accident and the nightmarish five years that had followed. Her true goal was to educate readers about the often-nefarious methods of insurance companies, lawyers and doctors, as well as to encourage people to fight back against injustice as she had.

Chapter 25

Treasured Vacations

Luisa wished more than anything to communicate hope to the future readers of her book, and she began searching out writers and others whose messages brought encouragement and support to those who had suffered tragedies in their lives.

Reflecting on the strong and potent words of the late Martin Luther King ' I have a Dream.' Luisa wanted so much so to follow this ever occurring dream within her.

One of the writers whose work had helped Luisa get through her ordeal was Jacques Weisal. In his 1992 book, Option From Within, Weisal wrote of the need to love yourself and be loved in turn. He also emphasized the importance of knowing yourself and being able to forgive yourself for mistakes, and of how vital laughter is in life.

Weisal's writings taught Luisa to nurture positive thoughts and to avoid being negative when she was interacting with her beloved daughters Rosanna and Carmella. She even learned to turn to the funny pages in her daily newspaper and start her day off right by chuckling at a cartoon.

Luisa wrote to Weisal, and the author wrote an encouraging letter back. Later, he warmed Luisa's heart by calling to wish her well in her book endeavor. Luisa considered Weisal to be a truly extraordinary motivator, and vowed to tell her readers about him in her book.

Luisa also found inspiration in the pages of Joyce Meyer's book *Battlefield of the Mind*, a work that emphasized the presence of a higher spirit guiding each person through the travails of daily life.

The well-known television personality Oprah often hosted guests with heartening stories that uplifted Luisa as well. She also recognized that the creations of Walt Disney – from his animated films to his theme parks – nurtured the human spirit through innocent fun and laughter.

One evening while mulling over the positive things she hoped to accomplish by writing her book, Luisa had an inspiration: She would use some of the proceeds from book sales to fund the art schools she planned to open in several cities.

She decided to name the enterprise the Cannoli Cultural Art Center, Inc and to open them to students of all ages. The teachers at the school would be interior designers, artists and writers, and there would be one teacher for every ten students.

Within days Luisa had begun to elaborate on her concept. An

essay of 250 words would be written on the power of prayer and friends in daily living as part of the application for acceptance into the Art Center. Each school term would be five weeks long and at the end of each session the artwork of the students would go on display during a graduation ceremony. Selected guest artists would highlight the ceremonies with short lectures.

Student projects would be available for sale with a percentage of the proceeds going to the individual artist and a percentage to the maintenance of the Cannoli Cultural Art Center Schools. She would create a web site www.cannoli.org which would show all of Luisa's dreams coming true for the world to see, and the artistic projects would be made available for the world to see and purchase to cherish for generations to come.

The Centers would also display famous art works from galleries throughout the world. Luisa hoped to show the works of such renowned artists as Rembrandt, Salvador Dali, Anthony Quinn and even Disney animators. She also planned to display Murano Glass creations, and homemade wooden items such as windmills, cuckoo clocks and carvings.

Luisa realized that she would need a lot of help to make her dream come true and she decided to form a committee of 15 Elite Club 450 members to oversee the schools and help foster their growth.

Fired up by her idea, Luisa soon contacted over a dozen artists and writers around the country and enlisted their help in organizing schools in their cities. Schools would open first in Kauai, Oahu, California, Georgia, Texas, Ohio, Kentucky, and Missouri. The interest was there and shared among these highly qualified individuals. They ask of Luisa to keep them informed when she was ready for the expansion into other locations. Luisa projected that to be a five-year plan. Her plans were to start in a rural area and prove the Cannoli Cultural Art Center to be a success.

Although Luisa was now spending most of her time rebuilding

her design career and working on her book, she also continued to wrestle with whether or not to pursue legal action and government involvement against the insurance company lawyers and operatives who had wronged her. It was a decision that would inevitably mean more legal battles, and she wasn't at all sure that she was ready to go to war again.

Luisa decided that she would postpone any further legal and possible government action until her book was published. She placed these unknown events and concerns into the wise guidance of the Holy Spirit and the Almighty God. One unfinished task was to obtain permission to incorporate the works of several writers, artists, designers and others in her manuscript.

She began by calling Alice Drake, Editor of a local home magazine, to ask permission to use a layout of last fall's Kitchen and Bath Show in her book. Alice graciously agreed and told Luisa that she was going to write an article about her book for the magazine.

This generous offer touched Luisa so much that – after thanking Alice and hanging up – she was overwhelmed with tears. She said a prayer of gratitude to the Lord for this first public mention of her book. It would still be at least ten months before her book was released but this early word on her work would undoubtedly stir up interest and perhaps bring in some orders.

When Alice's article came out in later April, Luisa was thrilled with the piece.

How A Life-Altering Motor Vehicle Accident Inspired A Novel

In 1997, award-winning designer Luisa Cannoli's life changed in an instant. In Luisa's own words, she shares the horrific experience: "I was hit by a weaving tractor-trailer on my driver's side forcing the total car to go sideways across I-75. As

I cried out, 'Lord I'm going to be crushed' a brilliant white light engulfed me as I went under the second tractor-trailer on 1-75 in Clarksville, Tennessee on July 22, 1997."

Unfortunately for Luisa, who has over 20 years of design experience, that was only the beginning of her traumatic saga. During the subsequent legal battle with insurance companies, it was discovered that the Cannoli's phone was illegally tapped for three years and a large sum of their possessions was stolen. Years and years of physical therapy and six surgeries have left Luisa and her family with mounting debt. Instead of giving in and remaining a victim of those dire cir-cumstances, Luisa decided to take control of her life.

In order to share her life-altering experiences, Luisa decided to pen a roman a clef, a novel in which actual people or places are depicted in a fictional guise, under the pseudonym Luisa Cannoli. The first edition of Violation, The Life of Luisa Cannoli, is expected to be self-published in spring 2004 with best-selling author Richard Moran serving as ghostwriter and editor. Some of the proceeds from the novel will go to establish scholarships for children to learn all ways to develop their art talents with their hands, not just with computers.

All her interior design venders donated materials for this award-winning interior designer booth at the Home Show in October 2002.

Following publication of Alice Drake's article, Luisa began winding up her current design projects and planning for the family's traditional week-long Mother's Day trip to Largo Mar Resort in Florida with her sisters.

Since flushing all 24 of her prescriptions down the toilet in August 2001, Luisa had lost over 100 pounds. Although she now exercised regularly and watched what she ate, Luisa attributed most of her weight loss to the return of her normal metabolism once she had given up drugs.

Luisa was certain that her doctors had known the harmful side effects of the drugs they were prescribing for her. Yet she doubted that Dr. Grizzly or Dr. Ba had filed FDA reports on the adverse reactions she had suffered. She resolved to warn the readers of her book about the unprofessional manner in which some physicians overmedicated their patients.

In mid-May 2003 Luisa packed for her vacation at the Largo Mar Resort in Ft. Lauderdale with her mother and sisters. Her sister Roxanne coordinated the week. Sophia was the only one who could not attend because of her children's activities.

Luisa, Alexia, Anna and Roxanne were treating their Mom for the week. The closeness of the siblings was always strong but as they became wives and mothers, they were not able to spend as much time together as in earlier years. Luisa was thrilled to finally be able to enjoy the company of her mother and sisters, for her medical treatments had prevented her from vacationing with them for the past five years.

The day of her departure for Florida, Anton and Luisa picked up her mother at home and headed for the airport. The flight was great and they were met at the Ft. Lauderdale Airport by Anna, who explained that Alexia and Roxanna were busy food shopping.

A half hour later they arrived at the beautiful Lago Mar resort, which Luisa remembered so well from previous visits. Alexia and Roxanne were back from grocery shopping for their week's stay and surprised Teresa and Luisa with wine, cheese and fruit.

Alexia added to the merriment by giving everyone fun party gifts. She even had a printed program of activities for the week – including the listing of a topless beach in south Miami. Knowing that the week ahead was going to be nonstop fun, Luisa felt a joyous freedom she hadn't known in years.

As soon as all the women were settled in, they decided to go shopping at the resort-clothing store. When they got to the store Luisa's sisters pointed out that she had recently lost over 100 pounds and insisted that she buy some new beach clothes.

Luisa happily agreed and picked out a new white top, a black bathing suit and black sandals to match. All the while they shopped her sisters kept up a steady stream of banter and jokes, and Luisa thought to herself, this is just like old times.

After their shopping spree, the women traveled to South Miami for a Luau at the Street Pub followed by dinner at Anthony's. The next day they decided to go shopping at the Shoe Inn in West Palm Beach as Luisa, Teresa and Roxanne were all in search of new shoes. From there they traveled to Miss Tilly's Hat Shop, then had dinner outside by the fountain at the West Palm's well-known Bellagio restaurant. They ended their wonderful day by having cheese and wine back at their beach resort.

The women spent the rest of the week soaking up sun, shopping, sightseeing and sharing delicious meals together. During their time at Largo Mar Luisa shared her plans for her upcoming book with many of the friendly people she met and found everyone she talked to supportive of her literary efforts.

Perhaps her most enthusiastic supporters were four women she met in the beautiful Foyer at Largo Mar. It turned that they were designers like Luisa. Their mutual occupation made them connect immediately and Luisa decided to tell them her story.

"I'm a survivor of a major automobile accident," she told them, and went on to relate the horrifying details of her long ordeal.

"Doctors and lawyers certainly do like to line their pockets," one of the women commented. "A lot of them would rather make money than help people."

All the women were appalled by the atrocities of the insurance company defense. They told Luisa to keep in touch with them and exchanged names and addresses with her. They strongly advised Luisa to pursue her goals and were much interested in helping her with the Cannoli Art Cultural Center Inc.

Just then Alexia and Teresa showed up. Luisa made the introductions. One of the women asked Luisa's sisters if Luisa was always that energetic.

"Yes," Alexia said with a smile. "And she also loves to talk."

They all laughed, then said goodbye with good wishes passed all around. The three sisters headed for the pool bar to enjoy summer drinks and snacks. As Luisa sipped her drink, she knew that the memories of this Mother's Day vacation with her mom and sisters would remain with her for life.

The next day the sisters and their mother packed their bags and took a taxi to the airport where they said their goodbyes. All arrived home safe, brimming with wonderful memories of their vacation together at Largo Mar.

Now Luisa had three weeks to get ready for her Hawaiian vacation with her family. She finished a small interior design job and had medical treatments to alleviate chest pain and numbness on her left side.

Her treatments included a gamma ray stress test and within a day Dr. Michael called to tell her the results. Luisa had grown to like the physician because he seemed to care about her as a person as well as a patient and would often ask her about her design career and her upcoming book.

"Your stress test showed that you have angina," he told Luisa. "I'm going to order an angiogram to try to pin down the origin of the problem."

"I'm leaving for Hawaii in a few days," Luisa said. "Will there be time for me to get an angiogram before I leave?"

"No, I'll have to schedule the test for after you return," Dr. Michael replied. "In the interim I want you to take a baby aspirin every day and avoid lifting anything heavy."

"Anything else I should do?"

"Yes, have a good time in Hawaii. Stress-free relaxation is the best medicine I can think of for your condition."

Luisa said goodbye to Dr. Michael and hung up. Angina! she

thought. That's just what I need. Another medical condition to worry about.

In the days that remained before her departure for Hawaii, Luisa prayed hard that everything would be all right. After all, a heart problem was not something that she could afford to take lightly.

Finally the departure day for Hawaii arrived. Anton drove Luisa to the Greyhound Bus station to take a bus to Indianapolis where she would catch a flight to St. Louis. She would meet Rosanna in St. Louis and the two would then fly on to Hawaii. Anton, Carmella and Ashley would fly out the next day and be in Maui by that evening.

Luisa left all her worries behind as she boarded the bus and took a seat behind the driver. As it happened, the driver was new and a Greyhound supervisor, Joe Brown, had come along on the trip to help his new employee get used to the routine.

Luisa struck up a conversation with Joe and soon decided to share her story with him. She also gave him one of her book packets to read. His face showed his shock as he stared at the photo of the illegal telephone chip and learned of the thefts at her home. He could not believe how ruthless the Freedom Insurance investigators had been.

As Luisa went on with her story, her eyes filled with tears at the memory of the terrible violations she had suffered. Joe comforted her with a story of a young boy who survived a tornado.

The boy's home had been blown apart and he was found in the rubble. As his rescuers pulled him out of the wreckage, he told them that he had seen angels around him while he waited for help. The angels were very white, and he had felt safe despite being trapped. Tears rolled down Luisa's face as Joe told this beautiful story. He told Luisa to take care.

In response to Joe's kind words, Luisa opened up her heart as never before. She told Joe that for years she had prayed constantly to the Lord asking for guidance. She went on to reveal that she loved using her creativity and the gifts that God gave her to help others. He expressed to Luisa that even though she believed in God before this horrific accident on 7-22-97, that she was indeed a reborn Christian. His eyes shined as he spoke to Luisa with his deep and caring voice, that she had not found her purpose in life until she was propelled by these inner driven powers to share her experiences in her upcoming book.

Joe told Luisa that he would pray for her and her family.

Sheer wonder of the earth's grand design, and the "recycling process" was in Luisa's thoughts for over twenty years. Bringing those Earth Day rallys to mind, Luisa expressed her thoughts to Joe, as he sat there wide-eyed, focusing on her as she spoke.

Luisa asked Joe about his thoughts about Reincarnation and the meaning of recycling to him. "Do you think God's world involves Reincarnation of our souls into mortal beings?"

She further expressed her concerns about the role of money in daily living. Believing that one earns money by working for the good of all, Luisa was sorely disappointed by seeing many people over the years driven simply by the need of money. In running her own design business, she chose have a lower profit margin, and to continually develop her creative gifts given by God, and help others reach their goals.

Joe said that "he saw her as a true "reborn Christian" with her more realistic views now surfacing." " As a part of the tranformation process, she would continue to view life more honestly and openly now."

In hearing Joe speak of Tranformation, Luisa told Joe that she had recently become aware of the Tranformation Organization in her area. She had been attending the organization frequently, and had truly bonded with the others in the group. She was attending the Encampment of God Church during the Lenten season. There, Brother Charles discussed the many gifts that had been bestowed upon mankind, received in what he called in "the mailbox from the Lord."

This mailbox also holds the the outgoing gifts and contributions donated by the congragation - benefitting each and every member . Brother Charles spoke firmly in a loud and convincing voice , " I am," and " I am part of the Lord." Hearing these words of inner transformation had just touched Luisa's heart and soul, and she told recalled this special moment to Joe. She told him that she felt that she had been reborn to help spread the Lord's message of tranformation to others. Tears welled up in Joe's eyes as he heard these heartfelt statements, and they sat for a moment, holding hands and sharing this new outlook on life.

When they reached Indianapolis, Joe carried Luisa's suitcase to the taxi stand where she could catch a cab to the airport. Luisa asked Joe to have his picture taken with her and he obliged. He also gave Luisa his address and asked her to stay in touch.

When Luisa got to the airport she went to the American Airlines arrivals area to wait for Rosanna, only to discover that daughter's plane had had mechanical problems and had returned to Boston. American Airlines informed Luisa that Rosanna would be on a direct flight to Hawaii early the next morning. The news upset Luisa but she consoled herself with the thought that Rosanna's safety was paramount.

The long bus ride had taken its toll on Luisa and she was now suffering terrible physical pain. She called Anton and asked him what to do. He told her to buy Bayer Aspirin.

After hanging up, Luisa went to the gift shop and purchased 12 packets of Bayer and a bottle of water. Unfortunately, she then found that she could not open her bottle of water nor the Bayer packets.

A young beautiful blond wearing a jean bib overall stood to Luisa's right and came to her aid. Luisa thanked her and told her that body massages help pregnant woman.

Giggling, the young blond told Luisa that she was not pregnant, although she admitted that the baggy overalls made her look like she was.

Luisa told her that she was in a great deal of pain and told her about her automobile accident and its aftermath. She then explained that she was writing a book about it.

The young blond asked Luisa if she had any information with her about her project. Luisa did and gave her a packet of information about her book. The woman gave Luisa her business card. She was with PBS and was its director of operations.

To Luisa's left stood a large African-American gentleman. He was very well dressed in a brown metallic suit with gold necktie and wide brimmed hat.

He said to Luisa, "You must have a whopper of a headache to need all those Bayer aspirins."

Then he gave Luisa his business card. He was a Minister. He said, "Send me your book packet too. I'll help you."

The clerk said the same. Once again, in time of need, others came to help and listen. Luisa took the Bayer aspirins and thanked them all most graciously.

An hour later, Luisa boarded her plane for Hawaii and settled in for the long trip. The flight went smoothly and as the plane approached Hawaii Luisa gazed down enraptured with the beautiful island below.

The connecting flight to Maui took only twenty minutes and her baggage was ready when she arrived. She took a shuttle to go to Dollar Car Rental and picked up the car reserved for them. She then drove to the Maui Banyon Beach Resort situated on a beautiful beach.

The night went fast and Luisa arose early to meet her family at Maui Airport. The two-week vacation was beginning.

After Anton, Rosanna, Carmella and Ashley had checked into the hotel, they decided to drive to nearby Lahaina. There they visited shops and priced snorkeling and surfing equipment rentals. They also shopped for groceries.

Then she and Anton looked over artwork and jewelry in several local shops. They strolled into Fine Jewelry and met Taresha the owner. She shared with the Cannolis' the difference in the pearls. Her knowledge and most fair pricing convinced Anton to purchase the treasured pearl for his beautiful and most deserving wife. Luisa wanted a genuine Tahitian black pearl from the South Pacific as a souvenir of their visit and Anton agreed to buy her one. He also selected pearls for Christmas gifts for Rosanna and Carmella. In an art shop he bought a print of Lahaina to hang in their home as a treasured memento of their vacation.

The Cannolis and Ashley had lunch at the historic Pioneer Inn. During lunch, the waitress told them that Mark Twain had stayed there and recommended that they visit the garden area and see the tattered old mailbox where the great writer had once received his mail.

That week the Cannolis played at the Beach and went to the Royal a Hawaiian Luau where they enjoyed plenty of Hawaiian food, including a delicious roasted pig. During the luau, everyone wore colorful leis and sang Hawaiian love songs.

During the days that followed, the girls went snorkeling and surfing and everyone traveled to Black Beach where Luisa found small black stones for jewelry and Christmas gifts.

Next they decided to drive to Hana and Macapens Mt. Surprise. Anton surprised his harem of girls by renting a convertible for this driving excursion and for the remainder of the week. They drove all over to see the volcanic mountains and enjoyed the sight of numerous rainbows throughout the day. They all ended that first week with beautiful tans and so many wonderful memories.

To everyone's delight, Carmella's friends from school had invented a Hawaiian scavenger hunt for the traveling group to hunt out items, people and places, which added so much color to their two-week adventure.

They headed next to Kauai, the garden island, for a three-day stay at an ocean front resort. There they enjoyed picnics on the beach, a boat ride, sleepy afternoons relaxing in hammocks and leisurely dinners at a wonderful restaurant called Ono.

The headwaiter Luis served them personally, sharing with the Cannolis his special chicken breast dish along with delicious soups and desserts. He gave Luisa his chicken breast recipe with macadamia nuts, Dijon mustard, cognac, poultry seasonings and olive oil.

The Cannolis also took a riverboat cruise to the Fern Grotto. The tour guide told the tourist group that many weddings were performed at the grotto with the couples being serenaded with the beautiful Hawaiian Wedding song sung by a native quartet accompanied by a ukulele.

Anton next took the girls on a tour of the surrounding waterfalls that tumbled from the green mountains. At one waterfall, they met a local artist named Moti who told them that he had moved to Hawaii from the West Coast many years ago to find peace in "God's haven."

Moti told Luisa that he liked to read a lot. One book in particular that he recommended was The Seat of the Soul by Gary Zukav. He explained that the book spoke of the five senses of humans and how one can evolve into a multi-sensory person.

Moti went on to tell Luisa that human perception and the inner discovery of ourselves allows us to sacrifice our lives for a greater purpose. If we have the teachings of Christ, Buddha, Krishna, Karma, and Ganhdi in our lives, we can achieve this multi-sensory level and the awareness that our immortal souls live on forever.

Luisa understood what Moti was saying and shared with him her readings and her experience teaching mid-eastern culture to high school classes.

After Luisa briefly told him the story of her tragic car accident and the horrible aftermath, Moti said that he too had suffered tragedies in his life and that surviving adversity had enlightened both their lives. He further shared with Luisa of having severe PTSD and those never experiencing it often cannot truly understand all that they have gone through. The flashbacks of his life – threatening experience remains in his mind also as she has in hers.

At the close of their conversation, Moti gave Luisa one of his oil watercolors to have as a token of their shared friendship. Luisa expressed sincere gratitude for his friendship and his gift and promised to read The Seat of the Soul upon her return to the mainland. She told Moti that his beautiful oil painting would hang proudly in her great room for all to see and admire.

From Kauai the Cannolis went to Kona where they saw an active volcano at night. Dressed in ponchos and carrying flashlights they spent hours crossing miles of hardened lava very gingerly holding hands with each other in the pitch black hours of the night with only a half moon to illuminate the harsh landscape.

Although Luisa wanted to share the entire adventure with the others, she felt an anxiety attack building and had to stop after four miles. She sat on a lava ledge to wait for her family to return. The next day they headed to Oahu for two days of sun and surfing at Waikiki Beach.

All too soon, their two-week vacation in the islands was over. It had been a dream come true, and everyone boarded the plane for their flight home brimming with wonderful memories of magical Hawaii.

Chapter 26

The Future Beckons

Following the Cannoli's trip to Hawaii, Luisa was still having chest pains. Since July 22, 1997, the pains – initially diagnosed as angina - had gotten worse.

Dr. Luken at the Cardiology Center recommended that Luisa have an angiocardiography as soon as possible. The nurse, Valerie, scheduled it immediately at North Lakeland Hospital.

The test revealed a blockage that was causing a shortage of oxygen to half of her heart. The shoulder seatbelt harness that had compressed her chest on July 22, 1997 was determined to be the cause.

Luisa was relieved to finally learn why she was having chest pains, and she was heartened by the concern of the caring doctors who actually listened when she told them of her symptoms. Although Dr. Ted Grizzly had heard the same complaints from Luisa for many years, he had chosen to ignore the recurring symptoms.

For some time now the chest pains had become worse when she lifted or carried items. She also experienced overall physical weakness for hours before the feeling subsided. In addition, her left hand turned white during her heart episodes.

Now she realized the cause of the severe body pain she had suffered on the way to Hawaii, and she would never forget the kindness of the people at the airport who had helped her get relief for her pain.

In July 2003, Luisa took Carmella on a trip to visit various sites in the northeast. They first flew to Boston to meet Rosanna, who was attending summer classes at the prestigious Master Tech University.

Luisa brought along some promotion material on her book *Violation* as she was in the midst of preparing a mailer to be sent to prospective buyers.

After an uneventful flight, they landed at Logan International Airport and found the weather in Boston to be rainy and dismal. Luisa's body pain flared up. A combination of Aleve and baby aspirin – along with relaxation techniques and prayers – finally brought her welcome relief.

Carmella told her mother that she looked forward to seeing Rosanna and the Boston Red Sox. The teenage girl was obviously ready for fun. They knew the Boston area well from previous visits to Rosanna and quickly found their way to the Italian district downtown.

They walked to Guidallo's – a restaurant they knew well – and were greeted by the owner, a friendly Italian man named Tony. He showed them the menu and they chose soup and salad and a pepperoni and mushroom pizza. Tony brought them cannolis for dessert and hot cocoa to warm them against the damp chilly weather outside.

After lunch they called Rosanna who told them that she had classes until 5:00 PM. To pass the time, she suggested that they catch the movie *Bad Boys II* at a theatre nearby. She would meet them after the showing.

After 5:00, Luisa and Carmella met Rosanna and drove to her home to have dinner. By now the weather had cleared and Rosanna had arranged for Boston Red Sox baseball tickets for that night.

Dressed in Red Sox shirts and hats, they thoroughly enjoyed

the game, which the Sox won. Afterward Rosanna took her Mom back to her apartment to rest while she and Carmella went out to meet Rosanna's friends. It was a fun and fast day.

The next morning the three of them rose early for the three-hour drive to the Oak'n Spruce Resort in the foothills of the Berkshire Mountains in Stockbridge, Massachusetts. They were all in a festive mood, for the sun was shining brightly and the beautiful countryside was cloaked in summer green.

As they entered Stockbridge the sight of the 18th Century colonial buildings reminded Luisa of the U.S. presidents who had stayed at the town's famous Red Lion Inn. That evening Luisa treated her daughters to dinner at the Inn.

The Oak 'n Spruce Resort was rustic in appearance and surrounded by stately trees and flowering azaleas and magnolias. The sights of the colonial era resort made Luisa think of her years teaching American history.

Wanting to give her students an authentic taste of early America, at Thanksgiving she had often served them meals of wild turkey, Indian succotash, cranberries and homemade pumpkin pies. She even had them make costumes and write scripts for the Thanksgiving exchange between the Indians and Colonists. Both Rosanna and Carmella had picked up their mother's love of history and often pointed out historic points of interest during their frequent travels.

Luisa discussed with her daughters the importance of being proactive like the Patriots of the Boston Tea Party did when they were treated unfairly by taxation without representation.

Rosanna suggested as a Dean Scholar to be proactive one should get involved in the politics and the way lobbying affects our daily lives without thinking about it.

Luisa who had studied American History and the lives of the leaders of our country shared her thoughts with possibly contacting the US Congressmen to investigate insurance companies using intimidation to get people to settle for such low amounts like in the San Francisco Earthquake from the early 1990's.

Carmella mentioned that when she was in the 4th grade that she ran for Class President and now she was going to enter the third year of high school to study World Cultures. Both girls liked this suggestion. Collectively, they scribbled some notes for a letter to go to the US Congress and one to go to the President.

With the election year around the corner, that to tackle insurance companies and to wake up the country to speak up would take a lot of effort. For those facing insurance companies, lawyers and doctors, a united front of

Emailing, faxing and writing the entire US Congress could possibly start a modern day Boston Tea Party in our country.

Luisa prayed that all her readers of her book would do the same for the future of the children and their children for generations to come.

The Cannolis' decided to express their opinions and forward their letter upon return home. Upon leaving the Red Lion Inn, they spoke to the headwaiter, James, to express their gratitude for the fine dinner and atmosphere. The waiter provided the Cannolis' the General Manager's business card, Mr. Finn. Luisa expressed to James her goals for the book and school. He supported Luisa and mentioned to tell Mr. Finn about it upon her return home. Luisa was swelling inside with that welcomed news. The full moonlight shone over them as they walked to their car to start their journey back to their resort.

A highlight of their trip to Stockbridge was a visit to the home of Norman Rockwell, where many of the late artist's paintings and illustrations were displayed. Luisa had long studied Rockwell's work, and the authentic detail of his paintings constantly amazed her.

After their two-day stay in the Berkshires, Luisa, Rosanna and Carmella rose early on a Monday morning and drove to Falmouth on the Massachusetts coast where Luisa and Carmella planned to catch the Ferry to Martha's Vineyard. Rosanna had classes to attend and would pick them up at the ferry after their three-day visit to the island.

Luisa and Carmella took the early Ferry to Martha's Vineyard. They checked into a Bed and Breakfast on Main Street in Oak Bluffs and set off to explore the quaint if weathered town.

The next day was July 22 – the sixth anniversary of Luisa's life-altering accident – and she took a long early morning walk alone. Getting through the anniversaries of her accident was always terribly hard for Luisa because of the painful memories that always came flooding back on these days.

As Luisa walked she thanked the Lord for all the new friends she had met and asked Him to help her hide her pain from Carmella. When she finally returned from her four-mile trek, she was feeling better, and Carmella didn't seem to sense her mother's inner turmoil.

They had lunch at Pompora's Italian Restaurant and then spent the rest of the afternoon window-shopping and buying souvenirs in town. That evening Luisa and Carmella decided to take the island bus to Edgartown and attend a chamber music recital in the Town Meeting Church. The recital was a memorial for the victims of 9/11 and Luisa and Carmella returned to their room in the bed and breakfast in a somewhat somber mood.

The next morning Luisa went to a quaint little island restaurant called Biscuits for a carryout breakfast of French toast, bacon and sunny-side-up eggs. After breakfast Carmella insisted that they go shopping. She had her heart set on a gray Martha's Vineyard sweatshirt and they browsed the shops until they finally found exactly the right one. In one of the shops Luisa discovered a royal blue bathing suit that she adored. It was reasonably priced and just the right size, so she splurged and bought it.

She wore her new suit to the beach that day and Carmella complimented her on how good she looked now that she had lost so much weight. Luisa beamed, pumped up by the return of her long absent self-esteem.

After sunbathing for several hours, mother and daughter returned to their room and packed for the trip back to Boston. As they were boarding the ferry, Luisa reflected that the photos they had taken of the beautiful and peaceful island would long remind them both of their most enjoyable visit.

Rosanna met them at the ferry dock in Falmouth and drove them back to Boston. That evening Rosanna was scheduled to play in a baseball game and Carmella tagged along to watch her play while Luisa stayed home to rest.

At 5:00 AM the next morning Luisa, Rosanna and Carmella took a taxi drove her mother and sister to the train station for their rail trip to New York City. She would join them in a couple of days. Luisa and Carmella said goodbye and departed Boston at 6:00 AM. Before noon they arrived at the Soho Suites Hotel in Manhattan where they would be staying.

Carmella could not believe how large and bustling New York was. Putting her arm through Luisa's she said, "You know, Mom, these skyscrapers and huge crowds are awesome, but to tell you the truth I prefer small towns."

"I agree," Luisa said. "New York is an exciting place to visit, but I don't think I could live here full-time. It's too impersonal."

"I've been thinking of going into either interior design or journalism when I graduate from college," Carmella said. "Can you imagine how competitive both those professions would be in a city this size? I'd rather work in a slower paced environment like East Hill Valley or Cincinnati."

Rosanna soon joined them as planned and everyone had a wonderful time. Luisa found herself bonding more solidly than ever with her two fast-growing daughters. The week went fast and soon it was time for them to say goodbye and head home.

Before they parted they all went to St. Patrick's Cathedral to say prayers of gratitude both for Luisa's continuing recovery and for the wonderful time they had all had together in New York.

That afternoon Luisa and Carmella taxied to JFK Airport for their flight home. Rosanna would fly back to Boston later that day to resume her college classes.

Luisa and Carmella arrived home safely. The Cannoli house was getting painted so Luisa stayed home to supervise the work. She also used the time to catch up on her reading. Fortunately, Mr. & Mrs. Cruise signed a contract with Luisa to have their bathroom redecorated the following September. The job, although small, would bring in much needed income for Luisa.

A week later Freedom Insurance finally contacted Luisa – six long years after her automobile accident and 1/12 years after the forced out of court settlement – and arranged to send her a check for $5,765 in payment for the car their client had destroyed that fateful day on the freeway. This came as surprise to Luisa but a letter about a check for half of the car's value raised questions in Luisa's mind. What about the rest of the money due? She called 2/3rd BANK and was advised to contact Freedom Insurance directly. She did, and the northern office advised her that the payment would be sent immediately to her. She asked the claims supervisor for his name, and he told her it was Mr. Goodman.

Luisa told Mr. Goodman about all that had occurred and how upset she was with Lee Sleazer and his team of investigators. She asked for the investigators' names, but Mr. Goodman told her she'd have to contact Lee Sleazer directly, as he had hired and paid them himself. He advised Luisa to find an attorney and prosecute Lee Sleazer for his involvement in the felonious crimes of his investigators.

Mr. Goodman expressed between his local office and the stall check office that 80,000 checks had to be sent to claimants within 10 days. That news appalled Luisa that all these people possibly had been violated such as she.

Mr. Goodman asked Luisa if Freedom Insurance was now off the hook. Luisa told him that she had contacted a powerful attorney to look into that matter. She told him that the FBI was aware of the matter and what they decided to do would not involve her. They hung up the telephone, and the checks arrived that week.

In late August Luisa flew to Chicago to meet with Richard Moran, who was nearing the end of ghostwriting her manuscript. Luisa spent an intense four days with him, going over the book and pointing out where new material should be inserted so that he could finalize her manuscript. They discussed the impact this story could have on other people as they learned of the underhandedness of powerful insurance companies and the investigators they hired, and the difficulty in fighting against them.

When Luisa flew home to Tennesse, she was confident that Violation would be based on the true story of her terrible automobile accident and the years of physical pain and emotional anguish that had followed.

Through the rest of the fall Luisa divided her time between working on her book and reinvigorating her design business. She created exhibits of her work for the new upcoming Home show and finalized the Cruise bathroom project.

Unfortunately, she continued to suffer from Post Traumatic Stress Disorder and received another speeding ticket. This time it was because a black semi on I-75 near Kentucky came speeding along and suddenly the driver put his right turn signal on. When he started moving into Luisa's lane, Luisa accelerated and her Lexus sped to get away.

A blue light came on and a brown-suited policeman stopped Luisa. He heard her story and could see the panic in her eyes. He gave her a ticket but told her that the prosecutor would understand. He gave Luisa a phone number to contact the prosecutor.

Luisa did, and the prosecutor lowered her ticket to no points. The driving difficulty due to PSTD came on so unexpectedly and Luisa continued to hope that it would get better with each new driving experience.

During the Home show, several old friends approached Luisa and told her that she "looked radiant." Her friend Terry Sue told her that to glow as she did, she must be very happy inside. Luisa thought the daily application of Lancome lotion Tresor also helped.

Reflecting on Terry Sue's remark, Luisa realized that she had indeed regained her joyous love of life. After six years of torture, she had rediscovered her creativity, her passion for helping others and her deep love of her husband and daughters.

With her life whole again and her book coming out in the first quarter of 2004, Luisa Cannoli looked forward to a wondrously fulfilling future.

That fall, her many friends helped her organize a golf outing at Kenton Golf Course, Independence, Kentucky with Dave and Dan. Wendy's and TFIG provided salads and wings. Eric, at Wyoming Pastry's, Wyoming, Ohio provided the scrumptious cannolis. Mardis and Meyer, along with the Sandwich Deli, provided the sandwiches and other dishes.

Jake provided good-looking models from Wings Model Agency. The models - Jimmy, Kendra, Marie, Kerry, Robin, Rachel and Jake - provided a super fashion show modeling clothes by Talbot's and Joseph C. Banks. The groups of golfers cheered the models through their stage presentations as Frank Sinatra and Shane provided the music. Soundwaves, on Kemper Road, in Cincinnati, provided the music and CD Warehouse provided the CDs.

Many donations were received to give to the guests. To name a few, Cherie Shannon of the Antique Ferguson Mall donated an original artwork from the 1940s, and 2/3rd bank donated Tupperware for many to receive. There were lights from the Light House and Interiors Store, and Designs for your Entire Home donated floral arrangements. Beer, wine and liquor came from Cork 'n Bottle, toys from Deals for many children, and a Vera

Bradley purse came from Crabtree and Evelyn.

In late November, Anton saw an article for a part-time job in the Saturday local newspaper. It was for an after school Art Enrichment School in the nearby city of Massone.

Luisa called the Art Director, Kathy Dickerson, and they set up an interview for the 1st Thursday in December. At that meeting, Kathy introduced Luisa to another teacher and close friend of Ms. Dickerson, Sally Flagstone.

The three of them discussed the art school program. Luisa gave them her resume, along with photos of her interior design projects, and showed them the watercolor for her book. Since Luisa wanted to focus on the art job, she told Sally and Kathy a little bit of her story but kept it brief. As it turned out, when Sally heard Luisa's story, she had a most compelling story to tell Luisa.

The story was that in 1984 her sister-in-law was killed instantly by a tractor-trailer on I-75 in southern Kentucky. The accident was witnessed by her two surviving children of the precious ages of four and seven years old.

Luisa had tears in her eyes as Sally spoke, as she had heard this story in June upon her return from Hawaii. When Sally paused for a moment, Luisa asked her if the husband's name was Paul, a remodeling specialist.

He was. Then Sally continued, telling Luisa and Kathy that, 20 years ago, the insurance company had done the same thing to her family as they had to Luisa's. They denied responsibility for the injuries of the two children and the death of her sister-in–law.

The battle went on for four years. During that time, the stress to the family was incredible. The surviving husband was hospitalized a number of times during the legal hassles by the lawyers. The climax was a few days before the jury trial. The husband received a most ruthless and heart-piercing letter from the insurance claims adjuster, stating that the surviving mother would never miss their children, as they were too young to remember her.

Upon receipt of the letter, the surviving husband was hospitalized again and the personal injury case was dropped, leaving the family with only memories of the horrific death of their precious loved one.

Tears rolled down Kathy and Luisa's faces as they heard this emotional story. They hugged and comforted Sally. Luisa asked Sally how the two children managed as they grew up. Sally explained the difficulties they had without their mother to share their happy and sad moments.

They were now 25 and 23 years old. The young boy speaks of his Mom and how he has missed her since he was four years old. His sister is beginning to get her young adult life together and starting a business career in sales. For the husband, the loss will always remain.

Luisa told Kathy and Sally that she hoped her book would help victims and wake up potential readers to take a proactive stand against the wealthy insurance companies and hoped they would contact their Washington representatives in emails, faxes and letters of their own insurance stories.

Sally bought the book that afternoon, and Luisa signed the watercolor for them. Luisa was hired and her job will begin when the school has enough students for the program.

She thanked them both and followed up with a most sincere thank you note to each of them. Luisa was thrilled with the golden opportunity that had been presented to her, and was grateful to Anton for pointing out the ad to her.

Luisa contacted the City of Massone, Tennesse and that same day the contract to rent the Community Center was in the mail. Luisa was thrilled that her ten-year dream to go back into teaching and continue to work with award-winning interiors would be fulfilled.

Disciple Church of Christ was also contacted. The church minister and board of trustees welcomed Luisa and her Cannoli

Cultural Art Center so much, that Luisa chose them to place her art program into place sometime in late winter 2005 with the 2004 year devoted to an extensive book tour with book signings and parties to spread the power of prayer, and the need to fight back and stand tall against lawyers, insurance companies, doctors and prescribed drugs.

The raging tempest that had almost destroyed her was over, the black clouds of pain and suffering had passed, and a rainbow arched over her road ahead.

Looking ahead to the holidays, the Cannolis began getting their home ready for the season. Rosanna would be home for Thanksgiving.

They all dusted and rearranged their bedrooms. To Luisa's utter surprise, the Disney Stock certificates were found buried underneath some clothing in the girls' closets. The closets had not been cleaned for a number of years. Luisa thought about the many games of cat and mouse played during 2000 and 2001 and decided that probably during one of their trips, the snakes returned some of the items, but not all of them.

Now she thought she understood what was behind H.S. Witt accusing Anton of insurance fraud in December 2001. The Cannolis dropped the theft claim because of the way H.S. Witt treated Anton, and Freeby did not help Anton through that examination one bit.

Luisa had until December 17, 2003 to reopen that theft claim. With some of the items returned, she considered doing that, but Anton told Luisa that he was permanently bruised by H.S. Witt and did not care to reopen the claim.

Luisa made calls to Car Owners Insurance and the State of Tennessee Department of Insurance to request complaint forms she wanted to make against Freedom Insurance and Car Owners Insurance. Anton had no wish to talk to the insurance company representatives. Luisa called Marshall Kent to ask his advice.

Marshall was glad to hear from Luisa. They exchanged

pleasantries and caught up with each other's lives. Luisa explained her desire to reopen the claim with Car Owners Insurance but told him of Anton's adamant position not to reopen it.

Marshall reminded Luisa that he would help them, and told Luisa to tell Anton that he would go to meet the supervisor with both of them. They ended their friendly conversation with Luisa saying she would call him at the end of November.

Much to Luisa's disappointment, Anton would not be swayed and chose not to reopen the claim. Luisa called Marshall and told him of Anton's decision. She thanked Marshall for his genuine support and friendship during all the years since 1997, and he asked Luisa to keep in touch. She said she would, and hung up the telephone.

Luisa contacted the FBI and spoke to an agent named Kirland Ferguson. She briefly told him the story and was surprised to learn from him that agents always give their name to those who call. For Luisa, this further verified that the call to the FBI in July 2001 instead went to the defense attorney's snakes to prevent the truth from being heard.

Agent Ferguson advised Luisa to call the East Hill Valley police department to reopen the case. Luisa hung up and then called the non-emergency telephone number of the East Valley police. She briefly stated her business and requested that one of the detectives return her call.

Luisa never heard back from them. This did not surprise her, but the question remained unanswered for her. Why would they not try to stop criminal activity? What was behind their system not to see justice pursued?

Thanksgiving came with all the blessings and friendships of family getting together. Then it was time to get their home ready for Christmas. They all decided to have a Southern Living Christmas Holiday Open House.

Luisa watched her favorite show, Oprah Winfrey. Her Holiday Shows helped Luisa get her tables set for the Holiday

Open House. Luisa watched and listened to the show with Rod Stewart. He sang songs from his new CD, and his rendition of Bewitched melts your heart with his mellow words.

The Cannolis readied their home with Christmas lights and decorations. Johnny Mathis and Frank Sinatra Christmas tunes were heard throughout their home. Invitations with a picture of their English Tudor decorated with snow and lights were printed. Luisa had wanted to do this for a long time, and now finally it was happening. The invitations and Christmas cards were sent to many friends – new and old.

On Christmas Eve, the Cannolis went to Mass at their parish, St. Anthony Francis in East Hill Valley.

On Christmas Day, Luisa received the two new CDs by Rod Stewart - *As time goes by* and *the American Songbook*, along with the DVD *Seabiscuit* and an Elvis CD. Her loving husband gave her Lancome products.

Luisa's gifts to her family were the framed photos of their splendid Hawaii adventure along with stones from the Black Beach, which had been made into earrings and a necklace.

For her Anton, a new pair of brown corduroy slacks and sweater to match. They had a French toast breakfast with smores on the campfire. They drank vanilla and amaretto flavored hot chocolate. They said prayers to the Lord for the blessed year they had had.

That Saturday, January 3rd, the Cannolis went to Mass at St. Anthony Francis. The theme of this service was for peace as Saddam Hussein had just been captured. As the service came to a close, the pastor, Father Jason, asked the parishioners to read together, *A Prayer For Peace:*

> *O God, Lead our hearts*
> *In the ways of peace.*
> *Help us to be at peace with*

Ourselves, our families,
Friends and neighbors as
We face life's daily challenges.
May peace radiate from our hearts
Wherever we go.

Help us to be active peacemakers by conveying your love
And patience to those lives we touch.
Direct us by your spirit, that
Both our words and our actions may
Help the world be renewed in peace.

Amen

The church choir ended with the song Let there be peace and let it begin with me. This brought inner peace to Luisa as she finally forgave Frank Walker for the permanent harm the horrific accident on July 22, 1997 had done to her life and the way she was left to straighten it out.

The Cannolis had a wonderful dinner that evening with their daughters and their boyfriends at the 2/3rd's Banking Center with a complimentary Baked Alaskan dessert to celebrate her birthday.

Early the next early morning Luisa, began the grocery shopping at the Grocery Mart. It was fun, with Joe, the meat and dairyman, helping locate the pig feet for the older guests. Tina helped with the breasts of chicken and Gladys helped keep an eye on the carts of groceries as Luisa loaded up yet another cart. There were three carts in all. The clerks, Dave, Stacie, Jennifer and Amber all helped Luisa load the groceries into the carts and into her car.

Rosanna, Carmella, and Rosanna's new beau, Maximillian, helped with all the cooking – homemade lasagna, pork tenderloin with sautéed mushrooms, crushed onions and a little poultry seasoning. Luis Hernendez's chicken recipe from Hawaii with macadamia nuts, honey Dijon mustard, cognac and olive oil was delicious. Appetizers were plentiful with pigs in a blanket, cheese and vegetable trays, taco dips, deviled eggs, and meatballs, just to mention a few. Desserts were homemade cookies, brownies, cannolis and cheesecakes.

They handed out white bags with candles as they greeted their guests. More than 60 guests came and went from afternoon on. Boom Paw Eddie Luella, Caroline, Suzanna and her husband Charles, Anne and her husband George, along with Luisa's family were there. Mary Ellen and her husband Phil came with a tray of brownies. Lynne and her husband Dave came with smiling Christmas cheer. Susan and Jerome brought a CD *Winter Solace* to bring the outside in with soft musical sounds.

Carol, Dave, Linda, Mike, Bennett, Marsha, Phil all met Anton's relatives and helped with keeping the food dishes and drinks flowing. Diana, Seth, Lynne and Arnold joined in with the making of the Tiramasu layered dessert laced with chocolate chips and Kahlaua.

Christmas songs by Johnny Mathis, Ray Charles and Frank Sinatra, along with Kenny G music, played in all the rooms. Luisa thought of two of her friends who had died in early December 2003. Stitch had been killed in a car accident in an intersection. Luisa recalled that it wasn't long before the accident that he had measured her kitchen table for the replacement glass it needed after having been cracked by Anton in August 1999. Luisa remembered when he had proudly told her that he had made the curved glass top that fit perfectly on her table.

She had also been shocked to learn that her friend Tommy B. had lost his battle with cancer. Tommy B. had counseled Luisa many times over the past few years when she had visited his café on the river in the Valley of Greenville, Kentucky. Luisa cherished his kind and supporting words.

She sent his family a token of condolences and a donation for a tree to be planted in his name. She enclosed a note, telling them that when her Cannoli Cultural Art Center was opened, a tree would be planted in Tommy's memory.

His family placed his smiling and happy face on a Billboard to honor his memory. Luisa took a photo of the billboard and planned to laminate it and then place under the tree when it was planted.

Their families and friends would never forget both of these terrific friends. They laughter and the songs they sang on this earth would be heard over and over again as they drifted from the heavens.

Luisa's cousins all joined in the festive evening. Anna and Mary brought more Christmas cheer into the festive atmosphere with stories of their kids who were now married. Carrie and her husband, Richard, brought some Holiday cheer to share with the fun group. Katie and Barbie brought laughter and ideas for Luisa's pottery class.

Jessica, Jimmy and Kelly egged on Boom Paw Eddie to tell more of his jokes. Sue and Bob, along with Bill and Pat, talked about their trip to Hawaii. Charlotte, Bev, Joyce and Phyllis shared their trip to Australia with Kate and Eddie. June and her family drove in from South Carolina and brought some delicious homemade Christmas cookies to share.

Patricia and Ray came with their four beautiful daughters, Regina, Felicia, Shawn and Yolanda, and their grandchildren. Patricia surprised everyone with pink packages of makeup supplies. Schalanod and her family drove from Florida bringing a beautiful fruit tray with oranges, pineapples, grapes and bananas, and the Christmas platter was trimmed with red and green crisp berries. Charlene and her family came from Phoenix, Arizona bringing the beautiful cactus Ochilla with the orange-red orchid like flower blooming.

Groups of people were in the great room for talking and joking. The men stood and sat by the player piano and drank their bottles of Rolling Rock, joking with their wives across the room, as pictures were taken. The many empty beer and wine bottles accounted for some of jolly and cheerful mood.

All shared conversations and laughter. The kids played foos ball and ping ball and listened to their music in the lower level. Brandon, Tom and Rob, Allison and Carmella played with Ally and Bennett.

As the evening drew to a close, there were many hugs and kisses as the guests departed. In the Southern Living way of entertaining, Luisa had little gift bags of potpourri and Santa Clauses filled with colorful candy for her guests. More pictures were taken at the front door near the wall of Christmas cards the Cannolis had received.

After all the guests were gone, Rosanna, Max, Carmella and their other friends went downstairs to entertain themselves.

Anton went over to Luisa and hugged her tightly and kissed her most passionately. He thanked her for all the work she did in getting everything together for a most beautiful Christmas Holiday Open House. He told her it was the best party that they'd had in a good long time.

He put his hand around her waist and walked her into their great room. As they approached the green leather sofa, he said to her, "Let's just watch the fire go out."

As they lay on the sofa together, holding each other in one another's arms, Luisa spoke softly to Anton, "Do you remember when the girls were so little that we watched the Muppet Show every Saturday night at 7:30 p.m.? We laughed so hard at the jokes and comments by Waldorf and Statler."

Anton told that he remembered, and then asked if she remembered the name of the Swedish chef?

She thought for a minute, "I would have to think about that one, Anton."

Anton chuckled as he lightly kissed her. He told her that was his name, the Swedish Chef.

They laughed together as they listened to Rod Stewart and

Johnny Mathis, along with Christmas songs sung by Frank Sinatra.

They drank their glasses of Marilyn Merlot and clinked their wine glasses together. They shared with each other a slice of chocolate cheesecake from Annette's Cheesecakes

They lay on the sofa together for hours into the night sharing fond memories of the past year and the true friendships of family and the friends that had stuck by them since July 22, 1997. They kissed each other passionately as the fire crackled in the night. She was reminded of verses she had found in Nonnie's memoirs:

Per piacere amami poco se vuio amarmi a lungo - Love me a little as long as you love me long.

As Luisa drifted off to sleep, she was also reminded of a poem from *The Treasury of Italian Love Poems, Quotations and Proverbs*, titled *The Glorious End to the Adventurous Journey.*

By permission of John L. Hart FLP, and Creative Syndicate, Inc.

Bibliography

Fodor's 98 Europe, New York: Fodor's Travel Publications, Inc., 1998

Tea Time with God, Tulsa: Honor Books, 1996

Ban Breathnach, Sarah, *Simple Abundance*, New York: Warner Books, Inc. 1995

Ban Breathnach, Sarah, *Something More*, New York: Warner Books, Inc. 1998

Branyon, Rcichard A., *Treasury of Italian Love Poems*, Quotations, and Proverbs, New York: Hippocrene Books, 1995

Brockovich, Erin with Mark Elliot, *Take It From Me*, New York: McGraw-Hill, 2002

Caudill, Margaret A., *Managing Pain Befoe It Manages You*, New York: The Guilford Press, 1995

Covey, Stephen R., *The 7 Habits of Highly Effective People*, New York: Fireside, 1990

Eadie, Betty J., *Embraced By The Light*, New York: Bantam Books, 1994

Fried, Stephen, *Biter Pills,* New York: Bantam Books, 1998

Kissing, Steve, *Running from the Devil*, New York: The Crossland Publishing Company, 2003

Mohr Catalano, Ellen and Kimeron N. Hardin, *The Chronic Pain Control Workbook (second edition)*, Oakand: New Harbinger Publications, Inc., 1996

Moran, Richard, *Doomsday*, Indianapolis: Alpha Books, 2003

Peters, Thomas J. and Robert H. Waterman, Jr., *In Search of Excellence*, New York: Warnerbooks, Inc., 1982

Sparks, Nicholas, *A Walk To Remember,* New York: Warner Books, Inc., 1999

Sparks, Nicholas, *Message in a Bottle*, New York: Warner Books, Inc., 1998

Sparks, Nicholas, *The Notebook*, New York: Warner Books, Inc., 1998

Weisel, Jacques, *Bloom Where You're Planted*, Deerfield Beach: Health Communications, Inc., 1996

Whitall Smith, Hannah, *A Christian's Secret of a Happy Life*, Springdale: Whitaker House, 1983

Williamson, Marianne, *Illuminata*, New York: Random House, 1994

Zukav, Gary, *The Seat of the Soul*, New York: Fireside, 1990